WELCOME T

New York is a vibrant, larger-th
cosmopolitan city with unflagg
and a competitive streak, whe
Street or in the arts. It grew up vertically on
a handful of islands watched over by the
Statue of Liberty, amid noise and frenzied
activity, ever intent on doing things bigger
and faster. Manhattan stretches from the
East River to the Hudson, a checkerboard
of narrow glass canyons and shady streets
of townhouses.

It has many faces: sophisticated along
Fifth Avenue, bohemian and intellectual
in Greenwich Village, bustling on Times
Square and Broadway, bucolic in Central
Park, artistic in Chelsea, trendsetting
in TriBeCa, SoHo and NoLlta. Visitors
have an infinite choice of things to do:
museums, music, art galleries, theater –
Broadway and off. The borough of Brooklyn,
Manhattan's sprawling neighbor, is no
less fascinating, with its diverse, lively
'villages' (DUMBO, Williamsburg, Cobble
Hill), a mix of elegant brownstones, lofts
and warehouses taken over by artists
and writers. Further on, the melting pot
of Queens is home to Greek, Chinese and
Hispanic communities, and many more.

The city is dotted with neighborhood
cafés, lounge bars, diners, restaurants
serving food from all over the globe,
flea markets, boutiques, jazz clubs, arts
venues… Come and discover all the magic
New York has to offer with this MapGuide.

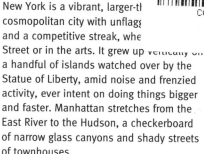

C000056160

CONTENTS

Unmissable sights

✪ Statue of Liberty / Ellis Island

Icons of the New World

STATUE OF LIBERTY (A A4)

→ *Ferry from battery Park*
Tel. (877) 523 9849; statuecruises.com
Summer: Daily 8.30am–4.30pm; Winter: Daily 9.30am–3.30pm; Admission $18.50–21.50 (ferry included)
Originally created to mark Franco-American friendship, the Statue of Liberty Enlightening the World has now become an internationally recognized emblem of both New York and the United States.

Visit
The most popular monument in the city receives some 4 million visitors every year. Such levels of popularity were unimaginable in 1886, when France completed the delivery of this allegorical statue as a gift to the United States. (The head and torch-bearing arm had already been constructed and exhibited in American fairs.) It was shipped across the Atlantic in no less than 270 crates.

The Statue of Liberty was designed by the sculptor Frédéric Bartholdi, in collaboration with Gustave Eiffel, who provided an interior metal framework to stabilize the giant 150-ft figure (305 ft including the pedestal). Inside, an exhibition traces its history, while the 10th floor (at the level of its crown) offers stunning views of the southernmost tip of Manhattan.

ELLIS ISLAND (A A4)

→ *Ferry from Battery Park*
Less than half a mile from the Statue of Liberty, Ellis Island served as an immigrant inspection station for 12 million people from 1892 to 1954. The station was transferred here in 1890 from its original site in Manhattan. By then, there had been a huge increase in applications to migrate to the US, which was in need of manpower to build its cities and industries: some days as many as 5,000 people landed on this small island (formerly a munitions depot). In 1900 the old wooden shacks were replaced by a neo-Renaissance building that now serves as an immigration museum paying tribute to the crucial contributions made by this influx of newcomers: 40% of today's Americans have at least one forebear who passed through here. The island's other buildings (only open to guided tours) include the hospital, morgue, quarantine quarters and offices.

Ellis Island Immigration Museum
→ *Tel. (877) 523 9849*
Summer: Daily 8.30am–4.30pm
Winter: Daily 9.30am–3.30pm
Admission free (ferry ticket $13)
This museum spread over three floors explores the hopefuls who passed through Ellis Island as well as American immigration as a whole. The ground floor displays the luggage carried by the migrants, and screens documentaries (tickets issued in the entrance hall). The Great Hall on the second floor immortalizes the crowds that once gathered to await an inspection of 3–7 hours that would decide their fate and filter out the sick. On the third floor, the exhibition *Treasures from Home* presents 2,000 objects that those aspiring Americans brought with them.

✪ World Trade Center

Finance and remembrance at
the foot of the towers

THE SITE (A C3)
→ Church / Vesey / West / Liberty Sts

The Twin Towers, the targets of the terrorist
attacks of September 11, 2001, were the heart of
the World Trade Center, but now new skyscrapers
have been put up and high finance is once again
in full swing in the neighborhood, albeit with an
added vocation to be a site of remembrance and
contemplation.

The history

The World Trade Center opened in 1973 and for
almost 30 years it was the nexus of the financial
district, with more than 50,000 people working
there and a further 200,000 visiting it every
month. Then, in a space of less than 20 minutes
on September 11, 2001 (9/11), two hijacked
airplanes hurtled into the two towers that
symbolized American prosperity and brought
them to the ground. After years of construction
work (still incomplete), the business community
has honored the promise made just hours after
the attack by the then mayor of New York,
Rudolph Giuliani: 'We will rebuild'. Since 2016,
the striking Oculus, a spectacular white bird
with an undeniable allegorical impact, designed
by the Spanish architect Santiago Calatrava,
has covered the new public transport hub
serving the site (after 15 years of a provisional
station).

9/11 MEMORIAL (A C3)
→ 180 Greenwich St
Tel. (212) 267 2047; 911memorial.org
Daily 7.30am–9pm
Admission free

In place of the Twin Towers, *Reflecting Absence*
(2011), created by Michael Arad, pays tribute to
their spirit, as well as their former location, via
two pools hollowed out of the ground, with water
running continually down their walls. The names
of the attack's 3,000-odd victims are engraved
on the parapet. The memorial is linked to the
rest of the city by the gardens that surround it,
under the name of the Memorial Plaza.

9/11 MEMORIAL MUSEUM (A C3)
→ Church St / Vesey St / West St / Liberty Sts
Tel. (212) 266 5211; 911memorial.org
Daily 9am–8pm (9pm Fri-Sat); Admission $24

This underground museum below the site of the
9/11 attacks pays homage to its victims and to
all those who risked their lives to save others
(particularly the firefighters: nearly 350 were
killed in the rescue operation). Photos, eye-
witness accounts and items salvaged from the
rubble poignantly convey the human drama of
that day.

ONE WORLD TRADE CENTER (1WTC) (A C3)
→ 285 Fulton St / West St
Tel. (844) 696 1776; oneworldobservatory.com
Daily 9am (8am May-Aug)–9pm (closed Jan-early Feb)
Admission $34

The attack left Manhattan with a gaping hole
in its emblematic skyline, and new towers have
been put up to help fill it (with others still under
construction). Since 2013, the One World Trade
Center, designed by David Childs, has dominated
this cluster of skyscrapers, due to its 408-ft
antenna and overall height (unsurpassed
in the US) of 1,776 ft (in honor of the year of the
Declaration of Independence). Clad entirely in
glass, the Freedom Tower, as it is known, has an
observatory with dizzying views of the city on its
100th floor, a full 1,246 ft above ground level.

✪ Empire State Building

The legendary skyscraper with incomparable views

EMPIRE STATE BUILDING (E A5)
→ *350 5th Ave / W 33rd St*
Tel. (212) 736 3100; esbnyc.com
Daily 8am–2am (last elevator to 86th floor at 1.15am)
Admission $34 (86th floor), $54 (102nd floor)

Ever since 1931, the year of its opening, this has been the best vantage point for an overview of Manhattan. Its unmistakable silhouette, topped with a thin antenna, became the stuff of legends in 1933 when King Kong planted Fay Wray on its peak. Its terrace, and its breathtaking panoramic vista of the city, has featured in countless romantic movies, such as *An Affair to Remember* (1957), with Cary Grant and Deborah Kerr.

Construction

Its summit, at 1,250 ft (or almost 1,475 ft counting the antenna), enabled the Empire State Building (ESB) to hold the title of the world's highest building for almost 40 years. It was dreamed up in the golden years of the 1920s but opened on May 1, 1931, during the Great Depression. Its subsequent lack of tenants gave rise to the nickname of the Empty State Building. But, its imposing size, mythical status in popular culture and attraction to tourists allowed it to stay afloat until the economic tide turned. Its construction, undertaken by the architectural firm of Shreve, Lamb and Harmon, was a prodigious feat in itself, as its rate of 4.5 floors a week (excluding the foundations) meant that it was completed in a mere 13 months. The ESB's refurbishment some 80 years later would require more time, but it did succeed in considerably reducing the building's energy consumption: an exhibition on the 2nd floor illustrates the changes that were made.

The lobby

THE ESB is a legend from top to bottom; the lobby sets the tone with a ceiling covered with Art-Deco frescos. On the back wall, the image in relief of the glowing ESB emanating rays of light is maybe even more well-known than that of the building itself.

Exhibition

On the 80th floor, the exhibition *Dare to Dream* traces the evolution of the building from the initial design to its completion. Sketches, notes and photos document this adventure, which involved 3,400 workers, including the famous 'sky boys' who were responsible for riveting the metal frame at vertiginous heights without any safety precautions at all.

Observation posts

The main observation platform on the 86th floor encircles the building and thus offers a 360° view of New York and beyond. Manhattan itself can be read like a map, with landmarks like Central Park, the nearby Chrysler Building and Brooklyn Bridge instantly recognizable. Closer inspection, using the grid system for guidance, makes it possible to pinpoint less prominent reference points. Visitors with a good head for heights can take a final elevator to another observation post on the 102nd floor (although it is debatable whether it is worth paying an extra $20 for views that are essentially very similar).

The multicolored skyscraper

The ESB serves not only as a geographical landmark but also as a calendar. The colors of its illumination change with the seasons: from red, white and blue for Independence Day to red and green at Christmas time and green alone for St Patrick's Day – and, when required, it remains plunged in darkness to mark a tragic event.

✪ The High Line

An architectural and botanical stroll along the tracks

THE GREENWAY (B A3)

→ *Between Gansevoort St and W 34th St*
Entrance by steps: 14th St, 16th St, 18th St,
20th St, 23rd St, 26th St, 28th St, 30th St and 34th St
Entrance by elevator or ramp: 14th St, 16th St, 23rd St,
30th St and 34th St
thehighline.org
June-Sep: Daily 7am–11pm; Oct-Nov, April-May:
Daily 7am–10pm; Dec-March: Daily 7am–7pm
Admission free

This unique public garden is perched 33 ft above ground level and stretches for 1.5 miles alongside an old railroad track. It is highly appreciated by New Yorkers as an architecturally diverse stroll, with abundant greenery and fine views of the Hudson.

Turning a railroad into a garden

In 1980 the growth of trucking led to the closure of the aerial train line linking Gansevoort Market with Chelsea and 34th St. In subsequent years the tracks became overrun with vegetation but in 1999 a neighborhood association set about transforming them into a park inspired by the Coulée Verte in Paris. Construction work began in 2006 and one section opened to the public in 2009 – with two others following in 2011 and 2014.

Nature

The choice of plants was largely determined by the species that had established themselves in the 25 years in which the railroad fell into disuse, although their textures and colors were also taken into account. Flowers and shrubs predominate up to 20th St but the park then acquires more substantial trees and lawn areas up to 30th St before ceding to wild grass in the upper reaches. These diverse settings can be appreciated from a range of belvederes and benches, or from the sunbeds available at 14th St (the best views of sunset are from here!).

Culture

The High Line is also decorated with works of art: fifteen temporary installations are spread along its route. High Line activities include: meditation, Tai chi for beginners, a honey harvest from High Line bees, Art & Design tours, experimental performances, Latin music and more. See *art.thehighline.org* for details.

Architecture

The raised walkway winds through such an array of buildings that it provides a veritable cross-section of modern architectural styles. The glazed belvedere at the junction of 10th Ave and 17th St, for example, reveals Manhattan's second-highest office block, 30 Hudson Yards (2019), while the white waves of Frank Gehry's IAC Building (2007) can be fully appreciated at 555 W 18th St. Just behind it, the distinctive façade of Jean Nouvel's block at 100 11th Ave (2010) has 1,600 glass panels, all tilted at different angles. At W 23rd St, Neil Denari's HL23 (2012) seems to be hovering above the High Line, while the section to the north, between 30th St and 34th St, is the stage for one of the city's most ambitious urban renewal projects. By 2025 the Hudson Yards is predicted to include 4,000 homes, around 100 stores and the HQs of several top-ranking corporations – all revolving around Thomas Heatherwick's *Vessel* (2018), a beehive-like structure incorporating 150 staircases (with a grand total of 2,500 steps!).

⭐ Fifth Avenue

Grandeur and festivities on the most famous avenue in the world

FIFTH AVENUE (**E** A1-A6, **G** C1-C4)
The legendary Fifth Avenue divides Manhattan down the middle, running for over 5 miles and crossing more than 130 streets between Washington Square (**B** C4) and Harlem (**H** C1). It is lined by some of New York's most emblematic buildings.

Architecture
Going northward, the first architectural reference point is the triangular Flatiron Building (**B** D1) at no. 175, followed by the Empire State Building (**E** A5) at no. 350. Further up, at no. 455, is the New York Public Library (**E** A4)), guarded by sculpted lions. Many other architectural wonders are located only a short walk from Fifth Avenue: the imposing railroad station of Grand Central Terminal (**E** B4), and the Chrysler and Chanin Buildings (**E** B4), both veritable Art-Deco masterpieces. Back on the Avenue, the approach to Central Park (**G** B2) coincides with St Patrick's Cathedral (**E** A2), near 50th St, and the Trump Tower (**E** A1), at no. 725. Further north, on the Upper East Side, the Museum Mile boasts

nine major museums, as well as early 20th-century mansions competing with each other in levels of ostentation.

Museums
The Museum Mile is the stretch of Fifth Avenue running from 70th St to 104th St. The flagships are the Metropolitan Museum of Art (**G** C1), at no. 1000, and the Guggenheim Museum (**G** C1) at no. 1071, but they should not be allowed to overshadow their smaller but equally prestigious neighbors: at E 70th St, the Frick Collection (**G** C3) houses the collection of an industrialist with exquisite good taste (Bellini, Vermeer, Goya); at no. 1048, the Neue Galerie (**G** C1) has an extraordinary selection of German and Austrian art from the period 1890–1940 (the Jugendstil, Blaue Reiter and Bauhaus movements). Superb work is also on show at the Cooper-Hewitt Design Museum (**H** C6) at 91st St; the cultural and historical Jewish Museum (**H** C6) at no. 1109; and at no. 1230 the vibrant Museo del Barrio (**H** C5), explores art from Puerto Rico and the rest of Latin America.

Shopping
The world's most important brands are always represented on Fifth Avenue (Nike, Apple, Louis Vuitton). At no. 727, the up-market jewelry store Tiffany & Co. (**E** A1) that so entranced Audrey Hepburn in *Breakfast at Tiffany's* still provides a dazzling spectacle today, with pieces such as the Tiffany Diamond on the main floor and the more accessibly priced 'fantasy jewelry' on the 3rd floor. Not to be missed is the department store Saks (**E** A2), which set up shop at no. 611 nearly a century ago; and Bergdorf Goodman at 59th and Fifth Ave (**E** A1) is a smaller department store but well-curated.

Festivities
Fifth Avenue often provides a stage on which New Yorkers gather to celebrate special occasions. Two million people assemble here on March 17 for the St Patrick Day's Parade, while the Hispanic communities organize a procession on the second Sunday of October, followed the next day by Columbus Day celebrations that exuberantly assert Italian-American identity. Other parades are organized for Easter and Gay Pride Day (see **Diary of Events** in the *Practicalities* section, page 19).

✪ The Museum of Modern Art (MoMA)

Art for our times

MUSEUM OF MODERN ART (MoMA) (D F1)
→ *11 W 53rd St (between 5th Ave and 6th Ave)*
Tel. (212) 708 9400; moma.org
Daily 10.30am–5.30pm (8pm Thu)
Admission $25 (free Fri 4–8pm)

Abby Aldrich Rockefeller, Lillie P. Bliss and Mary Quinn Sullivan, three visionary women who were intent on freeing art from an image that they considered overly conservative, provided the impulse to establish what was then the first museum exclusively devoted to contemporary and modern art. It opened its doors on November 7, 1929, a mere nine days after the Stock Market Crash, but nevertheless, the museum met with immediate success: in the first ten years it had to move to bigger premises three times because its collection expanded so rapidly.

The building
MoMA has occupied its present site since 1939 but it has been repeatedly enlarged. In 2004 Yoshio Taniguchi doubled its size with a major renovation. In 2019, further expansion designed by the architects Diller Scofidio + Renfro provides 50,000 square feet of new gallery space.

Painting and sculpture
MoMA's painting and sculpture collection is so wide-ranging that it cannot be adequately summarized. It comprises some 3,600 artworks dating from the late nineteenth century to the present, including Van Gogh's *Starry Night*, Matisse's *Red Studio*, Picasso's *Demoiselles d'Avignon*, Duchamp's *Bicycle Wheel*, Warhol's *Campbell's Soup Cans* and several of Jackson Pollock's drip paintings. This mind-boggling depth and diversity is complemented by meticulously curated temporary exhibitions.

Drawing
The drawing department owns 10,000 artworks created on paper in pencil, charcoal, ink, gouache, watercolor and collage.

Architecture and design
The first museum department ever devoted to architecture and design was launched in 1932

on the premise that these two art forms are inextricably linked. All the major trends from the Arts and Crafts movement (mid-19th century) to the present day are represented through plans, models, sketches and objects.

Photography
MoMA was one of the first museums to take this discipline seriously and it now has an archive of 25,000 photos, taken by major figures like Brassaï, Man Ray and Cindy Sherman but also by journalists, scientists and amateurs. The biannual New Photography exhibition (late Sep-early Jan) sets out to promote new talent.

Contemporary art
The protean nature of contemporary art is reflected in the diversity of media on show here. This line of enquiry can be continued in Queens: a ticket to MoMA provides the holder with free access, within 30 days, to MoMA PS1 (J C3), which is entirely devoted to contemporary art.

Sculpture Garden
The garden designed by the architect Philip Johnson in 1953 and reconfigured in 2004 is dotted with pieces by Calder, Matisse, Picasso, Maillol, etc.

Film/cinema
The film collection covers a broad range of periods and styles that are explored through themed exhibitions and screenings.

✪ Central Park

A vast green space amidst the hubbub of the city

CENTRAL PARK (G B2)
→ *centralparknyc.org*
Daily 6am–1am

This marvelous green space surrounded on three sides by apartment buildings and hotels is New York's lung, an unlikely luxury in a densely populated city devoted to real estate. Its huge expanse (875 yards wide and 2.5 miles long) includes ponds, wooded hills, hidden paths, elegant esplanades and vast lawns.

Origins

In 1857, when New York's population had reached around 200,000, the need arose for a green space. The city organized a competition for proposals to landscape marshland that was in its possession and the winners were Frederick Law Olmsted and Calvert Vaux. Over the course of 16 years they cleared and drained a swamp, before backfilling it and introducing vegetation to create an inviting, romantic garden space.

Sports facilities

Many New Yorkers use the park to go skate boarding, jogging or cycling but there are also areas specifically designated for sports: a skating rink, a swimming pool and tennis, basketball and volleyball courts. Less energetic citizens content themselves with chess and backgammon in the Visitor Center (**G** B4), or enjoy the tranquility and views of the skyline from Sheep Meadow (**G** B3), which was grazed by sheep until 1934.

A wildlife refuge

Central Park is home to many animal species, with countless rabbits, groundhogs and squirrels. It also serves as a sanctuary and stopover for migratory birds: the specially chosen plants in the North Meadow Butterfly Gardens (**H** B5) attract not only butterflies and countless other insects but birds on their way to or from Mexico. Peregrine falcons and Red-tail hawks are around too. Other animals live here in captivity: more exotic specimens in the Central Park Zoo (**G** C4) and more familiar farmyard species in the Tisch Children's Zoo (**G** C3). Untouched Nature is evident along the craggy paths running through the Ramble (**G** B2) while formally laid-out beds can be seen in the Conservatory Garden (**H** C5).

Going with the flow

Waterfalls, fountains and bridges all contribute to the picture-postcard image of Central Park, along with three expanses of water. From south to north, these are the Pond (**G** C4), where the ducks seem to know how to pose for photos; the Lake (**G** B3), crossed since 1862 by the striking Bow Bridge (**G** B2), where visitors can rent a rowboat from the Loeb Boathouse (**G** C2) from April to October; and the Jacqueline Kennedy Onassis Reservoir (**G** B1), which can be walked around on a 1.5-mile footpath.

The arts, past and present

Central Park has provided inspiration for artists from many fields, and the Mall (**G** B3), the park's main thoroughfare, repays the compliment with the statues of writers and musicians set along its edges. Strawberry Fields (**F** D4) commemorates John Lennon, who lived nearby, while the Shakespeare Garden assembles plants cited in the Bard's plays – and these very plays are performed for free every summer in the open-air Delacorte Theater (**G** B2). Seasonal fine weather is also the cue for concerts on the SummerStage (**G** C3) and numerous performances on the Bethesda Terrace (**G** B3) at weekends.

✪ The Metropolitan Museum of Art (Met)

Five thousand years of art and history

THE METROPOLITAN MUSEUM OF ART (G C1)
→ 1,000 5th Ave/E 82nd St
Tel. (212) 535 7710; metmuseum.org
Daily 10am–5.30pm (9pm Fri-Sat)
Guided tours: Daily 10.15am–4pm
(starts every 15 mins from the Great Hall)
Admission (for non-NY residents) $25
One of the world's great museums, organized into 21 departments, each one overflowing with masterpieces. Any comprehensive investigation would take three days (at least!), so it is advisable to decide on a particular focus beforehand.

History
The idea of a national institution devoted to the artistic education of the population was kindled in the mid-19th century in Paris, based on the model that had already emerged in European cities. The first Met opened its doors in 1870, in a temporary home (a brownstone at 681 5th Ave) but in 1880 Calvert Vaux constructed a redbrick building on a plot near Central Park, donated for this purpose by City Hall. The first extension was completed in 1888, while the Beaux-Arts façade and the Grand Hall serving as the museum's entrance were added in 1902. Subsequent expansions have had to do with the mushrooming of its collection.

Must-sees in the Met
On the main floor, the Egyptian section is particularly striking, with the remains of the Temple of Dendur, transported here from the banks of the Nile. Nearby, the American wing presents an exceptional selection of paintings, sculptures and decorative artworks, including Tiffany stained glass and an entire room designed by Frank Lloyd Wright. The arms and armor department has dazzling samurai tunics from the 16th–18th centuries. On the same floor, Greek and Roman arts, exhibited in natural light, are one of the highlights of the museum – as is the art from Africa, Oceania and the Americas; and on the second floor, from Asia, and the Islamic world. The collection of paintings is extraordinary, with countless masterpieces from various schools: the Renaissance (Fra Angelico, Botticelli), the Dutch masters (Vermeer, Rembrandt), the Cubists (Braque, Picasso), the Impressionists (Monet, Renoir), etc.

Met Breuer (**G** C2)
→ 945 Madison Ave (corner of E 75th St)
Tel. (212) 731 1675; Tue-Sun 10am–5.30pm (9pm Fri-Sat)
Admission (for non-NY residents) $25
(also valid in the Met/Cloisters for 3 days)
The department of modern and contemporary art displays work by many American pioneers: Edward Hopper, Norman Rockwell, Andy Warhol. Since 2016 it has been housed in the Breuer Building, a few blocks from the Met. There are also groundbreaking shows.

The Cloisters
→ Fort Tryon Park Subway, stop 190th St (A Line)
Tel. (212) 923 3700; March-Oct: Daily 10am–5.15pm
Nov-Feb: Daily 10am–4.45pm; Admission (for non-NY residents) $25 (also valid in the Met/Breuer for 3 days)
This museum of medieval art, high on a bluff with great views of the Hudson, opened in 1938 in what was then countryside, has assembled entire sections of churches, chapels and cloisters from various parts of Europe, along with tapestries, stained-glass windows and Limoges enamels.

✪ Guggenheim Museum

Not simply a museum...more a sculpture in its own right

THE GUGGENHEIM MUSEUM (G C1)
→ 1,071 5th Ave/E 89th St
Tel. (212) 423 3500
guggenheim.org
Fri-Wed 10am–5.45pm (7.45pm Sat)
Guided tours: Fri-Wed 2pm
Admission $25 (pay what you wish Sat 5.45–7.45pm)

This building has been startling visitors, both inside and outside, ever since it opened in 1959 and it is now generally considered a masterpiece of 20th-century architecture. The Guggenheim boasts a collection of some 5,000 works. These represent the main movements in modern and contemporary art but lack of space means that only 3% of them are on view at any one time. All exhibitions are reached via the sinuous ramp that winds its way round the museum's six floors.

The building
In 1939 the collector Solomon R. Guggenheim opened his 'museum of non-figurative painting' at 24 East 54th St (under the auspices of the foundation that bears his name). Four years later he commissioned Frank Lloyd Wright to design a

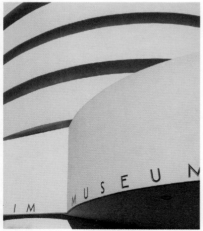

showcase worthy of the treasures he had amassed, but neither man would live to see the completed building. The entire creative process took 16 years in all, including three years of construction. In 1992 the museum was rounded off by an eight-story annex designed by Gwathmey Siegel, reflecting Wright's original intention – stymied by a lack of funds – to build a 10-floor tower behind the rotunda to provide office and storage space.

The galleries
The uninterrupted central space was designed, according to Wright himself, to avoid any 'meeting of the eye with angular or abrupt changes'. Natural light pours in from a height of 100 ft through a glass cupola, which is reached by a 440-yard spiral ramp lined with the works on show in the various temporary exhibitions. Even today, this remains a radically different approach to the presentation of art, as visitors can see works on various levels at the same time: this sets up dialogues not only between different artworks but also between them and their extraordinary setting. These powerful impressions are further enhanced by the hypnotic sight of a continuous parade of visitors walking up or down the ramp.

The collections
The more conventional rooms in the rectangular building play host to some of the 600 abstract paintings collected by the museum's founder, Solomon Guggenheim. These include works by Kandinsky, Bauer and Delaunay. Another of the museum's patrons, Justin K. Thannhauser (1892–1976) contributed works by the Impressionists and 20th-century painters, particularly the German Expressionists: Cézanne, Renoir, Degas, Manet, Picasso, Karl Nierendorf.

The Foundation
The Solomon R. Guggenheim Foundation is devoted to 'promoting the understanding and appreciation of art, primarily of the modern and contemporary periods'. After New York, it branched out: the Peggy Guggenheim Collection is housed in the Palazzo Venier del Leoni in Venice, while the Guggenheim museums in both Bilbao (1997) and Abu Dhabi (2019) occupy spectacular buildings designed by Frank Gehry.

✪ Brooklyn

This enormous borough conceals unexpected treasures

THE BOROUGH

Many visitors to New York imagine that the only attraction to be found on the other side of Brooklyn Bridge is a spectacular view of Manhattan Island. This is a serious underestimation of the sheer size of Brooklyn: in terms of population, its 2.5 million inhabitants would be sufficient to make it the fourth largest city in the whole of the United States. In fact, although Brooklyn was founded in 1646, it only became a part of New York City in 1898. It is now home to vibrant communities from Latin America, the Caribbean and Eastern Europe, as well as a hip under-30 working population, and has plenty to offer visitors on the cultural, artistic and architectural fronts.

The Neighborhoods

Brooklyn is bounded to the west by the East River, to the north by Queens and to the south by the Atlantic – its southwestern tip is occupied by Coney Island, with its legendary amusement park (see *Day Trips* pages (**L**). The borough's neighborhoods range from Brooklyn Heights, with its immaculate brownstones, to DUMBO, replete with art galleries, and the upmarket Park Slope, bordered by the enormous green space of Prospect Park. These days, however, Williamsburg has become the hotspot for locals, thanks to its countless shops and bars, particularly in the old industrial premises around Bedford Avenue.

BROOKLYN BRIDGE (I B1)

The utterly distinctive silhouette of the bridge's two massive gray stone towers has become one of New York's most enduring symbols. Its construction began in 1869, spurred by a drive to replace the slow and overcrowded steam boats which, at that time, were ferrying some 50 million people across the East River every year. Completed in 1883, it was the longest bridge of the age – and the highest – soaring 130 ft above the surface of the water. A walk or ride along its pedestrian or bike lanes in the early morning or evening provides some breathtaking views of

Manhattan, particularly the skyscrapers of the Financial District. Below it, the lawns of the Brooklyn Bridge Park (**I** B2) also offer a strategic, and more relaxed, vantage point.

BROOKLYN MUSEUM (I D5)

→ *200 Eastern Parkway*
Tel. (718) 638 5000; brooklynmuseum.org
Although the Brooklyn Museum, which opened in 1897, is slightly off the tourist trail it is more than a match for the Met with its huge collections of art from Egypt, Asia and Europe and, most particularly, Africa. Back in 1923 this museum became one of the first to exhibit African items for their artistic rather than ethnographic value and it now boasts one of the finest American collections in this field, covering more than 100 different cultures. The works range from Amazigh (Berber) jewelry to West African masks, from Ethiopian processional crosses to ceramics by the contemporary Kenyan artist Magdalene Odundo. Brooklyn Museum also puts on exciting retrospectives of contemporary New York artists (Keith Haring, Basquiat) and prioritizes the involvement of the local community. Every first Saturday of the month admission is free from 5–11pm and the exhibitions are complemented by guided tours, concerts, video screenings and performances. See the *Walks* pages (**K**), **On the Brooklyn Waterfront.**

New York in 3 days

Capture the essence of the city on a long weekend!

FRIDAY

9.30am
Before tackling Manhattan itself, take a trip outside, to the Ellis Island Immigration Museum (**A** A4), with a stopover at the Statue of Liberty (**A** A4), or, via a free round trip, to Staten Island, with its splendid views of Downtown. Back on land, visit another site full of historic significance: the World Trade Center (WTC) (**A** C3) and its museum and memorial paying homage to the victims of the attack on September 11, 2001.

11am
Head from the leafy paths of Battery Park (**A** C4), with its stunning views of the Hudson, to Wall St (**A** D3), where some of the narrowest streets in New York are flanked by vertiginous skyscrapers.

1pm
Take lunch alongside workers from the Financial District in one of the restaurants on Stone St: the terrace at Adrienne's Pizza Bar (**A** D3) is particularly pleasant in fine weather.

2.30pm
The East River is close by: at the South Street Seaport (**A** E3), the wooden deckchairs on the remodeled dock are ideal for a nap, or photos with the iconic outline of the Brooklyn Bridge (**I** B1) in the background.

3.30pm
Immerse yourself in another culture in Chinatown (**C** A6), where even the street signs are written in ideograms as well as English.

4.30pm
In SoHo, an architectural tour can be combined with window shopping, as many of the hippest stores have a classic wrought-iron façade. The best barometer of the latest trends is invariably the concept store Opening Ceremony (**B** D6).

5.30pm
Sit on a bench in Washington Square (**B** C4) and soak up the relaxing vibe, with chess players concentrating intently on their games, seemingly oblivious to the informal music-making in the background.

7pm
Dine in the heart of Greenwich Village for informal Indian fare at Baba Ji (**B** D3) or Italian at Via Carota (**B** B4).

8pm
Check out the rising stars at a concert in one of the city's legendary shrines of jazz: the Village Vanguard (**B** B3) or the Blue Note (**B** C4).

SATURDAY

8am
Take a bracing early-morning elevator ride to the 86th floor of the Empire State Building (**E** A5) and marvel at the breathtaking views of the city.

10am
Breakfast in one of the cafés in Macy's (**D** E4), one of the world's great department stores, with seven floors to explore.

11.30am
There is no need for a train journey to revel in the grandiose splendor of Grand Central Terminal (**E** B4). On the way there, its Art Deco neighbors, the Chanin and Chrysler Buildings (**E** B4), are equally imposing. For lunch, Cipriani Dolci (**E** B4) serves delicious Italian food; or try Grand Central Oyster Bar – sit at the bar for lower prices, or assemble a picnic from the Grand Central Market.(**E** B4). For dessert, delicious cakes from Lady M (**D** E3), eaten in the tranquility of Bryant Park (**D** E3).

1.30pm
There is a danger of sensory overload on Fifth Avenue, with the dazzling store windows below and some of the world's most famous skyscrapers soaring above.

2pm
There are always interesting temporary shows and many different kinds of art in the Museum of Modern Art (MoMA, **D** F1): Fauvism, Cubism, Surrealism, etc. On the way out, the MoMA Design Store (**D** E1) is worth a visit in its own right.

4.30pm
Rockefeller Plaza (**D** F2) is occupied by either a café terrace or a skating rink, depending on the season. At any time of year, however, Paul Manship's monumental sculpture of Prometheus is an impressive sight, while Rockefeller Center (**D** E2), a group of 19 buildings (14 from the 1930s), contains over 100 shops.

6pm
The Salon de Ning (**E** A2), 23 stories up, is an ideal setting for an evening drink. Choose between the rooftop terrace and the colorful interior.

7pm
This area abounds in economically priced eateries: Israeli Druze

specialties in Gazala Place (**D** C2), Japanese ramen in Ippudo (**D** D2).

8pm
Catch a smash-hit musical on Broadway: *Hamilton, Phantom of the Opera, Frozen...* having booked well in advance!

11pm
Check out Times Square (**D** E3) with its garish neon lights and buzzing energy. Have a nightcap at the nearby Joe Allen (**D** D2)

SUNDAY

9.30am
Enjoy a rousing start to the day with the gospel music that accompanies a service in the First Corinthian Baptist Church (**H** B4) in Harlem.

11am
Time for brunch at the Red Rooster (**H** C3) or Chez Lucienne (**H** C3).

12.30pm
Get into the swing of New York life by taking part in the ritual of a Sunday stroll in Central Park (**G** B2). Alternatives to walking are provided by bicycles and horse-drawn carriages.

2pm
Stop at the stunning Guggenheim Museum (**G** C1) on the way to the Metropolitan Museum of Art (**G** C1) – then allow at least two hours to get a taste of the treasures on display in its 21 different

departments. (If you want to avoid crowds, go in the morning.)

4pm
Time to cross the river and head to Williamsburg, currently Brooklyn's most fashionable neighbourhood, a mere 45 minutes away on the subway (line 4 or 5 to 14th St, then the L Line to Bedford Ave). Or you may prefer to explore DUMBO and Brooklyn Heights on the other side of Manhattan Bridge. See also *Walks* pages (**K**).

5pm
Check out the men's and women's vintage clothing at 10 ft by Stella Dallas (**J** B6) or at Antoinette (**J** B6).

6pm
Relax with a drink in the Ides Bar (**J** B5) on the 6th floor of the Wythe Hotel, and enjoy stunning views of Manhattan.

7pm
Dinner at Lilia (**J** B5), for veal bolognese with pappardelle.

8pm
Take in a rock concert at the Knitting Factory (**J** B6), and then hang out in the bar afterwards. Or head back to Manhattan to Arlene's Grocery (**C** B4) to listen to some new bands.

AN EXTRA DAY?

An opportunity to stray from the beaten path...
Governors Island
→ *Ferry from Battery Park May-Oct: Daily 10am–6pm (7pm Sat-Sun) govisland.com*
On fine days, this tiny island off the southern tip of Manhattan is a perfect getaway: a great place to bike or take in a seasonal art fair.
Meatpacking District (**B** A3)
Top fashion brands have set up shop in the former slaughterhouses on Greenwich Street, along with elegant bars and restaurants. The Whitney Museum of American Art, which specializes in work from the 20th–21st centuries, is also in this neighbourhood.
The High Line (**B** A3)
Take a stroll 33 ft above ground level along a former railroad track, now a lush park.
See also p. 5.
United Nations (**E** D3)
The United Nations HQ is the workplace of 5,000 delegates from 193 member states.
Frick Collection (**G** C3)
The masterpieces collected by Henry Clay Frick, on show in his neoclassical palace (Goya, Rembrandt, Turner).
Brooklyn Museum (**I** D5)
Breathtaking collections over 12 departments in a museum on a par with the Met. *See also page 11.*

MACY'S

Do as the locals do

Photograph Manhattan

Join a long line of renowned photographers and take your camera onto the streets of New York to capture fleeting moments, architectural details and striking design. For urban landscapes, head to Williamsburg Bridge (**J** A6) or cross Brooklyn Bridge (**I** B1) and station yourself in Brooklyn Bridge Park (**I** B2).

Eat on the hoof in Chelsea Market (**B** A2)

This highly distinctive food market, set in a superbly restored Nabisco factory, offers cupcakes in every color imaginable, lobster sandwiches, artisanal bread, chocolates and other typically American fare, but also delicious Thai curries and Italian ice cream.

→ *Avoid the weekend crush (or arrive early)*

Discount clothes

Fashion victims on the lookout for bargains flock to Century 21 (**A** C3) and often emerge dressed from head to toe by big-name brands (Ralph Lauren, Marc Jacobs, Calvin Klein, etc.), having saved from 40 to 85% on the usual cost. Allow plenty of time for a good rummage: the shoe department alone has 20,000 pairs to choose from!

→ *Arrive early (7.45am) to avoid the crowds*

Explore Street Art

New York street art did not stop with Jean-Michel Basquiat and Keith Haring. It renews itself constantly – think Banksy – as murals, graffiti, stencils and collages in several lively neighborhoods, particularly the East Village (**C**), Harlem (**H**) and Williamsburg (**J**).

→ *Be sure to check out the quieter streets*

Delight in Asian food

New York's Asian communities are steeped in sophisticated culinary traditions. The aroma of Beijing duck hangs in the air in Chinatown, while elsewhere there is an abundance of Malaysian, Japanese, Korean, Indian, Cambodian, etc. stores and restaurants.

→ *Momofuku Noodle Bar (**C** B3), Hangawi (**E** A6)*

Stroll along the banks of the Hudson River

New York has a tradition of open-air activities that serve as a respite from its buzzing intensity. The sound of waves gently lapping against the piers on the Hudson to the north of Battery Park (**A** C4) are a reminder of the proximity of the sea. There are unexpected gardens, marinas and benches strategically placed to enjoy the sun setting over New Jersey, just across the water.

Enjoy a burger in Chelsea

Not all burgers are

OF INTEREST...

Rooftops
Rise above the hubbub of the city while enjoying spectacular views and a leisurely drink. **SixtyFive at Rainbow Room** (**D** E2), **230 Fifth** (**B** C1).

Banks of the East River
The promenades on these riverbanks are popular spots for picnics. Views of the Manhattan skyline from **Brooklyn Bridge Park** (**I** B2) and **Gantry Plaza State Park** (**J** B3).

Cycling
With its City Bikes (*see p. 24*), cycling lanes, hip bike stores and Summer Streets program (*see Diary of Events, p. 19*),

New York has become a very bicycle-friendly city.

Flea markets
Spot the latest trends at the Brooklyn Flea Markets (**I**) et (**J**).

→ *brooklynflea.com Sat-Sun 10am–5pm/6pm*

Local produce
Support Zero Kilometer food by eating in restaurants using ingredients grown close to the city and by shopping in organic stores supplied by local farmers. **Union Square Greenmarket** (**B** D2), **Community Food & Juice** (**H** A4), **Egg** (**J** B6).

Food trucks
Around Washington Square (**B** C4) or see *nyctruckfood.com*

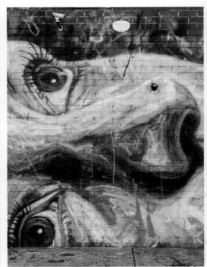

EXPLORE STREET ART

made equal....stop off at Cookshop (**B** A2) on Tenth Ave at 20th St in the heart of Chelsea's gallery district and order a delicious grass-fed burger in this light-filled room near the High Line. Great for people-watching if you sit outside when the weather is warm.

Sip a cocktail
Cocktails are big in New York! They can add a touch of glamor to a romantic encounter or mark the sealing of a business deal, and they can be enjoyed in various atmospheric settings: in a fashionable club with a stunning view, in the Ascent Lounge (**F** C6), on an elegant couch at the B Bar in the Baccarat Hotel (**D** F1), or in the extremely upmarket King Cole Bar (**E** A2). While you are downtown check out Le Bain on the 18th floor of The Standard (**B** A3) or Mr Purple on the 15th floor of the Hotel Indigo (171 Ludlow St, **C** B4) or The Roof at Public (215 Chrystie St, **C** B4).

See a show on Broadway (**D** D1)
Musicals, from *Hamilton* to *The Book of Mormon* and *Harry Potter and the Cursed Child*, have long been the lifeblood of the New York theater scene. Broadway is lined with famous theaters, and they also overflow on to Times Square, which is ablaze with garish neon signs.
→ *Cut-price tickets at the TKTS Broadway kiosk* (**D** E2)

Take in a jazz concert
Jazz was born in New Orleans and spread to New York's black community in the 1930s. The tradition continues to thrive today in Harlem, at the legendary Apollo Theater (**H** B3) and clubs such as Smoke (**H** A4) and Showman's (**H** B3), but the Village has developed equally flourishing venues: the historic Village Vanguard (**B** B3) and Blue Note (**B** C4).
→ *Consult the programs and book in advance*

Browse art in Chelsea or the Lower East Side
On a weekday or a Saturday, join art mavens browsing shows in the more than 350 art galleries in the blocks from 18th to 29th Sts between Tenth and the highway or Eleventh Avenues. Equally, check out the 75 galleries below East Houston. *See Art Galleries: best picks, p. 27.*

Take to the water
Being on the water off Manhattan is thrilling at sunset. In fine weather, ride the giant speedboat, *The Beast* (no toddlers allowed) for half an hour in the harbor. Or cruise the more sedate Circle Line around Manhattan.
→ *Cruises leave from Pier 83 (W 42nd) and 12th Ave*
→ *circleline42.com*

SIP A COCKTAIL

...AND EVEN ON SUNDAYS

Brunch
→ *Generally $10–30*
A New York institution. Bubby's (**A** B1), Buttermilk Channel (**I** B4)

Museums
Of a very high standard; can be crowded.

Parks
Something for everyone: watch street performers, see open-air concerts, enjoy a hot dog or ice cream...or simply lounge around on the grass. Central Park (**G** B2), Prospect Park (**I** D5)

Flea markets
Aside from the big names, there is a wealth of small impromptu markets: behind a church, on an empty lot, in a park...

Shopping
→ *Generally 10am–7pm*
Stores stay open in SoHo (**B**), Midtown (**E**), DUMBO (**I**) and Williamsburg (**J**)

Spectacles
The city that never sleeps has jazz clubs, concert halls and theaters that are as busy as ever. Village Vanguard (**B** B3), The Iridium (**D** D2), Beacon Theatre (**F** B3), Minton's (**H** B3), Ginny's Supper Club (**H** C3)

New York on a budget

Tips for enjoying the city for less!

FREE

Open-air cinema
Spectators bring their own rug to sit on the grass and watch a movie under the stars: McCarren Park (**J** B5) during the SummerScreen (*summerscreen.org*); Bryant Park (**D** E3), for the HBO Bryant Park Summer Film Festival (*bryantpark.org*).

Ferries
→ *siferry.com*
→ *govisland.com*
A return trip to Staten Island in the company of local commuters offers splendid views of Downtown. The boat trip to Governors Island is free Sat-Sun before 11.30am ($2 otherwise).

Art galleries
→ *artcards.cc*
→ *artcat.com*
→ *artslant.com*
Chelsea (**B** A1) offers contemporary art shows. Free drinks are sometimes available at exhibition openings on Thursday evenings. There are also major shows in galleries on 57th between Park and Sixth, on Madison between 76th and 79th, on 79th between Fifth and Madison, on 67th, 69th and 78th between Park and Madison, among others.

Open-air swimming pools
→ *Lasker Rink Central Park Tel. (212) 534 7639 Brooklyn Bridge Park Pop-Up Pool Pier 2*
Tel. (718) 222 9939
nycgovparks.org
Free swimming from July to Sep in pools in Central Park (**G** B2) and Brooklyn Bridge Park (**I** B2).

Concerts
Music open to all: Mon-night jam sessions in the Smoke Jazz and Supper Club (**H** A4), gospel services in the First Corinthian Baptist Church (**H** B4) and the SummerStage in Central Park (**G** B2).

Internet connection
Free Wi-Fi connection in public libraries.

EASY ON THE WALLET

City Pass
→ *citypass.com*
On sale in the box offices of participating museums and monuments.
Adults $126; 6-17 years $104; valid for 9 days
The pass provides access to several attractions: the Empire State Building, the Statue of Liberty, the Met, the Guggenheim Museum, the American Museum of Natural History, MoMA...

Museums
Free entry or pay-what-you-wish admission to some museums at certain times:
MoMA
→ *Free, Fridays 4–8pm*
Guggenheim Museum
→ *pay-what-you-wish, Saturdays 5.45–7.45pm*
The Frick Collection
→ *Free first Fri of the month; pay what you wish, Wed 2–6pm*
See page 21 for a full listing or consult each museum's website.

TKTS Broadway (**D** E2)
→ *Broadway / W 42nd St Daily 3–8pm (evenings); Wed, Sat 10am–2pm; Sun 11am–3pm (matinées)*
Discounts of 25–50% for Broadway shows (plus $3 booking fee) on the day of the performance (cash only).

Shopping
Fashionwear with reductions of up to 85% is available at Century 21 (**A** C3) and assorted bargains in the Hell's Kitchen Flea Market (**D** C3), the Dumbo Flea Market (**I** B1) and Beacon's Closet (**J** B5). The Front General Store (**I** B2) has good prices for both new and vintage articles.

Citi Bike
→ *citibikenyc.com*
Visitors can sign on for the residents' bike rental service for 24 hours ($12) or 3 days ($24), available in Manhattan, Brooklyn, Queens and Jersey City (first 30 mins free).

BYOB
Many restaurants have a policy of 'Bring Your Own Bottle' for wine (for example, Lucali, **I** A4), although some charge a corkage fee.

OPEN-AIR CINEMA

The city's neighborhoods

Each one with its own character and atmosphere...

Downtown (A)
This piece of land jutting out of south Manhattan seems to be reaching toward the Statue of Liberty. At its heart, Wall Street famously embodies the financial sector, but Downtown is also defined by water, as it is flanked by the Hudson River (to the west) and the East River. A stroll along their attractively renovated banks in Battery Park or in the old docks on South Street offers a respite from the fast pace of the city.

TriBeCa, Soho (A, B)
New York loves its acronyms! TriBeCa (Triangle Below Canal) is one of the oldest, referring to an area with an industrial past that can still be detected in its converted buildings. SoHo (South of Houston) was home to many artists in the 1960s but is now a hipster stronghold. Its wrought-iron façades, familiar from countless movies, conceal wonderful shopping opportunities, particularly in fashionwear and furniture.

Greenwich Village, Chelsea (B)
Greenwich Village extends around Washington Square Park. The winding streets are known by names rather than numbers, evoking the Bohemian spirit associated with the Village, home to many celebrated 20th-century writers and artists, which played a prominent role in the emergence of the Gay Liberation movement. Going toward Chelsea, the grid system re-establishes itself, complete with numbered streets, and both the property market and the art scene are clearly thriving, as evidenced by the countless galleries. To the west, Chelsea is bordered by the High Line.

Chinatown, Little Italy, NoLIta (C)
Chinatown offers a total immersion in another culture, but its neighbor, Little Italy, has retained only a few streets imbued with the ebullience of its original community, while NoLIta (North of Little Italy) was gentrified by the yuppie invasion of the 1990s.

Lower East Side (C)
This area's brownstone tenement blocks fitted with fire escapes had a reputation for violence and drug dealing as late as the 1990s but the Lower East Side has since been transformed with many fashionable stores, bars and restaurants.

East Village (C)
The East Village has preserved little of its alternative ethos, and its property prices are steadily rising. Secondhand stores, craft workshops and tattoo parlors line its main thoroughfare, the vibrant, leafy Saint Mark's Place (actually a street), which leads to Tompkins Square Park, the neighborhood's green lung. However, it too has hip and fashionable stores, bars, restaurants and art galleries.

Midtown (D, E)
In New York's pulsating core, between 42nd and 59th Streets, Midtown contains some of the most emblematic sights: Times Square, Broadway, the Rockefeller Center, the Empire State Building... Central Park, Upper West Side, Upper East Side (F, G). The sheer expanse (840 acres) of Central Park makes it a neighborhood in its own right. It also marks the frontiers of the upmarket residential districts of the Upper West and Upper East Sides. The latter also plays host to some of the city's most prestigious museums.

Harlem (H)
The name itself evokes the essence of African American culture, although a young, white population has also moved in. The former ghetto has given way to a laidback neighborhood that offers visitors gospel concerts and soul food restaurants. East Harlem has a significant Hispanic community.

Brooklyn (I, J)
Only Brooklyn occupies the area on the other side of the East River. Artists, millennials and young families have settled here, forced out of Manhattan by the high rents, and many new trends now setting the city alight can trace their origins back to Brooklyn.

MIDTOWN

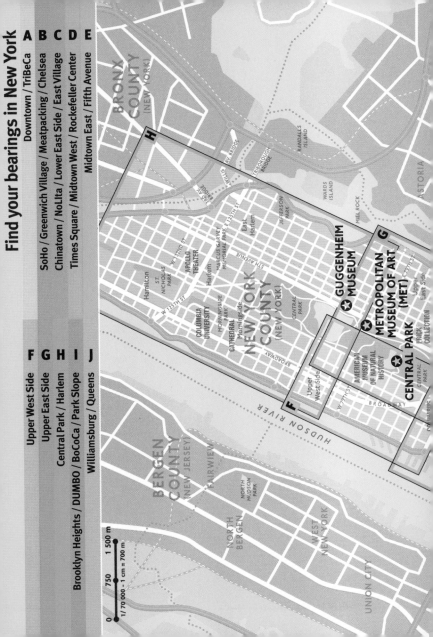

Find your bearings in New York

A Downtown / TriBeCa

B SoHo / Greenwich Village / Meatpacking / Chelsea

C Chinatown / NoLIta / Lower East Side / East Village

D Times Square / Midtown West / Rockefeller Center

E Midtown East / Fifth Avenue

F Upper West Side

G Upper East Side

H Central Park / Harlem

I Brooklyn Heights / DUMBO / BoCoCa / Park Slope

J Williamsburg / Queens

MAGNOLIA BAKERY

VILLAGE VANGUARD

ABC CARPET & HOME

Thu-Fri); Sat 5.30–11.30pm
Jean-Georges serves only
non-GMO, plant-based,
organic farm produce.
$9–18.

CAFÉS, TEAROOMS

City Bakery (C2) **10**
→ 3 W 18th St (Fifth)
Tel. (212) 366 1414
Mon-Fri 7.30am–6pm; Sat
8am–6pm; Sun 9am–6pm
Cookies and salads
from the Union Square
Greenmarket.

Buvette (B4) **11**
→ 42 Grove St (Bleecker)
Tel. (212) 255 3590
Daily 7am (8am
Sat-Sun)–2am
Tiny bistro for breakfast,
lunch and dinner;
delicious madeleines,
croque monsieurs and
tartines.

Eataly (C1) **12**
→ 200 Fifth Ave (23rd)
Tel. (212) 229 2560
Daily 9am–11pm
With 14 places to eat,
this market sells meat,
fish, greens, cheese and
more. La Birreria beer
garden is on the rooftop.

Ladurée (D5) **13**
→ 398 W Broadway
(Spring and Broome)
Tel. (646) 392 7868
Daily 8am (9am Sat-Sun)
–9pm (10pm Fri-Sat)
Have tea, breakfast,

lunch or dinner; also an
outdoor terrace, macaron
and pastry shop.

La Mercerie (D6) **14**
→ 53 Howard St
Tel. (212) 852 9099
Daily 9am–10pm
This cafe, bakery,
restaurant serves simple,
refined French food in a
beautiful setting.

BARS, CLUBS, CONCERTS

Balthazar (D5) **15**
→ 80 Spring St (Crosby)
Tel. (212) 965 1414
Mon-Fri 7.30am–midnight
(1am Fri); Sat-Sun 8am–
1am (midnight Sun)
Keith McNally's brasserie
has a vast bar for scene-
watching.

Jimmy (C5) **16**
→ 15 Thompson St (Grand)
Tel. (212) 201 9118; Daily
5pm–1am (2am Thu-Sat)
On the 18th floor of the
James Hotel: great views,
a fireplace and an out-
door pool on a teak deck.

**Village
Vanguard** (B3) **17**
→ 178 Seventh Ave
South (Perry and 11th)
Tel. (212) 255 4037
Sets: 8.30pm, 10.30pm daily
For over 60 years the best
names have played here.
Cover charge $30.

Blue Note (C4) **18**

→ 131 W 3rd St (MacDougal)
Tel. (212) 475 8592
Concerts daily 8pm, 10.30pm
(also 12.30am Fri-Sat); Sun
brunch at 11.30am, 1.30pm
A legendary address
in the jazz world, with
world-class artists.

**The Jane Hotel
Ballroom** (A3) **19**
→ 113 Jane St (West)
Tel. (212) 924 6700
A vast fireplace, stuffed
trophies and leather and
velvet couches add to the
old-world atmosphere.

Empire Diner (A2) **20**
→ 210 10th Ave (22nd St)
Tel. (212) 335 2277
Daily 5pm–1am
Fun for drinks and small
plates.

SHOPPING

All the following shops
are open daily
Greenwich Village
(B3-D4) **21**
James Perse
→ 368 Bleecker St
Intermix
→ 365 Bleecker St
Screaming Mimi's
→ 240 W 14th
**Meatpacking
District** (B3) **22**
→ 14th St and Abingdon Sq.
Chic shopping, eating and
living in this former meat
market neighborhood.
Jeffrey

→ 449 W 14th St (Tenth)
Vince
→ 833 Washington
St (W 12th)
SoHo (D5) **23**
→ Between Grand, Prince,
Thompson and Lafayette Sts
Galleries and boutiques.
Uniqlo
→ 546 Broadway (Spring);
flagship at 666 Fifth Ave
Alexander Wang
→ 103 Grand St
Prada
→ 575 Broadway (Prince)
**ABC Carpet
& Home** (D2) **24**
→ 888 Broadway (E 19th)
Tel. (212) 473 3000
Mon-Sat 10am–7pm (8pm
Thu); Sun 11am–6.30pm
China, glassware,
pillows, toys, jewelry
and furniture.
Barneys (C2) **25**
→ 101 7th Ave (16th & 17th)
Tel. (646) 264 6400
Daily 10am (11am
Sun)–7pm (8pm Wed-Sat)
Five floors of men's
and women's clothing;
and Fred's restaurant.
Chelsea Market
(A2) **26**
→ 75 Ninth Ave
Daily 7am (8am
Sun)–2am (10pm Sun)
This vast former Nabisco
factory has many shops
and restaurants,
including the sushi bar
at The Lobster Place.

▲ Map C

CUSHMAN ROW

THE HIGH LINE

▲ Map E

CENTER FOR ARCHITECTURE

NEW YORK UNIVERSITY

WASHINGTON SQUARE

Washington Square

ASTOR LIBRARY

COLONNADE ROW

NEW YORK UNIVERSITY

WASHINGTON CENTENNIAL MEMORIAL ARCH

WASH. MEWS

Waverly Place

Washington Place

GREENWICH VILLAGE

WEST 10TH ST

WEST 9TH ST

WEST 11TH ST

WEST 12TH ST

WEST 13TH ST

WEST 14TH ST

EAST 14TH ST

CONSOLIDATED EDISON BUILDING

Union Square

UNION SQUARE PARK

IRVING PLACE

PARK AVENUE

THEODORE ROOSEVELT HOUSE

GRAMERCY PARK

FLATIRON BUILDING

MADISON SQUARE PARK

METROPOLITAN LIFE TOWER

RUBIN MUSEUM OF ART

AVE. OF THE AMERICAS

NEW YORK LIFE INSURANCE BUILDING

MADISON AVENUE

LEXINGTON AVE.

BROADWAY

5TH AVENUE (FIFTH AVENUE)

4TH AVE.

UNIVERSITY PLACE

LAFAYETTE ST

BROADWAY

EAST 8TH ST

EAST 13TH ST

EAST 12TH ST

EAST 11TH ST

EAST 10TH ST

EAST 15TH ST

EAST 16TH ST

EAST 17TH ST

EAST 18TH ST

EAST 19TH ST

EAST 20TH ST

EAST 21ST ST

EAST 22ND ST

EAST 23RD ST

EAST 24TH ST

EAST 25TH ST

EAST 26TH ST

EAST 27TH ST

EAST 28TH ST

EAST 29TH ST

WEST 13TH ST

WEST 16TH ST

WEST 17TH ST

WEST 18TH ST

WEST 19TH ST

WEST 20TH ST

WEST 21ST ST

WEST 23RD ST

23RD STREET

24TH

25TH

26TH

27TH

28TH STREET

6TH AVENUE

(6TH AVENUE)

4TH ST

N ST

MINETTA LA

CORNELIA ST

JONES ST

BLEECKER ST

MADISON SQUARE PARK

THE MUSEUM AT FIT

◀ Map A ▶

---

arly morning or sunset.
also page 5.

:ushman Row (A2)
›06-418 W 20th St
· of the best examples
·reek Revival
·houses. The exteriors
·e from 1840 (cornicing,
· windows on the attic
·r decorated with laurel
·ands), all characteristic
·owhouses – identical,
·active red-brick houses.
:allery
·trict (A1)
·etween 21st and 29th
·10th and 11th)
·-June: Tue-Sat 11am–6pm
· 350-plus art
·eries located in former
·ehouses are the places

to see contemporary art.
Thursday is opening night
and the streets are festive.

★ **Flatiron Building** (D1)

→ *175 Fifth Ave; Open to visitors during office hours*
Erected in 1902 to house
the Fuller Construction
Company, this was the first
skyscraper in New York. It
resembles a flatiron, but its
triangular shape is due to
the layout of Broadway.
The first four floors are clad
with limestone and Italian
Renaissance motifs;
terracotta is used for the
upper stories. Until 1909 it
was the tallest building in
the world (285 ft).

★ **The Museum at FIT** (B1)

→ *Seventh Ave (27th); Tue-Fri noon–8pm; Sat 10am–5pm*
Attached to the prestigious
Fashion Institute of
Technology, where Calvin
Klein and other famous
American designers were
trained, this museum
presents excellent
exhibitions on themes
around fashion, muses
and designers.

★ **Whitney Museum of American Art** (A3)

→ *99 Gansevoort St (Washington St); Wed-Mon 10.30am–6pm (10pm Fri-Sat)*
Designed by Renzo Piano,
the 220,000 square feet

encompass a theater on
the 3rd floor, a permanent
collection on the 6th and
7th, temporary shows on
the 8th, as well as Danny
Meyer's Studio Café; his
restaurant, Untitled, is
on ground level.

★ **Madison Square Park** (D1)

→ *23rd St (Fifth)*
A beautiful, lush park with
a great view of the Empire
State Building to the north
and the Flatiron to the
south. Crowds line up
at the Shake Shack in
the middle of the park
for its famous burgers,
reputed to be amongst
the best in the city.

THE MUSEUM AT ELDRIDGE ST

**LOWER EAST SIDE
TENEMENT MUSEUM**

Map content

WEST 🅜 HOUSTON ST — CENTER OF PHOTOGRAPHY

★ ST. PATRICK'S OLD CATHEDRAL ★

NEW MUSEUM OF CONTEMPORARY A

PRINCE ST — PRINCE ST
NOLITA
18

SPRING ST — SPRING STREET
FREEMAN ALLEY
ESSEX ST
15

BOWERY ST
KENMARE ST
HAUGHWOUT BUILDING
1
17
8
3

LOWER EAST TENEMENT MU

BROOME ST — BROOME STREET — LITTLE ITALY
12

GRAND STREET
POLICE HEADQUARTERS
GRAND ★ ST — GRAND ST

HOWARD ST — **★ MUSEUM OF CHINESE IN AMERICA**
HESTER ST — HESTER ST

CANAL ST — **CANAL STREET** — CANAL ST

WALKER ST

WHITE STREET
CHINATOWN

BAYARD ST
THE MUSEUM A ELDRIDGE STRE

CHINATOWN

LEONARD STREET
CHURCH OF TRANSFIGURATION
Confucius Plaza
DIVISION ST
E BROADWAY

WORTH STREET
COLUMBUS PARK
DOYERS ST
HENRY STREET

CIVIC CENTER
Foley Square
N.Y. COUNTY COURT HOUSE
Chatham Square
PARK ROW
MADISON ST

A — **B**

Article text

★ **Chinatown** (A6)
→ Around Confucius Plaza (Bowery and Division)
Pagoda-shaped roofs, Buddhist temples, stalls, restaurants with their signs in Chinese... this is a very lively area during Chinese New Year.

★ **The Museum at Eldridge Street** (B6)
→ 12 Eldridge St
Tel. (212) 219 0302
Sun–Fri 10am–5pm (3pm Fri)
Guided tour of synagogue and museum every hour (last tour 4pm)
This first Eastern European Ashkenazic synagogue in America was built in 1887 by Russian and Polish Jewish immigrants. The interior has beautiful carved wood balconies and magnificent chandeliers. A small museum traces the history of the Jewish community in Manhattan.

★ **Little Italy** (A5)
Mulberry Street was the stronghold of the New York-Italian community before it moved to the Bronx and Brooklyn. Today, busy trattorias and pizzerias mostly cater to tourists.

★ **Museum of Chinese in America (MOCA)** (A5)
→ 211-215 Centre St (Grand); Tel. (855) 955 6622
Tue–Sun 11am–6pm (9pm Thu)
In this musuem, the history of Chinese immigration in Manhattan is traced through artifacts, photos and audio tapes.

★ **Lower East Side Tenement Museum** (B5)
→ 103 Orchard St
Tel. (877) 975 3786
Guided tours only: Daily 10am–6pm (last tour 5pm)
These small, plain tenement buildings were once home to immigrant families living in the most deplorable conditions. Guided tours of the restored apartments offer insights into the life of an Irish couple in 1869, or an Italian Catholic family

during the Depression.
★ **St Mark's Place** (E
Tompkins Square, whic
welcomed the sit-in
protesters in the sixties
marks the starting poin
this long street lined wi
trees and brownstones.
At the junction of Secor
Avenue and 10th St is
St Mark's Church-in-the
Bowery. On this site the
was once a chapel whic
marked the boundaries
the Bowery farm belong
to Peter Stuyvesant, las
governor of the colony
New Amsterdam. The
current church, a sober
elegant neoclassical-st
construction, was erect

MUSEUM OF CHINESE IN AMERICA

CHINATOWN

Destination of successive waves of immigrants, this area stretches north from Fulton and Franklin Streets, with Chinese, Italian and Central European communities eager to express their culture and traditions. Chinatown, Little Italy, Lower East Side... you can take a world tour minutes from the corporate skyscrapers of Wall Street. Further north, in the East Village, hub of the Beat Generation of the 1950s, and now the millennials, are many fashionable bars and restaurants.

MOMOFUKU NOODLE BAR

KATZ'S DELI

RESTAURANTS

La Esquina (A5) 🍴🅾️
→ 114 Kenmare St (Lafayette)
Tel. (646) 613 7100
Daily 11am–2am
A fake taco-stand front has a door that leads to the basement restaurant for delicious Mexican food. Dishes $6–37; outposts also at 200 W 55th St (**D** E1) and 1402 2nd Ave (**G** E3).

Momofuku Noodle Bar (B3) 🍴②
→ 171 First Ave; Tel. (212) 777 7773; Daily noon–4.30pm (4pm Sat-Sun), 5.30–11pm (1am Fri-Sat)
Star chef David Chang's noodle bar. Don't miss his famous BBQ pork buns and fried rice cakes. Seven other spots: Ssäm Bar, Ko, Milk Bar, Má Pêche, Nishi, Fuku +. Dishes $12–18. No reservations.

Pasquale Jones (A5) 🍴③
→ 187 Mulberry St (Kenmare); Daily 5.30–11pm (10pm Sun); lunch Fri-Sun noon–3pm
Italian food and small plates, with creative wood-fired pizzas in an elegant, modern space. Dishes $21–65.

Ivan Ramen (C4) 🍴④
→ 25 Clinton St (Stanton)

Tel. (646) 678 3859
Daily noon–3.30pm, 5.30pm–midnight
A storefront space with two counters and two small dining areas: try the spicy red chili ramen and triple pork, triple garlic mazemen. Dishes $15–16.

Katz's Deli (B4) 🍴⑤
→ 205 E Houston St (Ludlow)
Tel. (212) 254 2246; Mon-Fri 8am–10.45pm (2.45am Thu, midnight Fri); Sat open 24hrs; Sun noon–10.45pm
One of New York's most famous delis, opened in 1888. $4–30.

Il Buco Alimentari & Vineria (A4) 🍴⑥
→ 53 Great Jones St (Bowery and Lafayette)
Tel. (212) 837 2622; Daily 8am (9am Sat-Sun)–11pm (midnight Fri-Sat).
A rustic bakery, food shop and trattoria. Dishes $19–34. Try the original Il Buco at 47 Bond St (Bowery).

Prune (B4) 🍴⑦
→ 54 E First St (First and Second Ave)
Tel. (212) 677 6221
Daily 5.30–11pm (also 10am–3.30pm Sat-Sun)
Chef Gabrielle Hamilton's tiny restaurant serves fantastic brunch and dinner; brunch is worth the wait. Dishes $16–33.

ERY BALLROOM **MANHATTAN PORTAGE** **A-1 RECORDS**

De Maria (A5)
→ 19 Kenmare St
(Elizabeth and Bowery)
Tel. (212) 966 3058
Daily 8.30am (9am
Sat-Sun)–10pm (11pm
Sat-Sun)
Enjoy a local, seasonal
menu in a beautiful space
inspired by Walter de
Maria's studio; natural
wines and inventive
cocktails. Dishes $14–24.

TEAROOM, ICE-CREAM PARLOR

**sugar Sweet
sunshine** (C5)
→ 126 Rivington St (Norfolk)
Tel. (212) 995 1960
Mon-Fri 8am–10pm
(11pm Fri); Sat-Sun
10am–11pm (Sun 7pm)
Great variety of cupcakes,
cakes and cookies.

**Il Laboratorio
del Gelato** (B4)
→ 188 Ludlow St (Houston)
Tel. (212) 343 9922
Mon-Fri 7.30am–10pm
(midnight Fri); Sat-Sun
10am–10pm (midnight Sat)
Excellent artisanal gelati,
not too sweet, in flavors
that change seasonally.

BARS, CONCERTS

Lobby Bar (A4)
→ Bowery Hotel, 335
Bowery; Tel. (212) 505 9100

Daily 5pm–4am
(2am Sun-Wed)
Cozy, lively retro space
with a fire going in the
winter; for summer, try
the patio upstairs.

The Flower Shop
(B5)
→ 107 Eldridge St
Tel. (212) 257 4072
Mon-Fri 5pm–midnight
(2am Thu-Fri); Sat-Sun
11am–midnight (2am Sat)
Lively bar scene under
the cozy restaurant
upstairs.

Arlene's Grocery
(B4)
→ 95 Stanton St (Orchard)
Tel. (212) 358 1633; Daily
4pm (Sat-Sun)–4am
A former bodega, it
booked The Strokes
before they were known.
Don't miss Rock n' Roll
Karaoke Night.

Joe's Pub (A3)
→ 425 Lafayette St
(Astor Place); Tel. (212) 539
8500 Daily 6pm–2am
(11.30pm Sun)
A quirky supper club
with live performances
by actors, writers and
musicians.

**Bowery
Ballroom** (B5)
→ 6 Delancey St (Bowery)
Tel. (212) 533 2111
Daily from 8pm
A large music venue with
a varied program: world

music, rock, pop, etc; bar
area in the basement.

**Nuyorican
Poets Cafe** (C4)
→ 236 E Third St (Ave C)
Tel. (212) 780 9386
Hours vary according
to the program
A bastion of the Nuyorican
(New York + Puertorican)
art movement of the
1970s; theater, poetry,
slam (Fri 10pm), hip-hop,
jazz, salsa and more.

SHOPPING

**Shopping
in NoLIta** (A5)
→ Between Mulberry,
Houston, Elizabeth and
Kenmare Sts; the shops
below are open daily
(Sun from 11am or noon)
NoLIta stands for North
of Little Italy: the area
has many stores, bars
and restaurants.

The Study
→ 234 Mulberry St
Tel. (212) 219 2789
For the home office:
notebooks, prints, all
matter of desk supplies.

Manhattan Portage
→ 258 Elizabeth St
Tel. (212) 226 9655
More than 100 styles of
strap-on bags and totes.

**McNally Jackson
Books** (A5)
→ 52 Prince St

(Mulberry and Lafayette)
Tel. (212) 274 1160; Daily
10am–10pm (Sun 9pm)
A well-curated
bookstore, which also
sells magazines. Café.

A-1 Records (B3)
→ 439 E 6th St (Ave A)
Tel. (212) 473 2870
Daily 1-9pm
From rare to newly
released, vinyl records
cover genres as varied
as jazz and hip hop.

Reformation (B4)
→ 156 Ludlow St (Stanton)
Tel. (646) 448 4925
Daily noon–8pm (7pm Sun)
Hip, eco-conscious,
USA-made, inexpensive
women's clothing.
Also at 23 Howard
St (**B** D6).

John Derian (B4)
→ 6-10 E Second St
(Second Ave and Bowery)
Tel. (212) 677 3917
Tue-Sun 11am–7pm
Three small shops
packed with linens,
china, furniture, art by
Hugo Guinness, and
much more. Also at
18 Christopher St (**B** C3).

Xenomania (B3)
→ 206 E Sixth St
Tel. (646) 590 3211
Tue-Fri noon–7pm
Textiles, rugs, jewelry
and furniture from
India, Iran and
Uzbekistan.

NEW MUSEUM
OF CONTEMPORARY ART

ST PATRICK'S
OLD CATHEDRAL

EAST RIVER

ROOSEVELT DRIVE (EAST RIVER DRIVE)

EAST HOUSTON STREET

EAST 14TH STREET

EAST 2ND ST
EAST 3RD ST
EAST 4TH ST
EAST 6TH ST
EAST 7TH ST
ST. MARK'S PLACE
EAST 9TH ST
EAST 10TH ST
EAST 13TH ST
EAST 15TH ST
E 16TH ST

AVENUE B
AVENUE C
AVENUE D

Kamie's
Place

HAVEN
PLACE

SZOLD
PLACE

JOHN
J. MURPHY
PARK

EAST RIVER STAT
FRANKLIN DELANO ROO
Baruch

16

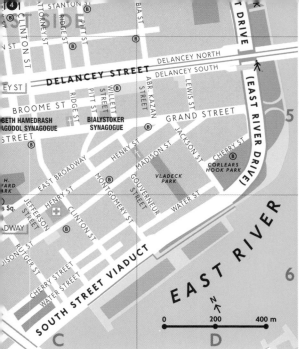

ST MARK'S PLACE

COOPER UNION

799, in the heart of
e Ukraine. Its Greek
val steeple was added
828 and the Italianate
ico in 1858.

**New Museum of
temporary Art** (B5)
35 Bowery (Stanton
Rivington)
212) 219 1222; Tue-Sun
n–6pm (9pm Thu)
uyo Sejima and Ryue
izawa of the Tokyo
SANNA designed this
en-story, 60,000-sq.-ft
ce clad in opaque zinc-
ted steel, made up
ree main gallery
rs, a 182-seat theater
e basement and a
house. Contemporary

exhibitions.

★ **St Patrick's
Old Cathedral** (A4)
→ 263 Mulberry St
Tel. (212) 226 8075
Daily 8am–6pm (8pm Sun)
This is the second oldest
Catholic church in the city.
From 1809 to 1879 it served
as New York's Archdiocese
church, up until the
construction of St Patrick's
Cathedral on Fifth Avenue.
Its austere façade hides
a Gothic Revival interior.

★ **Merchant's House
Museum** (A4)
→ 29 E Fourth St
Tel. (212) 777 1089
Thu-Mon noon–5pm
(8pm Thu)

Built in 1832 for the rich
merchant Seabury Tredwell,
this Greek Revival-style
rowhouse became a
museum in 1936. The
original furniture and
layout has been retained,
proviving a reflection on the
lives of the upper classes
in 19th-century New York.

★ **Cooper Union** (A3)
→ 41 Cooper Square
(Astor Place); no visits
Peter Cooper, millionnaire
and philanthropist, wished
for a co-education school
of art and techniques
that would be open to
all, regardless of class,
sex or racial background. It
opened in 1859 in a superb

Italianate brownstone
building. Today it is one
of the oldest steel-beamed
buildings still standing.

★ **International Center
of Photography** (A4)
→ 250 Bowery (Prince)
Tel. (212) 857 0003
Tue-Sun 10am–6pm
The Gwathmey Siegel
space has two floors
and three galleries for
exhibitions; their vast
archive of over 60,000
photographs includes
the work of Henri Cartier-
Bresson, Robert Capa, Eve
Arnold, Weegee, Dorothea
Lange, and even images
of Oppenheimer and the
Bomb. Café and bookstore.

PIER 78
NEW JERSEY
FERRY

HUDSON RIVER WALK

12TH AVENUE

JACOB
K. JAVITS
CONVENTION
CENTER

(ELEVENTH AVENUE)

WEST 38TH ST

WEST 37TH

WEST 36TH

WEST 35TH

(TENTH AVENUE)

DYER AVENUE

ST

ST

ST

ST

WEST 34TH ST

WEST

11TH AVENUE

33RD

34TH ST
HUDSON YARDS

HUDSON
YARDS

10TH AVENUE

S

THE HIGH LINE

WEST

30TH

ST

HELIPORT

4

N

0   100   200 m

A

B

C

INTREPID SEA, AIR AND SPACE MUSEUM

ROCKEFELLER CENTER

TOP OF THE ROCK

★ General Post Office (D4)

→ *Eighth Ave (31st and 33rd)*
Tel. (212) 330 3296
Mon-Fri 7am–10pm; Sat 9am–9pm; Sun 11am–7pm
Work is finally underway to convert the building into a new concourse of Amtrak (expected late 2020). This huge 1933 McKim, Mead & White building is inspired by a neoclassical temple.

★ Bryant Park (E3)

→ *Sixth Ave (42nd)*
This formally planted oasis behind the main branch of the New York Public Library shows classic films in the summer. Get a snack from Tom Colicchio's 'wichcraft

outlet, in an outdoor kiosk.

★ Times Square (E3)

→ *Broadway (Seventh)*
Surrounded by state-of-the-art illuminated billboards, Times Square is a hub of activity. The nerve center of the Theater District, it is best seen at night when the huge video screens are lit.

★ Madame Tussauds (D3)

→ *234 W 42nd St (Seventh and Eighth)*
Tel. (866) 841 3505; Daily 10am–8pm (10pm Fri-Sat)
Angelina Jolie, Brad Pitt, Fidel Castro and Bob Dylan are among the realistic wax figures of over 200 of the

world's top celebrities set in themed areas with interactive exhibits; check out the gift shop.

★ Rockefeller Center (E2)

→ *Rockefeller Plaza (49th)*
This is one of the world's first commercial complexes (1931–39) designed by the leading light of the American Art Deco movement, architect Raymond Hood. The 19 buildings within the complex are arranged in a gridiron pattern, laid out around the famous Rockefeller Plaza.

Rockefeller Plaza (F2)
→ *W 49th St / W 50th St*

From Fifth Avenue, the Channel Gardens lead to the lower plaza, an ice ri in winter, overlooked by gilded bronze statue of Prometheus by Paul Manship. At Christmas a enormous 130-ft Christm tree is placed behind it.

Top of the Rock (E2)
→ *Daily 8am–midnight*
From the GE Building (no. 30) are stunning vi of the city from the Top the Rock observatory.

Radio City Music Hall (
→ *1260 Sixth Ave (50th)*
Tel. (866) 858 0007 for sh / (212) 247 4777 for guide tours (daily 11am–3pm, e 30 mins). Box office:

D

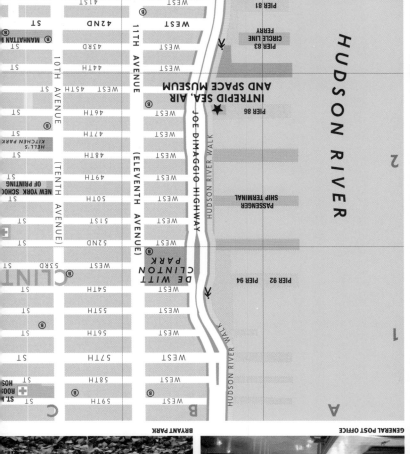

HUDSON RIVER

PIER 81

PIER 83
CIRCLE LINE
FERRY

INTREPID SEA, AIR
AND SPACE MUSEUM

PIER 86

JOE DIMAGGIO HIGHWAY

HUDSON RIVER WALK

PASSENGER
SHIP TERMINAL

DE WITT
CLINTON
PARK

PIER 92   PIER 94

HUDSON RIVER WALK

11TH AVENUE

(ELEVENTH AVENUE)

10TH AVENUE

(TENTH AVENUE)

HELL'S
KITCHEN PARK

NEW YORK SCHOOL
OF PRINTING

CLINT

MANHATTAN

WEST 41ST
42ND ST
43RD
WEST 44TH
WEST 45TH ST
WEST 46TH
WEST 47TH
WEST 48TH
WEST 49TH
50TH
WEST 51ST
52ND ST
WEST 53RD ST
WEST 54TH
WEST 55TH
WEST 56TH
WEST 57TH
WEST 58TH
WEST 59TH

ST, ROOS
HOS

GENERAL POST OFFICE

BRYANT PARK

In the heart of the Theater District is Times Square, more brightly lit than ever before, with giant billboards, huge neon signs and illuminated newsboards. Of course, there's as much to see on the streets as on stage. On New Year's Eve hundreds of thousands of people congregate here to watch the crystal ball drop 77 feet at midnight. Further east on 42nd, behind the Public Library, is Bryant Park; in the summer, bring a blanket and watch a movie on the 20 by 40 ft screen.

GAZALA'S

IPPUDO

RESTAURANTS

Joe Allen (D2) 🍴❶
→ 326 W 46th St (Eighth and Ninth); Tel. (212) 581 6464; Daily noon (11.30am Wed, Sat-Sun)–11.45pm (midnight Fri-Sat)
Posters hang on the brick walls of this spot which caters to actors and theater-goers alike. Hamburgers, steaks, spare-ribs and fish are served in a cozy room with a big bar. Burgers $15; dishes $20–36.

Gazala's (C2) 🍴❷
→ 709 Ninth Ave (49th) Tel. (212) 245 0709 Daily 11am–11pm (11.30pm Fri-Sat)
Chef/owner Gazala Halabi cooks up her native Druze cuisine. Also at 380 Columbus Ave (78th). Dishes $12.50–19.50.

Orso (D2) 🍴❸
→ 322 W 46th St (Eighth and Ninth); Tel. (212) 489 7212; Daily noon (11.30am Wed, Sat-Sun)–11pm (10pm Sat-Sun)
This small northern Italian restaurant often has a Broadway star or director after the show. The crisp pizza bread with garlic is irresistible, as are the small crunchy pizzas

and pan-roasted chicken. Service is quick and friendly. Dishes $15–29.

DB Bistro Moderne (E2) 🍴❹
→ 55 W 44th St (Fifth and Sixth); Tel. (212) 391 2400 Mon-Fri 7–10am, 11.30am-2.30pm, 5–11pm (10pm Mon); Sat-Sun 8am–2.30pm, 5–11pm (10pm Sun)
In the fancier back or in the casual front room, try the burger with foie gras and truffles. Three-course pre-theater set menu $50; dishes from $29.

Ippudo (D2) 🍴❺
→ 321 W 51st St (Eighth and Ninth) Tel. (212) 974 2500; Daily 11am–3.30pm, 5–11.30pm (12.30am Fri-Sat)
Delicious appetizers and ramen in this attractive setting of red banquettes set against brick walls or at the long, blond wood bar. Also at 65 Fourth Ave. Dishes $15–18.

The Modern (F1) 🍴❻
→ 9 W 53rd St (Fifth) Tel. (212) 333 1220; Mon-Sat noon–2pm, 5–10.30pm Bar Room: Daily 11.30am–10.30pm (9.30pm Sun)
Bauhaus meets Danish Modern in the formal Dining Room and in the casual Bar Room, where mixing your menu is part of the fun: spicy steak

DWAY THEATERS

MIDTOWN COMICS

ANTHROPOLOGIE

tartare with quail egg, for example. Small plates from $12 (Bar Room); set menu (dinner) $98–128.

CAFÉS, PATISSERIES

by CHLOE (F2) **7**
→ 1 Rockefeller Plaza
Tel. (646) 543 7181; Daily 7am (10am Sat-Sun)–10pm
A vegan restaurant with take-out; kale Caesar salad, burgers and avocado pesto pasta are just some favorites.

Amy's Bread (D2) **8**
→ 672 Ninth Ave (47th)
Tel. (212) 977 2670; Mon-Wed 7am–10pm (9pm Mon); Thu-Fri 7am–11pm; Sat-Sun 8am–11pm (9pm Sun)
A popular neighborhood bakery with great cookies and artisanal breads.

Lady M (E3) **9**
→ 36 W 40th St
Tel. (212) 452 2222
Mon-Fri 9am–8pm (10pm Fri); Sat- Sun 11am–10pm (6pm Sun)
Pattisserie renowned for its 'mille crêpes', cakes made up of 20 layers of wafer-thin crêpes and cream in a dizzying variety of flavors.

Maison Kayser (D1) **10**
→ 1800 Broadway (Columbus Circle); Tel. (212)

245 4100; Daily 7am–10pm
Ideal for a coffee or tea and a French pastry in their bright, cozy space.

THEATERS, BAR, CLUBS

Broadway theaters (D1-E3) **11**
They are on Broadway between 42nd and 53rd streets, or the side streets usually between Broadway and Eighth.

SixtyFive at the Rainbow Room (E2) **12**
→ 30 Rockefeller Plaza
Tel. (212) 632 5000
Mon-Fri 5pm–midnight
Enjoy the spectacular view and the spicy tuna tacos or the langoustine tartare with your drinks.

The Lambs Club (E3) **13**
→ 132 W 44th St (Broadway and Sixth)
Tel. (212) 997 5262
Daily 7am–2.30pm (3pm Sat-Sun), 5–11pm (9.30pm Sun-Mon)
Now the Chatwal Hotel, this 1905 Sanford White building once housed America's first theatrical club. The bar has an updated Deco look in red leather, metal and wood.

Café Un Deux Trois (E2) **14**

→ 123 W 44th St (Broadway and Sixth)
Tel. (212) 354 4148
Daily 7am–midnight
This bistro has a vast bar where you can get a snack too. Friendly service.

The Iridium (D2) **15**
→ 1650 Broadway (51st)
Tel. (212) 582 2121
Daily 7pm–midnight; nightly shows 8.30pm, 10.30pm
Excellent jazz club with American food. Cover charge $25–60.

SHOPPING

Macy's (E4) **16**
→ 151 W 34th St (Broadway)
Tel. (212) 695 4400
Mon-Sat 10am–10pm (9pm Sun)
This vast department store has the usual goods, but at reasonable prices.

B & H (D4) **17**
→ 420 Ninth Ave (34th)
Tel. (212) 615 8820
Mon-Fri 9am–7pm (2pm Fri); Sun 10am–6pm
The largest audiovisual shop in New York: video, photographic and computer goods at very reasonable prices.

Midtown Comics (E3) **18**
→ 200 W 40th St (Seventh)
Tel. (212) 302 8192

Mon-Sat 8am–midnight; Sun noon–8pm
Graphic novels, books, comics; also T-shirts, masks, models, costumes and videos.

Hell's Kitchen Flea Market (C3) **19**
→ W 39th St (Ninth Ave)
Sat-Sun 9am–5pm
There are finds: clothes, vintage jewelry, antiques.

Anthropologie (F2) **20**
→ 50 Rockefeller Plaza
Tel. (212) 246 0386
Daily 10am–9pm (8pm Sun)
Ethnic-inspired fashion: colorful clothes, jewelry, perfume, candles, shoes, bags and accessories.

MoMA Design Store (E1) **21**
→ 44 W 53rd St (Fifth and Sixth)
Tel. (212) 767 1050; Daily 9.30am–6.30pm (9pm Fri)
State-of-the-art gadgets and art posters from the 1940s–70s; also crockery and some furniture. Also at 81 Spring St.

Anne Fontaine (F2) **22**
→ 610 Fifth Ave (Rockefeller Center)
Tel. (212) 489 1554
Mon-Fri 10am–7pm; Sat 11am–6pm; Sun noon–5pm
In case you need an iconic white blouse, this is the place to get it. Also at 873 Madison Ave and 93 Greene St.

WEST	(EIGHTH)	38TH	ST
WEST		37TH	ST
WEST	(SEVENTH AVE)	36TH	ST
WEST		35TH	ST

Map content (top):

GARMENT DISTRICT

WEST 38TH ST — BROADWAY — WEST 38TH ST — EAST 38TH ST — PARK AVENUE
EAST 37TH ST — THE MORGAN LIBRARY
WEST 37TH ST
WEST 36TH ST — EAST 36TH ST
34TH ST — WEST 35TH ST — EAST 35TH ST

OFFICIAL NYC INFORMATION CENTER 16
34TH ST — Herald Square — WEST 34TH ST — EAST 34TH ST — 33RD ST
EMPIRE STATE BUILDING
WEST 33RD ST — EAST 33RD ST

GENERAL POST OFFICE ★
MADISON SQUARE GARDEN
PENN STATION
WEST 32ND ST — EAST 32ND ST — 5TH AVENUE — MADISON AVE — PARK AVE. SOUTH
WEST 31ST ST — EAST 31ST ST
WEST 30TH ST — EAST 30TH ST

8TH AVENUE — 7TH AVENUE — AVENUE OF — 5TH AVE

D — E — F

▼ Map B

MUSEUM OF MODERN ART / MOMA

CARNEGIE HALL

Sat 10am–6pm
...ned in 1932 in the
...ence of Charlie
...lin, Clark Gable and
...o Toscanini, Radio
...with its 5,800-seat
...torium, is one of the
...t dramatic spaces in
York. The restored
...ior of the building is
...rt Deco masterpiece.

**★ trepid Sea, Air and
...ce Museum** (B2)
...er 86, 12th Ave
... St); Tel. (212) 245 0072
10am–5pm
... Sat-Sun from April-Oct)
..., F-16s, planes from
...d War Two and Hueys
... Vietnam are part of
...estored aircraft carrier

museum; don't miss the
Concorde or the Space
Shuttle. Many interactive
exhibits.

**★ Museum of Modern
Art (MoMA)** (F1)
→ 11 W 53rd St
Tel. (212) 708 9400
Daily 10.30am–5.30pm
(8pm Fri)
Yoshio Taniguchi's
rebuilding of the museum
has doubled the space of
this great collection, which
includes masterpieces
of Fauvism, post-
Impressionism, Cubism
and Surrealism, as well as
of photography and design.
See also page 7.

★ Carnegie Hall (E1)

→ 881 Seventh Ave (57th)
Tel. (212) 247 7800
Guided tours: Oct-June:
Mon-Fri 11.30am, 12.30pm,
2pm, 3pm; Sat 11.30am,
12.30pm; Sun 12.30pm
(varies by week,
check beforehand)
Built for steel magnate
Andrew Carnegie, this is
New York's oldest concert
hall and its most perfect,
acoustically. It opened in
1891 with Tchaikovsky
conducting. Some of the
biggest names in music
have performed here, from
Caruso, Toscanini and Von
Karajan to The Beatles.
The smaller Zankel Hall
is on the lower level.

**★ Discovery
Times Square** (D3)
→ 226 W 44th (Broadway
and Eighth Ave); Tel. (866)
987 9692; Daily 10am–7pm
(8pm Wed-Thu; 9pm Fri-Sat)
A vast 60,000 sq-ft
museum-like space with
educational, entertaining
and interactive exhibitions
such as: Titanic, Leonardo
da Vinci's Workshop, King
Tut, Terracotta Warriors
and The Hunger Games.

★ Hudson Yards (C4)
→ 30-34th St (10th Ave)
Thomas Heatherwick's
Vessel that rises to 15
stories, filled with 2,500
steps to climb in the 5-acre
garden and plaza.

GRAND CENTRAL TERMINAL

CHRYSLER BUILDING

Map area labels:

WEST 39TH ST — EAST 39TH ST
WEST 38TH ST — EAST 38TH ST
WEST 37TH ST — EAST 37TH ST
WEST 36TH ST — EAST 36TH ST
WEST 35TH ST — EAST 35TH ST
34TH ST — EAST 34TH ST
WEST 33RD ST — EAST 33RD ST — 33RD ST
WEST 32ND ST — EAST 32ND
WEST 31ST ST — EAST 31ST
WEST 30TH ST — EAST 30TH
WEST 29TH ST — EAST 29TH
28TH STREET — EAST 28TH ST — 28TH STREET

(FIFTH AVENUE) · AVENUE (6TH AVENUE) · MADISON · PARK AVENUE · BROADWAY · AVENUE OF THE AMERICAS · 5TH AVENUE · MADISON AVENUE · PARK AVE. SOUTH

THE MORGAN LIBRARY ★

EMPIRE STATE BUILDING ★

A · **B** · **5** · **6** · **E**

★ **Empire State Building** (A5)
→ 350 Fifth Ave
Tel. (212) 736 3100
Daily 8am–2am
The construction of this legendary skyscraper in 1930 – then the highest ever man-made building – took 411 days and cost $42 million. The top mast initially served as a mooring place for airships. Until 1 WTC, it was the tallest building in the city (at 1,454 ft) and it still draws over 3.6 million visitors a year who come to see the views of downtown Manhattan and Central Park from its observatories on the 86th and 102nd floors. See also page 4.

★ **New York Public Library** (A4)
→ Fifth Ave / W 42nd St
Tel. (917) 275 6975
Mon-Sat 10am–6pm
(8pm Tue-Wed); Sun 1–5pm
With 11 million books catalogued, this is the third largest public library in the US, after Washington's Library of Congress and Boston. Designed by the Beaux Arts architects John M. Carrère and Thomas Hastings, it opened in 1911. The stairway of this stunning building, guarded by two stone lions, is a favorite meeting place.

★ **Villard Mansions** (B2)
→ 451–457 Madison Ave (50th and 51st)
These buildings, with the look of a Renaissance palace, were built in 1885 to fulfill the grand dreams of Henry Villard, founder of the Northern Pacific Railway. They are now part of the Palace Hotel.

★ **The Morgan Library** (B5)
→ 225 Madison Ave (36th)
Tel. (212) 685 0008
Tue-Fri 10.30am–5pm
(9pm Fri); Sat-Sun 10am
(11am Sun)–6pm
Renzo Piano redesigned part of this space with its marvelous collection of medieval and Renaiss manuscripts, rare boo and old master drawin financier J. Pierpont M (1837–1913), on displa a neo-Renaissance pa dating from 1906.

★ **Grand Central Terminal** (B4)
→ 42nd St (Park Ave)
This Beaux Arts buildi completed in 1913, br the railway right into the heart of Manhatta and now over 750,000 commuters pass throu every day. The specta main marble hall (375 long, 120 ft wide) has gorgeous ceiling with

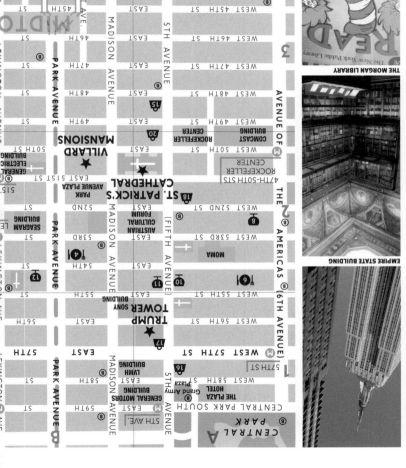

THE MORGAN LIBRARY

EMPIRE STATE BUILDING

From the Morgan Library & Museum on 36th and Madison, designed by Charles McKim with a Renzo Piano addition, stroll over to Fifth Avenue past the lions in front of The New York Public Library and take a right on 42nd Street to see Art Deco Chanin and Chrysler Buildings on Lexington Avenue. Walk through Grand Central Station, with its many shops, over to Fifth Avenue past the Channel Gardens of Rockefeller Center and up to the shopping district beyond the spires of St Patrick's Cathedral.

PONGAL

GRAND CENTRAL OYSTER BAR

RESTAURANTS

Pongal (B6) 🍴❶
→ 110 Lexington Ave (27th and 28th)
Tel. (212) 696 9458
Daily noon–10.30pm (11pm Fri-Sat)
A cozy restaurant offering authentic vegetarian cuisine from the south of India. Dishes $9–13.

Sushi Yasuda (C4) 🍴❷
→ 204 E 43rd St (Second and Third); Tel. (212) 972 1001; Mon-Fri noon–2.15pm, 6–10.15pm; Sat 6–10.15pm
An elegant floor-to-ceiling bamboo space with great sushi. Dishes $20–38.

Mr. Chow (C1) 🍴❸
→ 324 E 57th St (First and Second); Tel. (212) 751 9030
Daily 6–11.30pm
A sunken dining room, all mirrors and black lacquer, makes a stylish setting for eating Chinese food. Noodles $13; other dishes $27. Also at 121 Hudson St.

Casa Lever (B2) 🍴❹
→ 390 Park Ave (54th St)
Tel. (212) 888 2700; Daily 7am (5.30pm Sat)–11pm
In a room with Warhol portraits, sink into a booth for Milanese fare; weather permitting, have a drink or eat outside. Dishes $29–49.

Grand Central Oyster Bar (B4) 🍴❺
→ Grand Central Terminal, lower level
Tel. (212) 490 6650
Mon-Sat 11.30am–9.30pm
Seafood specialties in a spectacular Beaux Arts vaulted, tiled underground space. Dishes $18–42.

Michael's (A2) 🍴❻
→ 24 W 55th St (Sixth)
Tel. (212) 767 0555
Mon-Fri 7.30–9.30am, noon–2.30pm, 5.30–9.30pm; Sat 5.30–9.30pm
Enjoy upscale Californian cuisine at this airy power spot with unparalleled people-watching. Dishes $18–48.

Agern (B4) 🍴❼
→ Grand Central Terminal, at 42nd and Vanderbilt
Tel.(646) 568 4018; Mon-Fri 11.30am–2.30pm; 5.30pm–10pm; Sat 5.30–10pm
Locally farmed and wild ingredients made into seasonal Nordic dishes; stylish space. Dishes $24–45.

BARS

B Bar at Baccarat Hotel (A2) ❽
→ 28 West 53rd (Fifth and Sixth)
Tel. 212 790 8800
Daily 4pm–11.30pm
Under crystal chandeliers

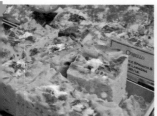

ND CENTRAL MARKET

BERGDORF GOODMAN

NIKE TOWN

enjoy drinks with spicy tuna tartare, truffled French fries, foie gras or desserts; has an outside terrace and the Salon for drinks or tea.

P. J. Clarke's (C1) **9**
→ 915 3rd Ave (55th)
Tel. (212) 317 1616
Daily 11.30am (10.30am Sat–Sun)–2am (kitchen 1am)
Since 1884, a lively bar now famous for its hamburgers and cheesecake.

Salon de Ning (A2) **10**
→ The Peninsula Hotel, 700 Fifth Ave (55th)
Tel. (212) 903 3097; Daily 5pm–1am (midnight Sun)
On the 23rd floor of the Peninsula Hotel, this bar evokes 1930s Shanghai inside and outdoors; Asian-inspired light fare and a great view.

King Cole Bar & Salon (A2) **11**
→ The St Regis Hotel, 2 E 55th St (Fifth)
Tel. (212) 339 6857
Mon–Sat 11.30am–1am; Sun noon–midnight
This bar, with the famous Maxfield Parrish mural, has been expanded into a lounge where you can also get breakfast, lunch and dinner.

Monkey Bar (B2) **12**
→ 60 East 54th St (Park Ave); Tel. (212) 288 1010

Mon–Fri 11.30am–1am; Sat 5.30pm–1am
A cozy bar with the original monkey murals, at banquettes you can grab a bite off the main menu (dishes from $22).

The Campbell Apartment (B4) **13**
→ 15 Vanderbilt Ave (43rd St); Tel. (212) 297 1781
Daily noon–2am
This room with 25-foot ceilings channelling a 13th-century Florentine palazzo once owned by a 1920s tycoon is a great place to have a drink.

SHOPPING

Brooks Brothers (B3) **14**
→ 346 Madison Ave (44th)
Tel. (212) 682 8800
Mon–Fri 8am–8pm; Sat 9am–7pm; Sun 11am–7pm
The place for classic suits, ties, pajamas and shirts; also children's clothes (ages 5–16) and preppy women's clothing.

Saks Fifth Avenue (A3) **15**
→ 611 Fifth Ave (49th)
Tel. (212) 753 4000
Mon–Sat 10am–8.30pm; Sun 11am–7pm
The latest styles from the top designers and excellent cosmetics and accessories.

Bergdorf Goodman (A1) **16**
→ 754 Fifth Ave (58th)
Tel. (212) 753 7300
Mon–Sat 10am–8pm; Sun 11am–7pm
A luxurious department store selling American and international design: women's clothing (the men's store is across the street), baby clothes, antiques, linens and cosmetics.

Tiffany & Co (A1) **17**
→ 727 Fifth Ave (57th)
Tel. (212) 755 8000; Mon–Sat 10am–7pm; Sun noon–6pm
A New York institution since 1837, and forever linked with the image of Audrey Hepburn looking through its window. Fine jewelry, china, crystal and tableware are all here. Try the Blue Box Café on four – reserve through Resy.

Niketown (A2) **18**
→ 650 Fifth Ave (W 52nd)
Tel. (212) 891 6453; Daily 10am (11am Sun)–8pm
Four floors dedicated to Nike sportswear and shoes, with members only NikePlus on five.

Grand Central Market (B4) **19**
→ Lexington Ave (42nd)
Mon–Fri 7am–9pm; Sat 10am–7pm; Sun 11am–6pm
In one hall of the station, find food for picnics –

fully prepared – as well as cheeses, salamis and breads; also stores like L'Occitane, Swatch and Papyrus. Don't miss the Great Northern food hall.

Fifth Avenue stores (A1-5) **20**
Some of the popular shops here are:
H&M (nos 505 and 589)
→ Tel. (855) 466 7467
Uniqlo (no. 666)
→ Tel. (877) 486 4756
Zara (no. 666)
→ Tel. (212) 765 0477
Bottega Veneta (no. 697)
→ Tel. (212) 371 5511
Dolce & Gabbana (no. 717)
→ Tel. (212) 897 9653
Armani (no. 717)
→ Tel. (212) 209 3500
Abercrombie & Fitch (no. 720)
→ Tel. (212) 306 0936
Gucci (no. 725)
→ Tel. (212) 826 2600

Dover Street Market (B6) **21**
→ 160 Lexington Ave (30th St)
Tel. (646) 837 7750
Daily 11am–7pm (noon–6pm Sun)
Seven floors curated by Rei Kawakubo of Comme des Garcons, with a mix of hip young and established designers; Rose Bakery for breakfast or lunch.

▲ Map J

UNITED NATIONS

"EVERYONE ENTITLED TO A SOCIA INTERNATIONAL ORDE WHICH THE RIGHTS AND FREEDOMS SET FORTH IN THIS DECLARATION BE FULLY REALIZE"

CHANIN BUILDING

▲ Map G

EAST RIVER

QUEENS MIDTOWN TUNNEL

FRANKLIN DELANO ROOSEVELT DRIVE

UNITED NATIONS PLAZA

★ UNITED NATIONS

Tudor City Place

FORD FOUNDATION BUILDING

DAILY NEWS BUILDING

...YSLER ...DING

HAMMARSKJOLD PLAZA

Beekman Place
Mitchell Place
Sutton Place

EAST 41ST ST
EAST 42ND ST
EAST 43RD ST
44TH ST
45TH ST
46TH ST
47TH ST
48TH ST
49TH ST
50TH
51ST
52ND
53RD
54TH
55TH
56TH
EAST 57TH ST
58TH
59TH

1ST AVENUE (FIRST AVENUE)
2ND AVENUE (SECOND AVENUE)
3RD AVENUE (THIRD AVENUE)

EAST

QUEENSBORO BRIDGE

ROOSEVELT ISLAND TRAMWAY

...LE'S

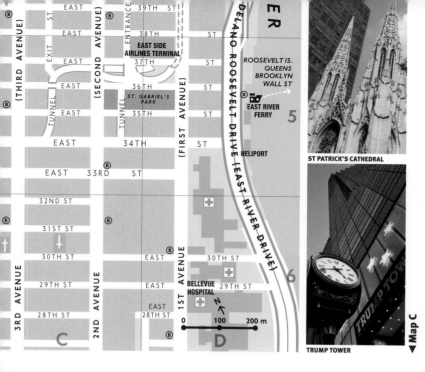

ST PATRICK'S CATHEDRAL

TRUMP TOWER

► Map C

stellations painted
Paul Helleu in 1912 –
ticularly impressive
ight when the stars
t up.

Chrysler Building (B4)
→ 05 Lexington Ave
n during office hours
steel spire of this
ding has become
of the symbols of New
k. Erected by William
Alen for the car
gnate Walter Chrysler,
flamboyant Art
o building (1930) is
ous for its gargoyles
tographed by Margaret
rke-White. Marble,
me-plated steel,
ite and wood inlaid

with floral motifs decorate
its splendid lobby.

★ United Nations (D3)
→ First Ave (46th)
Tel. (212) 963 4475
Mon-Fri 9am–4.45pm;
Sat-Sun 10am–4.45pm
(guided tours weekdays only)
John D. Rockefeller, Jr
donated 18 acres of land
running alongside the East
River, purchased for $8.5
million. The complex was
built after World War II
by a team of 11 architects,
including Le Corbusier. A
visit takes in the Security
Council Chamber, the
General Assembly Building
and more. Watch out for
Foucault's Pendulum,

Norman Rockwell's mosaic
and Chagall's stained-glass
window in the lobby.

★ Chanin Building (B4)
→ 122 E 42nd St (Lexington)
Another standout of New
York's Art Deco architecture,
this 1928 building is
embellished with
magnificent bronze friezes
on the theme of evolution.

**★ St Patrick's
Cathedral** (A2)
→ 50th St (Fifth Ave)
Tel. (212) 753 2261
Daily 6.30am–8.45pm
(no visits during services)
This Gothic building, the
largest Catholic cathedral
in the US (holds up to
2,400 people), was built

for New York's vast Irish
community and is now the
starting point for the city's
Easter and St Patrick's Day
parades.

★ Trump Tower (A1)
→ 725 Fifth Ave (57th)
Daily 8am–10pm
The work of real estate
developer, Donald Trump,
now President, this
68-story luxury tower
built in 1983 has an
Italian-marble paneled
atrium and an 80-ft
waterfall fountain. Heavy
security makes going
to the fifth floor for the
tree-planted terrace
hanging over the street
impossible.

LINCOLN CENTER

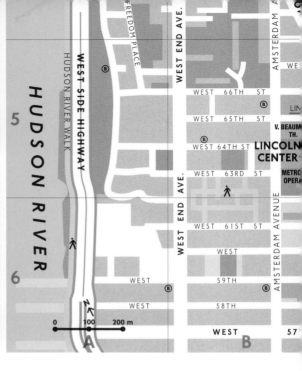

AMERICAN FOLK ART MUSEUM

F

★ Columbus Circle (C6)
→ *Southwest corner of Central Park*
The Time Warner building has changed the face of this area and draws visitors to its restaurants and mall with such stores as Stuart Weitzman and Diptyque.

★ Maine Memorial (D6)
→ *As above*
Sculpted by Attilio Piccirilli, this bronze and marble Beaux Arts monument was erected by press tycoon William R. Hearst in 1913 to commemorate the US battleship Maine, sunk by the Spanish in 1898 in the harbor of Havana, which marked the beginning of the Spanish-American War.

★ Museum of Arts and Design (MAD) (C6)
→ *2 Columbus Circle (58th) Tel. (212) 299 7777 Tue-Sun 10am–6pm (9pm Thu-Fri)*
Formerly the American Craft Museum designed by Edward Durrell-Stone, MAD recently moved to this building redesigned by Brad Cloepfil. The museum presents an overview of the latest trends in objects, furnishings and craft techniques. Great store for unusual gifts.

★ Lincoln Center (B5)
→ *70 Lincoln Plaza at Broadway (62nd and 65th) Tel. (212) 875 5456; Guided tours: Daily 10.30am–4.30pm (times vary)*
Diller Scofidio & Renfro brilliantly redid Alice Tully Hall, and many parts of this complex, also adding cinemas and a rooftop theater. The seven buildings hold up to 12,000 spectators. The main venues are the Metropolitan Opera House, David Geffen Hall (home to the New York Philharmonic orchestra), the Vivian Beaumont Theater, the David H. Koch Theater, Alice Tully Hall and the Juilliard School of Music.

★ American Folk Art Museum (C5)
→ *2 Lincoln Square (66th / Columbus Ave) Tel. (212) 595 9533 Tue-Sun 11.30am (noon F Sun)–7pm (7.30pm Fri, 6pm Sun)*
The fascinating permane collections and traveling exhibitions of American folk art: paintings, potte and fabrics from the 18 century to the present c

★ The Dakota (C4)
→ *72nd St (Central Park W* A prestigious address which has been home

MAINE MEMORIAL

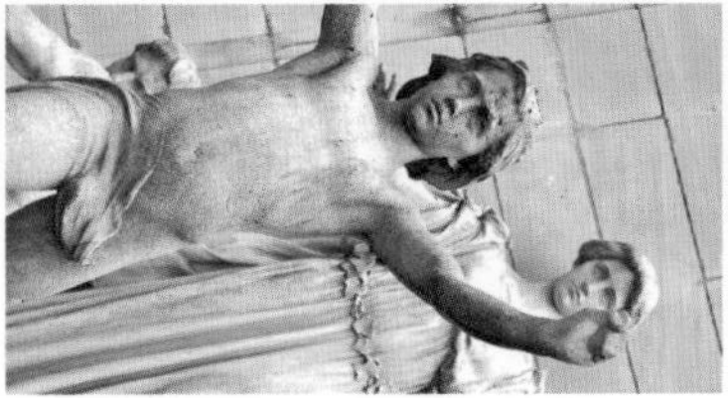

COLUMBUS CIRCLE

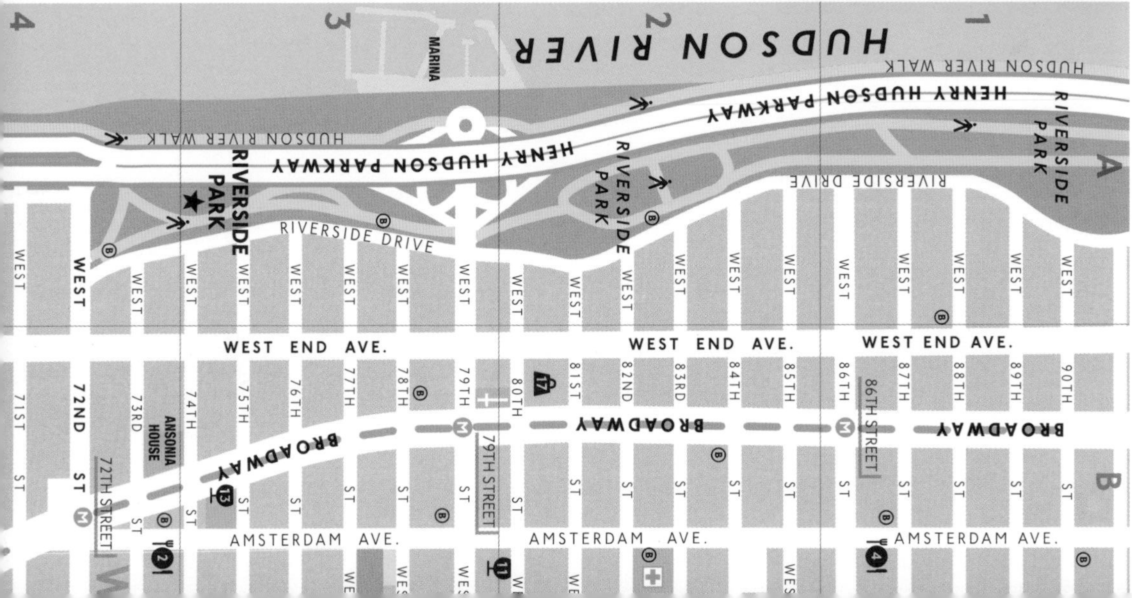

Upper West Side

Map Labels

Streets (West):
- WEST 71ST ST
- WEST 72ND ST
- WEST 73RD ST
- WEST 74TH ST
- WEST 75TH ST
- WEST 76TH ST
- WEST 77TH ST
- WEST 78TH ST
- WEST 79TH ST
- WEST 80TH ST
- WEST 81ST ST
- WEST 82ND ST
- WEST 83RD ST
- WEST 84TH ST
- WEST 85TH ST
- WEST 86TH ST
- WEST 87TH ST
- WEST 88TH ST
- WEST 89TH ST
- WEST 90TH ST

Avenues and Roads:
- AMSTERDAM AVE.
- BROADWAY
- WEST END AVE.
- RIVERSIDE DRIVE
- HENRY HUDSON PARKWAY
- HUDSON RIVER WALK
- HUDSON RIVER

Parks:
- RIVERSIDE PARK

Points of Interest:
- ANSONIA HOUSE
- MARINA

Subway Stations:
- 72ND STREET
- 79TH STREET
- 86TH STREET

Immortalized by West Side Story, the upper west side has greatly changed since the period when Lincoln Center was being built (1955–69). Many of the big names in show business seem to prefer this luxurious but lively district to its equivalent across the Park. From Columbus Circle to 96th Street there are many good restaurants and bars to visit after seeing a show. From Lincoln Center you can take a short walk and visit the spectacular Rose Center for Earth and Space.

BARNEY GREENGRASS

CAFÉ LUXEMBOURG

RESTAURANTS

Blue Ribbon Sushi Bar & Grill (C6) 🍴❶
→ 6 Columbus Hotel, 308 W 58th St (Eighth)
Tel. (212) 397 0404; Mon-Sat 7–10.30am, noon–2am; Sun noon–midnight
A beloved brand for classic sushi and cooked fish and meat. Downtown locations: 119 Sullivan St (**C** C5) and 187 Orchard St (**C** B4), and a brasserie at 30 Rockefeller Plaza (**D** E2). Dishes $15–33.

Salumeria Rosi (B4) 🍴❷
→ 283 Amsterdam Ave (74th); Tel. (212) 877 4800 Mon-Fri noon–10pm; Sat-Sun 11am–11pm
Eat at the bar or at tables in this small, elegant spot; every kind of salumi and delicious pâtés and grilled vegetables. Small plates or platters $9–17.

Bar Boulud (C5) 🍴❸
→ 1900 Broadway (63rd and 64th)
Tel. (212) 595 0303
Mon-Fri 11.30am–2.30pm, 5–11pm (midnight Fri); Sat-Sun 11am–4pm, 5–10pm (midnight Sat)
This modern bistro with booths serves terrines, pâtés and coq au vin; next door is Boulud Epicerie; on 64th is Boulud Sud for

Mediterranean cuisine. Sandwiches from $16; dishes from $23 at Bar Boulud and Boulud Sud.

Barney Greengrass (B1) 🍴❹
→ 541 Amsterdam Ave (86th and 87th)
Tel. (212) 724 4707
Tue-Sun 8am–6pm
A deli with formica tables and delicious smoked salmon, sturgeon bagels and East European specialties. From $11.

Café Luxembourg (B4) 🍴❺
→ 200 W 70th St (West End and Amsterdam)
Tel. (212) 873 7411
Daily 8am (9am Sat-Sun)– midnight (11pm Sun-Tue)
Lynn Wagenknecht's 1930s-style bistro with a classic menu and a lively crowd of actors and writers. Dishes $25–40.

Nougatine at Jean-Georges (C6) 🍴❻
→ 1 Central Park West (60th and 61st)
Tel. (212) 299 3900
Daily 7am (8am Sat-Sun)– 10.30am, 11.45am–3.30pm, 5.30pm (5pm Fri-Sat)–11pm
In this modern space with a view of the park enjoy a crispy shrimp and avocado salad with champagne dressing. Three-course set lunch $38; dinner tasting

BEACON THEATRE

ZABAR'S

menu $98.

Time Warner Center restaurants (C6) 🍴7

→ *10 Columbus Circle*

Among the nine restaurants are Masa, Bluebird and Thomas Keller's Bouchon Bakery where you can sample (or take out) a sublime pastry, quiche or French-style baguette. And Whole Foods in the basement has salads, sushi and other take-out.

Shun Lee West (C5) 🍴8

→ *43 W 65th St (Columbus and Central Park West)*
Tel. (212) 595 8895
Mon–Fri noon–midnight;
Sat–Sun noon–10.30pm
(midnight Sat)

Popular with the Lincoln Center crowd. Attached is the black-and-white Shun Lee Café serving dim sum. Dishes $17–38 ($17 in the café).

ICE-CREAM PARLOR, CAFÉS

Maison Kayser (D6) 9

→ *1800 Broadway (59th St)*
Tel. (212) 245 4100
Daily 7am–8pm

A cozy café ideal for lunch, with tartines, sandwiches and salads – inside or out – and pre-theater dinner with onion soup, beef *bourguinon* and roasted salmon; also breakfast and brunch.

Grom (D6) 10

→ *1796 Broadway (58th and 59th); Tel. (212) 974 3444*
Daily 11am–11.30pm
(12.30am Fri-Sat); opens noon Mon-Thu in winter

Extra-noir chocolate is just one of 20 ice-cream flavors from this Turin gelateria. Also at 233 Bleecker St (**B** C5).

Sarabeth's (B2) 11

→ *423 Amsterdam Ave (80th); Tel. (212) 496 6280*
Daily 8am–10pm

Great for breakfast, and the fruit juices are ambrosial.

BARS, CONCERTS

Lincoln Ristorante (B5) 12

→ *142 W 65th (Broadway and Amsterdam)*
Tel. (212) 359 6500
Mon-Tue 5–10.30pm;
Wed-Fri noon–2pm,
5–10.30pm (11pm Thu-Fri);
Sat-Sun 11.30am–2pm,
5–11pm (9.30pm Sun)

Have a drink in the bar of this glass pavilion designed by Diller Scofidio + Renfro at Lincoln Center; in warm weather sit outside by the reflecting pool.

Beacon Theatre (B3) 13

→ *2124 Broadway (74th)*
Tel. (212) 465 6500
beacontheatre.com

A beautiful Art Deco theater which has hosted performers as varied as Leonard Cohen, Bruce Springsteen and Sting; see the concert program for upcoming shows.

The Office (C6) 14

→ *80 Columbus Circle (60th); Tel. (212) 805 8800*
Tue-Sat 5.30–11.30pm
(1am Fri-Sat)

A small, intimate bar on the 35th floor of the Mandarin Oriental. The adjacent Aviary lobby lounge offers stunning views and inventive cocktails.

Jazz at Lincoln Center (C6) 15

→ *Time Warner Building, Frederick P. Rose Hall, (60th St and Broadway)*
Tickets from CenterCharge, daily 10am–9pm, tel. (212) 721 6500 or online: jazz.org

Special concerts at the Appel Room with its 50-ft glass wall overlooking the park (tickets $5–20 can be booked ahead). Listen to jazz nightly at:

Dizzy's Club Coca-Cola (C6) 16

→ *Tel. (212) 258 9595*
Concerts usually at 7.30pm

and 9.30pm daily; entrance $20–45 plus $10 min. per person for food and drinks

SHOPPING

Zabar's (B2) 17

→ *2245 Broadway (80th)*
Tel. (212) 787 2000
Mon-Sat 8am–7.30pm
(8pm Sat); Sun 9am–6pm

Gourmet food, ideal for picnics. Upstairs: kitchenware. Downstairs: fish, smoked meats, cheeses, pastries and rare teas.

J. Crew (C6) 18

→ *10 Columbus Circle*
Tel. (212) 823 9302
Daily 10am–9pm (7pm Sun)

Well-designed men's, women's and children's clothing, shoes and accessories.

Theory (C4) 19

→ *230 Columbus Ave (70th and 71st); Tel. (212) 362 3676*
Daily 10am (11am Sat)–7pm;
Sun noon–6pm

Classic, popular women's clothes that are well cut and easy to wear.

Rag & Bone (C4) 20

→ *182 Columbus Ave (68th and 69th)*
Tel. 212 362 7138
Daily 11am–7pm (Sun 7pm)

Great jeans and hip casual tops, jackets, day and night wear for women.

▼ Map G

STRAWBERRY FIELDS

IMAGINE

DAKOTA BUILDING

▼ Map H

STRAWBERRY FIELDS

BETHESDA FOUNTAIN

CHERRY HILL

★

BOW BRIDGE

THE LAKE

THE RAMBLE

CENTRAL PARK 3

TRANSVERSE ROAD N.2

BELVEDERE CASTLE
SHAKESPEARE GARDEN

DELACORTE THEATER

TURTLE POND

THE GREAT LAWN 2

SUMMIT ROCK

PINETUM

TRANSVERSE ROAD N.3

WEST DRIVE

WEST DRIVE

WEST DRIVE

JACQUELINE KENNEDY ONASSIS RESERVOIR

1

DAKOTA BUILDING

73RD ST

DAKOTA BUILDING

72ND STREET

72ND ST

71ST

71ST

NEW YORK HISTORICAL SOCIETY ★

AMERICAN MUSEUM OF NATURAL HISTORY ★

81ST ST MUSEUM OF NATURAL HISTORY

WEST 81ST ST

74TH ST

75TH ST

76TH ST

82ND ST

83RD ST

84TH ST

86TH STREET

87TH

88TH

89TH

90TH

COLUMBUS AVE.

COLUMBUS AVE.

COLUMBUS AVE.

CENTRAL PARK WEST

CENTRAL PARK WEST

CENTRAL PARK WEST

D

C

**AMERICAN MUSEUM
OF NATURAL HISTORY**

RIVERSIDE PARK

▲ Map D

number of American (Judy Garland, ...en Bacall, Boris Karloff, ...ard Bernstein...). ...in 1884 by Edward ..., president of Singer ...ng Machines, ...akota was one of ...York's first luxury ...tment buildings. ...er Beatle John ...on, who lived here, ...murdered just outside ...ecember 8, 1980.

**...rawberry
...s** (D4)
...nd St (Central Park West)
...s particularly bucolic
...er of Central Park
...r of The Dakota, a
...ic symbolizing peace,

called Imagine, evokes one of John Lennon's greatest hits. Many fans still gather there to pay respects to his memory.

★ **New York Historical
Society** (C3)
→ 170 Central Park
West (77th); Tel. (212) 873
3400; Tue-Sat 10am–6pm
(8pm Fri); Sun 11am–5pm
New York's oldest
museum, dating back to
1804, now renovated, has
such attractions as a
multimedia installation
about New York's past,
DiMenna's Children's
History Museum and an
Italian restaurant by
Stephen Starr.

★ **American Museum
of Natural History** (C3)
→ Central Park West (79th St)
(entrance by the Theodore
Roosevelt Memorial)
Tel. (212) 769 5100
Daily 10am–5.45pm
One of the largest natural
history museums in the
world has permanent
exhibitions on minerals,
dinosaurs, mammals,
birds, and African,
American-Indian and Asian
civilizations. There are
celebrated dioramas
and first-rate temporary
exhibits on everything
from diamonds to live frogs
and butterflies. Nature
films are shown on a giant

screen in the LeFrack
Theater. Don't miss the
fantastic planetarium next
door: the Rose Center for
Earth and Space.

★ **Riverside Park** (A3)
→ Riverside Drive
Running 86 blocks along
the Hudson River, this is
the second largest green
expanse in Manhattan
after Central Park.
Frederick Law Olmsted
followed the route of the
Hudson River Railroad
to create this vast park,
which includes the Boat
Basin Café at the end of
79th Street with an open-
air space overlooking
the marina.

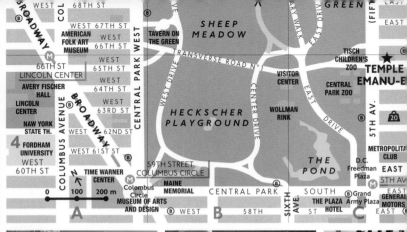

▲ Map D

WEST 68TH ST
BROADWAY
WEST 67TH ST
AMERICAN FOLK ART MUSEUM
WEST 66TH ST
TAVERN ON THE GREEN
SHEEP MEADOW
66TH ST LINCOLN CENTER
WEST 65TH ST
TRANSVERSE ROAD N°1
AVERY FISCHER HALL
WEST 64TH ST
VISITOR CENTER
TISCH CHILDREN'S ZOO
TEMPLE EMANU-E
LINCOLN CENTER
WEST 63RD ST
HECKSCHER PLAYGROUND
CENTRAL PARK ZOO
NAW YORK STATE TH.
WEST 62ND ST
WOLLMAN RINK
20
FORDHAM UNIVERSITY
WEST 61ST ST
METROPOLITA CLUB
WEST 60TH ST
COLUMBUS AVENUE
59TH STREET COLUMBUS CIRCLE
THE POND
D.C. Freedman Plaza
EAST 5TH AV
TIME WARNER CENTER
MAINE MEMORIAL
CENTRAL PARK
SOUTH
Grand Army Plaza
EAST GENERAL MOTORS
Columbus Circle MUSEUM OF ARTS AND DESIGN
WEST
58TH
THE PLAZA HOTEL
EAST
0   100   200 m
A   B   C

CENTRAL PARK

CENTRAL PARK ZOO

CENTRAL PARK / WOLLMAN

★ **Central Park** (B2)
→ *Visitor Center (65th St)*
Park open daily 6am–1am
Landscape architect Frederick Law Olmsted (1858–77) and Calvert Vaux designed the park in 1857. It took 20 years and 500,000 trees to create this 844-acre oasis in the middle of Manhattan. *See also page 8.*

Wollman Rink & Victorian Gardens (B4)
→ *East Drive (65th)*
Rink: Oct-April: Daily 10am–10pm (2.30pm Mon-Tue, 11pm Fri-Sat, 9pm Sun) Gardens: End May-mid Sep: Daily 10am–7pm (times vary)
victoriangardensnyc.com

A mini amusement park with rides, slides, a roller-coaster in summer and open-air ice-skating in winter. Don't miss the Carousel at 64th St.

Central Park Zoo (C4)
→ *Fifth Ave (64th)*
Tel. (212) 439 6500; Daily 10am–5pm (5.30pm Sat-Sun); closes 4.30pm Nov-March
More than 150 species over the Tropic Zone, the Polar Circle and the open-air Temperate Territory; there is also a children's zoo. Don't miss the grizzly bear and snow leopards.

★ **Roosevelt Island Tramway** (E4)
→ *E 60th St (Second); Daily 6am–2.30am (3.30am Fri-Sat)*
Float over the East River in the aerial cable car, taking in the breathtaking panorama of the city for the price of a subway ticket.

★ **Frick Collection** (C3)
→ *One E 70th St (Fifth)*
Tel. (212) 288 0700; Tue-Sat 10am–6pm; Sun 11am–5pm
For nearly 40 years Henry Clay Frick, an industrialist from Pittsburgh, amassed a unique collection of artworks housed in his mansion: enamels from Limoges, Renaissance bronzes, paintings by Vermeer, Fragonard, Ingres, Bellini, El Greco and Whistler; and a collection

of French royal furniture
★ **Mount Vernon Ho Museum & Garden** (
→ *421 E 61st St (First)*
Tel. (212) 838 6878; Tue-S 11am–4pm (last tour 3.30
Built in 1799, this Feder style nine-room museu with 19th-century perio furniture once belonge to President John Adam daughter. Summer conc

★ **Temple Emanu-El**
→ *One E 65th St (Fifth)*
Tel. (212) 744 1400
Sun-Thu 10am–4.30pm
Built in 1929, this large reformed synagogue in the world, a Byzantine-Romanesque-style tem covered with mosaics,

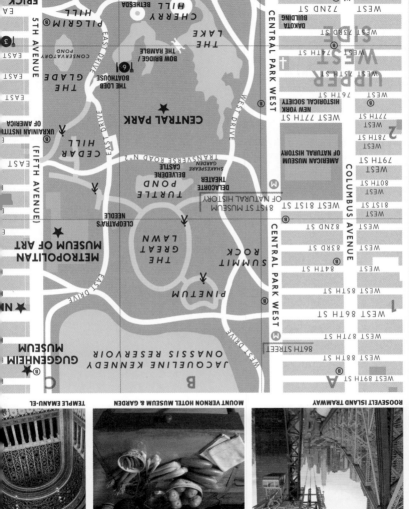

CENTRAL PARK

METROPOLITAN MUSEUM OF ART

GUGGENHEIM MUSEUM

FRICK COLLECTION

TEMPLE EMANU-EL

MOUNT VERNON HOTEL MUSEUM & GARDEN

ROOSEVELT ISLAND TRAMWAY

THE GREAT LAWN

PINETUM

SUMMIT ROCK

TURTLE POND

DELACORTE THEATER

SHAKESPEARE GARDEN

BELVEDERE CASTLE

TRANSVERSE ROAD N°2

CEDAR HILL

THE LOEB BOATHOUSE

THE GLADE

CONSERVATORY POND

EAST DRIVE

WEST DRIVE

CLEOPATRA'S NEEDLE

JACQUELINE KENNEDY ONASSIS RESERVOIR

UKRAINIAN INSTITUTE OF AMERICA

THE RAMBLE

BOW BRIDGE / THE LAKE

PILGRIM HILL

CHERRY HILL

BETHESDA FOUNTAIN / THE MALL

SUMMERSTAGE

BOWLING

The Mall

DAKOTA BUILDING

NEW YORK HISTORICAL SOCIETY

AMERICAN MUSEUM OF NATURAL HISTORY

81ST ST MUSEUM OF NATURAL HISTORY

CENTRAL PARK WEST

COLUMBUS AVENUE

5TH AVENUE

(FIFTH AVENUE)

EAST 72ND STREET

72ND STREET

WEST 70TH ST
WEST 71ST ST
WEST 72ND ST
WEST 73RD ST
WEST 74TH ST
WEST 75TH ST
WEST 76TH ST
WEST 77TH ST
WEST 78TH ST
WEST 79TH ST
WEST 80TH ST
WEST 81ST ST
WEST 82ND ST
WEST 83RD ST
WEST 84TH ST
WEST 85TH ST
WEST 86TH ST
WEST 87TH ST
86TH STREET
WEST 88TH ST
WEST 89TH ST

UPPER WEST SIDE

Historically the home of the well-heeled, the luxurious and rather formal upper east side spreads across eight major streets. From west to east the first three are: Fifth Avenue, famous for its major museums, apartments with views of the Park and some of New York's most exclusive stores; Madison Avenue, lined with boutiques of the leading names in fashion; and the largely residential Park Avenue, with its pre-war apartment buildings, each guarded by diligent doormen.

EJ'S LUNCHEONETTE

THE LOEB BOATHOUSE

RESTAURANTS

Sette Mezzo (D3) ①
→ 969 Lexington Ave (70th and 71st)
Tel. (212) 472 0400
Daily noon–3pm, 5–11pm
Daily specials in a bustling atmosphere of neighborhood regulars. Sister restaurant, Vico, is at 1302 Madison Ave (H D5). Dishes $25–43.

EJ's Luncheonette (D3) ②
→ 1271 3rd Ave (73rd)
Tel. (212) 472 0600
Daily 8am–10pm
This popular spot has a classic American diner menu. Dishes $8–19.

Via Quadronno (C3) ③
→ 25 E 73rd St (Madison)
Tel. (212) 650 9880
Mon–Sat 8am (9am Sat)–11pm; Sun 10am–9pm
This tiny Milanese restaurant has great espresso, delicious panini and salads. Panini from $7.50; dishes $20–38. Also at 1228 Madison Ave (H C6).

E. A. T. (C2) ④
→ 1064 Madison Ave (80th and 81st)
Tel. (212) 772 0022
Daily 7am–10pm
Refined deli food served in a soda fountain-style setting. Dishes $20–44.

The Mark Restaurant by Jean-Georges (C2) ⑤
→ The Mark Hotel, 25 E 77th St (Madison)
Tel. (212) 744 4300
Restaurant: Daily 7am–3.30pm, 5.30pm–1am
A lively bar leads to the restaurant where the favorites include black truffle pizza or the Mark cheeseburger; late dinner (until 1am). Dishes $29–58.

The Loeb Boathouse Central Park (B2) ⑥
→ Central Park Lake (East Park and 72nd)
Tel. (212) 517 2233; Mon–Fri noon–3.45pm, 5.30–9pm; Sat–Sun 9.30am–3.45pm, 6–9pm (not open for dinner Dec–March)
Have a meal on the terrace by the lake – great rock Cornish game hen or bronzino; lunch dinner or Sunday brunch. Dishes $24–47.

Sant Ambroeus (D2) ⑦
→ 1000 Madison Ave (78th)
Tel. (212) 570 2211
Daily 9am–11pm
This Milanese spot serves breakfast, lunch and dinner, with amazing cakes, sandwiches, cookies and ice cream to go and an espresso bar. Dishes $26–66. Also at

MACANUDO

ZITOMER

BLOOMINGDALE'S

61st St (Park and Madison) (**G** D4), 1136 3rd Ave (**G** D3), 259 West 4th St (**B** B3) and 265 Lafayette St (**C** A5).

CAFÉS, BARS, CONCERTS

Flora Bar (D2) **8**
→ *The Met Breuer, 945 Madison St (75th St) Tel. (646) 558 5383; Tue-Sun 11.30am–2.30pm, 5.30pm–10pm (9pm Fri-Sat)*
The partners of Café Altro Paradiso have created a lively space and outdoor patio. A light menu: some *crudo*, lambs' ribs with yogurt – among other offerings. Dishes $17–36.

Serendipity 3 (D4) **9**
→ *225 E 60th St (Second and Third); Tel. (212) 838 3531; Daily 11.30am–midnight (1am Fri-Sat)*
Enjoy chicken sandwiches, hot dogs and hamburgers; and for dessert, their frozen hot chocolate or Forbidden Broadway Sundae, in a playful setting crammed with gadgets and toys for sale. Dishes from $17.

Maison Kayser (D2) **10**
→ *1294 Third Ave (74th St) Tel. (212) 744 3100; Daily 7am–10pm (8pm Sat-Sun)*
This French bakery has

more than 20 kinds of pastries; breakfast, lunch and dinner are also served; seven other locations in the city. Sandwiches from $13.

Café Carlyle (C2) **11**
→ *35 E 76th St (Madison) Tel. (212) 744 1600 Mon-Sat 6.30–11pm (midnight Fri-Sat)*
Judy Collins and Woody Allen are among those who have performed at this small, elegant spot; Bemelmans Bar is across the hall.

Club Macanudo (C4) **12**
→ *26 E 63rd St (Madison) Tel. (212) 752 8200 Daily noon–1am (2am Wed-Sat, 10pm Sun)*
Ideal for an evening drink and a cigar; dinner menu and Sunday brunch.

Ty Bar (C4) **13**
→ *Four Seasons Hotel, 58 E 58th St (Madison and Park Ave); Tel. (212) 758 5700; Daily noon–1am (midnight Sun)*
Off the 57th Street lobby, a cozy setting with a fireplace.

Park Avenue Armory (D3) **14**
→ *643 Park Ave (66th and 67th); Tel. (212) 616 3030*
Built in 1861 as a military facility and social club, with rooms by Louis

Comfort Tiffany, Stanford White and the Herter brothers, its 55,000-ft drill hall hosts concerts, plays and opera – Robert Wilson, Laurie Anderson, art installations by Paul McCarthy and art fairs.

SHOPPING

Roberta Roller Rabbit (D3) **15**
→ *1019 Lexington Ave (73rd); Tel. (212) 772 7200 Mon-Sat 10am–6pm; Sun noon–5pm*
Colorful cotton tunics, dresses, beaded and woven bags, jewelry, curtains, bedding, tablemats and furniture – from India, South America and elsewhere.

Barneys (C4) **16**
→ *660 Madison Ave (61st) Tel. (212) 826 8900 Mon-Sat 10am–8pm (7pm Sat); Sun 11am–7pm*
Nine stories dedicated to fashion, with accessories and cosmetics.

Zitomer (C2) **17**
→ *969 Madison Ave (75th and 76th); Tel. (212) 737 5560; Mon-Sat 9am–8pm (7pm Sat); Sun 10am–6pm*
Great pharmacy with cosmetics on the main floor, accessories on the second and a toy store on the third.

Pretty Ballerinas (D2) **18**
→ *1034 Lexington Ave (74th) Tel. (212) 249 7844 Mon-Fri 10am–7pm; Sat 11am–6pm; Sun noon–5pm*
A playful selection of ballerina-style flats ranging from $219–459.

Bloomingdale's (D4) **19**
→ *1013 Lexington Ave (59th) Tel. (212) 705 2000 Mon-Sat 10am–8.30pm; Sun 11am–7pm*
This famous department store has everything, including day and evening wear, linens and hardware.

Fashion district (C4) **20**
The heart of shopping for fashion and accessories.
→ **On 57th Street**
Louis Vuitton (no. 1), Saint Laurent (no. 3), Burberry (no. 9), Miu Miu (no. 11), Chanel (no. 15), Christian Dior (no. 21).
→ **On Madison Avenue**
Fendi (no. 598), Hermès (nos. 690, 691), Jimmy Choo (no. 699), Alice + Olivia (no. 755), Dolce & Gabbana (no. 827), Prada (no. 841), Ralph Lauren (nos. 867, 878, 888), Celine (no. 870), Christian Louboutin (nos 965–67), Vince (no. 980), among many others.

RIVER

ELANO-ROOSEVELT-DRIVE

CORNELL
MEDICAL
CENTER

HOSPITAL

WALK

YORK AVENUE

EAST 70TH ST
EAST 71ST ST
EAST 72ND ST
EAST 73RD ST
EAST 74TH ST
EAST 75TH ST
EAST 76TH ST
EAST 77TH ST
EAST 78TH ST
EAST 79TH ST
EAST 80TH ST
EAST 81ST ST
EAST 82ND ST
EAST 83RD ST
EAST 84TH ST
EAST 85TH ST
EAST 86TH ST
EAST 87TH ST
EAST 88TH ST
EAST 89TH ST

(FIRST AVENUE)
(SECOND AVENUE)
(THIRD AVENUE)

1ST AVENUE
2ND AVENUE
3RD AVENUE

LEXINGTON AVENUE

PARK AVENUE

Cherokee Place

JOHN JAY PARK

BOBBY WAGNER WALK

EAST END AVENUE

CARL SCHURZ PARK

GRACIE MANSION

ASIA SOCIETY
UPPER EAST SIDE
FOX HILL HOSPITAL

FRICK COLLECTION

SOCIETY

◀ **Map E**

4

The map shows street grid with labels including: 68TH STREET HUNTER COLLEGE, CHINA HOUSE, ROCKEFELLER UNIVERSITY, MOUNT VERNON HOTEL MUSEUM & GARDEN, ROOSEVELT ISLAND, E 63RD ST FERRY, ROOSEVELT ISLAND TRAMWAY, BLOOMINGDALE'S, QUEENSBORO BRIDGE, BRIDGEMARKET, SUTTON PLACE, PARK AVENUE, LEXINGTON AVENUE, 3RD AVENUE, 2ND AVENUE, 1ST AVENUE, YORK AVENUE.

OPOLITAN MUSEUM OF ART

GUGGENHEIM MUSEUM

s 2,500.

sia Society (D3)
→ 5 Park Ave (70th)
212) 288 6400; Tue-Sun
–6pm (9pm Fri, except
through Labor Day)
e 300 pieces from John
ockefeller's superb
ction: artifacts and
s of art from Japan,
a and Afghanistan.
llent exhibitions.

eue Galerie (C1)
48 Fifth Ave (86th)
212) 628 6200
Mon 11am–6pm
Sabarsky: Wed-Mon
–6pm (9pm Thu-Sun)
ère & Hastings
gned this 1914
ling renovated as a

museum for early 20th-
century German and
Austrian art and design.
Klimt to the Wiener
Werkstätte to the Blaue
Reiter group are here.
Café Sabarsky is run by
the downtown restaurant
Wallsé. Great bookstore.

★ **Guggenheim
Museum** (C1)
→ 1071 Fifth Ave (89th)
Tel. (212) 423 3500; Fri-Wed
10am–5.45pm (7.45pm Sat)
Architect Frank Lloyd Wright
designed the 2,624-ft
gallery as a spiral climbing
gradually upward toward
the central dome. The
permanent works here
include the world's largest

collection of Kandinskys,
as well as an impressive
number of Impressionist,
Post-Impressionist and
early modern masterpieces
by Renoir, Degas, Monet,
Van Gogh, Picasso and
Léger; also sculptures by
Calder, Giacometti and
Brancusi. See also page 10.

★ **Metropolitan
Museum of Art** (C1)
→ 1000 Fifth Ave (E 82nd)
Tel. (212) 535 7710; Daily
10am–5.30pm (9pm Fri, Sat)
Opened in 1872, this vast
space holds more than two
million works of art, among
which great Italian works,
an amazing collection
of Egyptian and Roman

antiquities and American
art. The Temple of Dendur
was shipped from Egypt
and rebuilt stone by stone
in the museum. See the 15
Islamic galleries and the
renovated American Wing.
See also page 9.

★ **The Met Breuer** (D2)
→ 945 Madison Avenue (75th)
Tue-Sun 10am–5.30pm
(Fri -Sat 9pm)
metmuseum.org/metbreuer
The Metropolitan
Museum of Art is curating
contemporary exhibitions,
performance works and
interactive programs in
this 1966 Marcel Breuer
building, formerly the
Whitney. See also page 9.

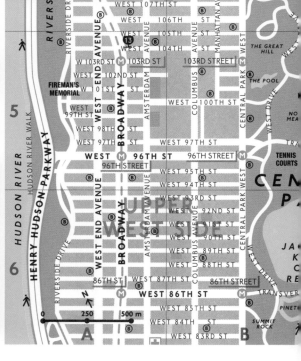

COMMON FISH OF CENTRAL PARK

HARLEM MEER

EAST HARLEM MURALS

★ Cooper Hewitt, Smithsonian Design Museum (C6)
→ 2 E 91st St (Fifth)
Tel. (212) 849 8400
Daily 10am–6pm (9pm Sat)
Once the property of Andrew Carnegie, now the national design museum, the collection includes everything from wallpaper to architectural drawings and furniture. Much of the collection can be viewed through interactive software; a Models & Prototypes gallery illustrates the importance of models for design. There is a shop and the Taralucci café on the main floor.

★ Museum of the City of New York (C5)
→ 1220 Fifth Ave (103rd)
Tel. (212) 534 1672
Daily 10am–6pm
A museum of the history and life of New York and its heroes, famous and unknown alike: historical documents, paintings, models, photos, posters, antique toys, famous dollhouses and costumes. Temporary exhibitions.

★ Museo del Barrio (C5)
→ 1230 Fifth Ave (104th)
Tel. (212) 831 7272; Wed-Sat 11am–6pm; Sun noon–5pm
Founded in 1969, this museum presents films, lectures, temporary exhibitions and concerts all relating to Latin-American art and culture. Very pleasant café.

★ St John the Divine Cathedral (A4)
→ 1047 Amsterdam Ave (112th); Tel. (212) 316 7540
Daily 7.30am–6pm (limited hours on Sundays)
Highlight tours: Mon 11am, 2pm; Tue-Sat 11am, 1pm; Sun 1pm (select weeks)
This enormous Gothic cathedral, begun in 1892, is still unfinished. Its central nave, a record 601 ft in length, leads to various chapels decorated by contemporary artists.

★ Columbia University (A3)
→ Entrance on W 116th St and Broadway
Tel. (212) 854 4900
Various tours offered Mon
The new 17-acre Manhattanville campus this university is being built, and the Jerome L. Green Science Center a the Lenfest Center for th Arts, both designed by Renzo Piano, are the fir projects to have been completed.

★ The Riverside Church (A3)
→ 490 Riverside Drive (12
Tel. (212) 870 6700
Daily 7am–10pm

H

MUSEUM OF THE CITY
OF NEW YORK

COOPER-HEWITT
DESIGN MUSEUM

Heading north along upper Fifth Avenue, Museum Mile is home to some of New York's most famous museums: the Metropolitan, the Guggenheim, El Museo del Barrio... On the west side, once past the Museum of Natural History, a short taxi ride will take you to Morningside Heights, home to Columbia University and the vast Cathedral of St John the Divine. Further north is Harlem, historically home to New York's Afro-American community, gospel, jazz and real Southern cooking.

MAX SOHA

RED ROOSTER

RESTAURANTS

Elio's (D6) 🍴❶
→ 1621 Second Ave (84th)
Tel. (212) 772 2242
Daily 5pm–midnight
This lively Italian restaurant serves a mean veal chop; frequented by writers and media/movie types. Dishes $18–35.

Chez Lucienne (C3) 🍴❷
→ 308 Malcolm X Blvd (125th and 126th); Tel. (212) 289 5555; Mon-Fri 11am–midnight (2am Fri); Sat-Sun 9am–2am (11pm Sun)
Settle into a banquette and enjoy French cooking – outside in fine weather. Live music on Saturdays. Dishes $14–26.

Max SoHa (A3) 🍴❸
→ 1274 Amsterdam Ave (123rd); Tel. (212) 531 2221
Daily noon–midnight
Columbia University students love this trattoria. Dishes $11–16.

Blvd Bistro (C3) 🍴❹
→ 239 Malcom X Blvd (122nd); Tel. (212) 678 6200
Tue-Fri 5–11pm; Sat 11am–11pm; Sun 10am–6pm
In a charming, rustic townhouse, French-American bistro cooking: lunch and a few daily specials for dinner, including a great rib-eye steak. Dishes $16–30.

Abyssinia Ethiopian Restaurant (B2) 🍴❺
→ 268 W 135th St (Frederick Douglas Blvd); Tel: (212) 281 2673; Daily 11am–10pm
Fantastic Ethiopian food cooked up by Daniel Rela and his wife in this 18-seat eatery. Dishes $13–21.

Lenox Saphire (C3) 🍴❻
→ 341 Lenox Ave (127th St)
Tel. (212) 866 9700
Daily 7am (8am Sat-Sun)–midnight (4am Fri-Sat)
On Thursdays listen to Phil Young's friends play fantastic jazz and blues while you enjoy Senegalese-American food: curries, stews or simply a burger or soul food. Dishes $11–16.

Sfoglia (D6) 🍴❼
→ 1402 Lexington Ave (92nd); Tel. (212) 831 1402
Daily 5.30–10.30pm (10pm Sun-Mon)
Rustic charm and Italian cooking; the fennel soup and squid ink risotto are memorable. Dishes $15–28.

Red Rooster (C3) 🍴❽
→ 310 Lenox Ave (126th)
Tel. (212) 792 9001
Mon-Fri 11.30am–3.30pm, 4.30–10.30pm (11.30pm Fri); Sat-Sun 10am–3pm, 4.30–11.30pm (10pm Sun)
Chef Marcus Samuelsson

RIAN PASTRY SHOP

APOLLO THEATER

BLUE TREE

serves up Swedish meatballs and fried yard chicken in this bustling spot. Dishes from $18. Live music in Ginny's Supper Club.

Streetbird Rotisserie (B4) 🍴9️⃣
→ 2149 Frederick Douglass Blvd (W 116th)
Tel. (212) 206 2557
Daily 11am–11pm
Chinese, Latin and El Barrio-influenced food in a setting inspired by 1970s–90s hip-hop. Dishes from $18.

Corner Social (C3) 🍴🔟
→ 321 Lenox Ave (Malcolm X Blvd.)
Tel. (212) 510 8552
Delicious grilled meats and fish and custom burgers. Inside by the fireplace or outside in warm weather. Dishes $17–$29.

CAFÉS, BARS, CONCERTS

Hungarian Pastry Shop (A4) 1️⃣1️⃣
→ 1030 Amsterdam Ave (111th); Tel. (212) 866 4230
Mon-Sat 8am–10.30pm;
Sun 8.30am–11pm
Columbia students like this café for its old-world pastries. Cash only.

Barawine (C3) 1️⃣2️⃣
→ 200 Malcolm X Blvd

(W 120th); Tel. (646) 756 4154; Mon-Fri 4–10pm (11pm Thu, Fri); Sat-Sun 11.30am–11pm (10pm Sun)
Enjoy a glass of wine and a niçoise salad or Black Angus carpaccio.

Smoke Jazz & Supper Club (A5) 1️⃣3️⃣
→ 2751 Broadway (105th)
Tel. (212) 864 6662
Mon-Sat 5.30pm–3am;
Sun 11am–3am
Cover charge $9–45
The jazz greats regularly play here.

Apollo Theater (B3) 1️⃣4️⃣
→ 253 W 125th St (Frederick Douglass Blvd)
Tel. (212) 531 5300
Guided tours: Mon,Tue, Thu, Fri 11am, 1pm, 3pm; Wed 11am; Sat-Sun 11am, 1pm
Many greats have performed here: Count Basie, Duke Ellington, Aretha Franklin, The Supremes and Stevie Wonder. 'Amateur night' on Wednesdays.

Showman's (B3) 1️⃣5️⃣
→ 375 W 125th St (Morningside Ave)
Tel. (212) 864 8941
Mon-Sat 1pm–4am
Concerts: Wed-Thu 8.30pm, 10pm, 11.30pm; Fri-Sat 9.30pm, 11.30pm, 1.30am
Since 1942, a great place to listen to live jazz. No cover charge; minimum

two drinks.

Noglu (C6) 1️⃣6️⃣
→ 1266 Madison Ave (90th and 91st)
Tel. (646) 895 9798; Mon-Sat 7.30am–6pm (7.30pm Sat);
Sun 9am–5pm
This tearoom-pâtisserie has organic and gluten-free cakes, tarts, sandwiches and quiches.

Minton's (B3) 1️⃣7️⃣
→ 206 W 118th St
Tel.(212) 866 1262
Daily 6pm–midnight
A stylish venue with great jazz and brilliant food from JJ Johnson, formerly of Cecil's. Dishes $19–$44.

Sexy Taco Dirty Cash (C3) 1️⃣8️⃣
→ 161 Malcolm X Blvd (118th); Tel. (212) 280 4700
Mon-Fri 3pm–midnight (2am Fri); Sat-Sun 11am–10pm (2am Sat)
A small, lively spot for a drink - margaritas, pacificos, wine and special cocktails.

SHOPPING

Carol's Daughter (C3) 1️⃣9️⃣
→ 24 W 125th St (Lenox and Fifth)
Tel. (212) 828 6757
Mon-Sat 10am–8pm; Sun 11am–6pm; several outlets
Lisa Price's cosmetics –

shampoos, soaps, oils, perfumes – made with natural ingredients.

Theory (C6) 2️⃣0️⃣
→ 1157 Madison (85th and 86th)
Tel. (212) 879 0265
Mon-Sat 10am (11am Sat)–7pm; Sun noon–6pm
Great selection of their signature women's clothing; also menswear.

Target (off D3) 2️⃣1️⃣
→ 517 E 117th St (East River)
Tel. (212) 835 0860
Daily 8am–midnight (11pm Sun)
Inexpensive wares, from furniture, kitchen and bath products to dried food, jeans and designer collections.

Blue Tree (C6) 2️⃣2️⃣
→ 1283 Madison Ave (92nd); Tel. (212) 369 2583
Mon-Sat 10am (11am Sat)–6pm
Actress Phoebe Cates's shop has women's clothing, jewelry and bath products.

Malcolm Shabazz Harlem Market (C4) 2️⃣3️⃣
→ 52 W 116th St (Lenox)
Tel. (212) 987 8131
Daily 10am–8pm
A colorful covered market in the heart of Harlem: masks, African craftwork, clothes, music and movie posters.

COLUMBIA UNIVERSITY

ALMA MATER

ST JOHN THE DIVINE CATHEDRAL

THE LIBRARY OF COLUMBIA

BRONX

WILLIS AVENUE

THOMAS JEFFERSON PARK

MADISON AVENUE

HARLEM RIVER DRIVE

ROBERT F. KENNEDY BRIDGE

LOUIS GUVILLIER PARK

HARLEM RIVER PARK

BRUCKNER BLVD

MAJOR DEEGAN EXPRESSWAY

GRAND CONCOURSE

EAST HARLEM

PARK AVENUE

FIFTH AVENUE

MOUNT MORRIS PARK WEST

MARCUS GARVEY MEMORIAL PARK

5TH AVENUE

NATIONAL JAZZ MUSEUM IN HARLEM

WILLIS AVE.

3RD AVE.

WILLIS AVENUE

MORRIS AVE.

RIDER AVENUE

CANAL PLACE

PARK AVENUE

WALTON AVENUE

GERARD AVENUE

GRAND CONCOURSE

HARLEM HOSPITAL CENTER

East 110th St — 111th St — 112th St
East 115th St — 116th St
East 117th St — 118th St — 119th St — 120th St — 121st St — 122nd St — 123rd St — 124th St
East 125th St — 126th St — 127th St — 128th St — 129th St — 130th St — 131st St — 132nd St — 133rd St

West 111th St — 112th St
West 115th St — 116th St
West 126th St — 127th St

E 129th St — 130th St — 131st St — 132nd St

W 133th St — E 135th St

West 131st St — 138th St — 139th St

East 138th St — 140th St — 141st St — 143rd St

138TH ST — 3RD AVENUE — 138TH STREET

138TH STREET — GRAND CONCOURSE

East 149th St — 150th St

149TH STREET — GRAND CONCOURSE

Flawley Circle

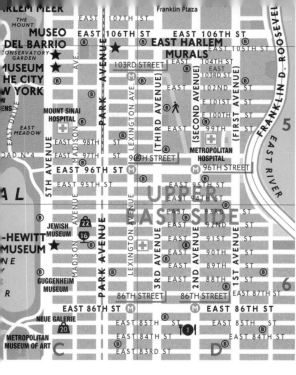

FIRST CORINTHIAN BAPTIST CHURCH

STUDIO MUSEUM IN HARLEM

▲ Map G

---

ded in 1930 on the
tive of J. D. Rockefeller,
iverside Church is
thic-style building
eled after Chartres
edral in France. Its
ntic 74-bell carillon
its five-octave range
e largest in the world.

**rst Corinthian
tist Church** (B4)
12 Adam Clayton
ll Jr Blvd (Seventh)
ces: Sun 7.30am,
am, 11.30am;
oon, 7pm
st ornate church in
ormer movie palace,
Regent (1913), which
nbles a Venetian
ce. Visit on Sunday

to attend services and
hear the glorious singing
of the 70-member choir.

★ **Studio Museum
in Harlem** (B3)
→ 144 W 125th St (Lenox Ave
and Adam C. Powell Jr Blvd)
Tel. (212) 864 4500
Thu–Sun noon (10am
Sat)–6pm (9pm Thu–Fri)
This terrific museum of
African-American arts
has a large collection
of paintings, sculpture
and photographs, the
latter including James Van
Der Zee's work from the
1920s–30s Harlem
Renaissance.

★ **Harlem Meer** (C4)
→ Central Park (106th / 110th)

***Charles A. Dana Discovery
Center:*** Daily 10am–5pm
This lake in Central Park
stretches from 106th to
110th Streets. There is
catch-and-release fishing
in summer and skating
in the winter. It is also a
good place to spot turtles
and night herons.

★ **East Harlem
Murals** (C5)
The walls of East Harlem
can speak. Numerous
colorful murals line the
streets and avenues, one
of the most famous being
the four-story work created
in the 1970s by Hank
Prussing and Manny Vega,
The Spirit of East Harlem

(Lexington and 104th St).
Also see the Graffiti Hall
of Fame (106th/Park Ave),
created in 1980, where
well-known street artists
display their skills on
schoolyard walls.

★ **National Jazz
Museum in Harlem** (C3)
→ 58 W 129th St
Tel. (212) 348 8300
Thu-Mon 11am–5pm
An exciting collection of
photographs, recordings,
books and documentary film
celebrating the jazz greats,
from Duke Ellington to John
Coltrane, via Charlie Parker.
There are 1,000 records
and DVDs available to
listen to.

BROOKLYN HEIGHTS PROMENADE

BROOKLYN HISTORICAL SOCIETY

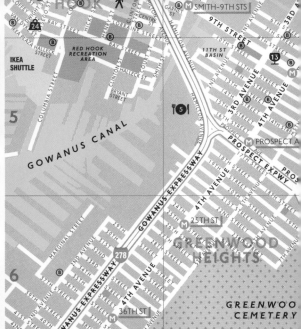

★ Manhattan Bridge (B1)
Manhattan's suspension bridge (1909, Leon Moisseiff) was the star of Sergio Leone's movie *Once Upon a Time in America*, and has a walkway and bikeway linking DUMBO to Chinatown.

★ Brooklyn Bridge (B1)
The initial plans, presented in 1855, seemed pure folly, and it wasn't until the end of the Civil War that the project saw the light of day. Some workers died during the 13 long years it took to build this steel suspension bridge, one of the longest and first of its kind in the world. A pedestrian walkway overlooks downtown, the East River and Brooklyn. *See also page 11.*

★ Brooklyn Heights Promenade (B2)
→ *Between Joralemon St and Grace Court*
This has to be the finest view of the Brooklyn Bridge and the skyscrapers of Lower Manhattan. Opened in 1950, the pedestrian walkway is a haven for joggers, artists looking for inspiration, and anyone admiring the sunset.

★ Brooklyn Bridge Park (B2)
→ *1 Main St; Daily 6am–1am*
An urban oasis located between the Brooklyn and Manhattan bridges, two riverside parks with views of the skyline. There are play areas, wild birds (with mulberry trees that attract them) and an old tobacco warehouse. Pier 1 has two large lawns and an imaginative children's playground.

★ Brooklyn Historical Society (B2)
→ *128 Pierrepont St (Clinton) Tel. (718) 222 4111 Wed–Sun noon–5pm*
Housed in a National Historic Landmark (1881) designed by George Post, with a fine, unglazed terracotta Queen Anne-style façade. The fourth floor is suspended, following the model of the Brooklyn Bridge. Inside, the museum documents Brooklyn's 400-year history.

★ New York Transit Museum (B3)
→ *Boerum Place (Schermerhorn); Tel. (718) 694 1600; Tue–Fri 10am–4pm; Sat-Sun 11am–5pm*
The entrance looks like an ordinary subway station, but inside is an exhibit tracing the history of the hundred-year-old network using photos, film footage and interactive

I

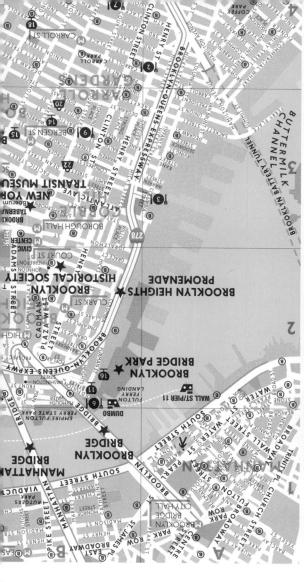

BROOKLYN BRIDGE

MANHATTAN BRIDGE

Brooklyn Heights, with its streets named after different fruit and its fine brownstone houses, has an old-fashioned provincial charm. To the north, DUMBO (Down Under the Manhattan Bridge Overpass) is home to a growing number of galleries and artistic communities housed in converted factories. To the east, young families and writers relax in cafés around BoCoCa (Boerum Hill, Cobble Hill and Carroll Gardens) and Park Slope, before heading off for a stroll in Prospect Park.

BUTTERMILK CHANNEL

RIVER CAFÉ

RESTAURANTS

Olmstead (D4) **① ❙**
→ 659 Vanderbilt Ave (Park & Prospect Place)
Tel. (718) 552 2610
Daily 5–10.30pm
Chef Greg Baxtrom has created a seasonal menu with greens and quail sourced from the garden out back. Dishes $13–24.

Lucali (A4) **② ❙**
→ 575 Henry St (Carroll)
Tel. (718) 858 4086
Wed-Mon 6–10pm
Seating 30, Mark Iacono serves up amazing pizza. No reservations; cash only. BYOB. Dishes $10–24.

Pok Pok (A3) **③ ❙**
→ 117 Columbia St (Kane)
Tel. (718) 923 9322; Daily 5.30 (Sat-Sun noon)–10pm
Authentic Thai food including Chiang Mai sausages. No reservations. Dishes from $15.

Fausto (D4) **④ ❙**
→ 348 Flatbush Ave (Sterling Pl and 8th Ave)
Tel. (917) 909 1427
Mon-Thu 5.30–11pm;
Fri noon– 2.30pm,
5.30–11pm; Sat- Sun noon–11.30pm (10pm Sun)
Rustic Italian dishes cooked in a wood-fired oven; great porgy, snapper *crudo*, roast chicken and homemade pestos. Dishes $18–26.

Buttermilk Channel (B4) **⑤ ❙**
→ 524 Court St (Huntington)
Tel. (718) 852 8490
Daily 11.30am (10am Sat-Sun)–3pm, 5–10pm (11pm Thu, midnight Fri)
Have the buttermilk-fried chicken with cheddar waffles in this light-filled room. Dishes $12–25.

River Café (B2) **⑥ ❙**
→ 1 Water St
Tel. (718) 522 5200; Mon-Fri 8.30–11.30am, 5.30–11pm;
Sat-Sun 11.30am–2.30pm, 5.30–11pm
On the river, with great views of the skyline; popular for Sunday brunch. Live piano at night. Set lunch $42; brunch $55; dishes $120.

Frankies Spuntino (B4) **⑦ ❙**
→ 457 Court St (4th Place and Luquer); Tel. (718) 403 0033; Daily 11am–11pm (midnight Fri-Sat)
A garden out back and modern Italian cooking. No reservations. Dishes $10–20. Also at 570 Hudson St (W 11th St) (B4). German Alpine cuisine nearby at Prime Meats (**C** B5).

Ganso Ramen (C3) **⑧ ❙**
→ 25 Bond St (Livingston)

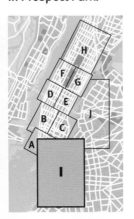

ER CLUB   STERLING PLACE   BIRD

Tel. (718) 403 0900
Daily 11.30am–10pm
(11pm Fri-Sat)
An open kitchen and a daily changing menu of perfect ramen. No reservations. Ramen $15–16.

La Vara (B3) 🍴**9**🍷
→ 268 Clinton St (Verandah Pl); Tel. (718) 422 0065
Mon-Fri 5–11pm (midnight Fri); Sat-Sun 11.30am–midnight (10pm Sun)
Delicious Spanish food drawing on Middle Eastern ingredients. Small plates from $3, large plates from $15.

Convivium Osteria (C4) 🍴**10**🍷
→ 68 5th Ave (Bergen)
Tel. (718) 857 1833
Mon-Fri noon–3pm, 5–11pm (11.30pm Fri); Sat-Sun 5–10pm (11.30pm Sat)
In three romantic, rustic rooms enjoy the cooking of Italy, Spain and Portugal. Dishes $18–35.

ICE-CREAM PARLORS, CAFÉ

Brooklyn Ice Cream Factory (B2) **11**
→ 1 Water St/Fulton Ferry
Tel. (718) 246 3963
Daily noon–10pm
Fabulous artisanal ice cream on the waterfront.

Ample Hills Creamery (D4) **12**
→ 623 Vanderbilt Ave (St Mark's)
Tel. (347) 240 3926
Daily noon–10pm (11pm Fri)
Delicious organic homemade ice-cream: try the salty hazelnut with chocolate covered sunflower seeds.

Four & Twenty Blackbirds (B5) **13**
→ 439 3rd Ave (8th)
Tel. (718) 499 2917
Mon-Sat 8am (9am Sat)–8pm; Sun 10am–7pm
A changing menu of pies to buy by the slice or whole; don't miss the salted caramel apple or lavender honey.

BARS, CONCERTS

Clover Club (B3) **14**
→ 210 Smith St (Baltic)
Tel. (718) 855 7939
Mon-Fri 4pm–2am (4am Fri); Sat-Sun 10.30am–4am (1am Sun)
Old-world charm with a trendy edge: bartenders in vests, chandeliers and a crackling fireplace.

Brooklyn Inn (B3) **15**
→ 148 Hoyt St (Bergen)
Tel. (718) 522 2525
Daily 4pm–4am
A former poets' hangout with an 1800s carved wood bar, stained-glass

windows and a juke box.

St Ann's Warehouse (B2) **16**
→ Tobacco Warehouse, Brooklyn Bridge Park
Tel. (718) 254 8779
Box office: Tue-Sat 1–7pm
Cutting-edge plays and performances – Wooster Group, Mabou Mines, Karen O among them.

Royal Palms (B4) **17**
→ 514 Union St (Nevins and 3rd Ave)
Tel. (347) 223 4410
Mon-Fri 6pm–midnight (2am Thu, Fri); Sat-Sun 2pm–midnight (2am Sat)
This expansive 1970s Palm Beach-themed bar houses ten shuffleboard courts, rotating food trucks and great drinks.

Lavender Lake (B4) **18**
→ 383 Carroll St (Bond)
Tel. (347) 799 2154
Daily 4pm–midnight (1am Thu, 2am Fri-Sat)
A converted carriage house, with inventive cocktails and a perfect menu; also a light-strung backyard.

Vinegar Hill House (C2) **19**
→ 72 Hudson Ave (Water St)
Tel. (718) 522 1018
Mon-Fri 6–11pm; Sat-Sun 10am-3.30pm, 6–11.30pm
A cozy bar area in this restaurant where you can find natural wines.

SHOPPING

Bird (B3) **20**
→ 220 Smith St (Butler)
Tel. (718) 797 3774
Mon-Fri noon–8pm;
Sat-Sun 11am–7pm
Women's and men's clothing and accessories – Phillip Lim, A.P.C. and Thakoon among them.

Sterling Place (C3) **21**
→ 363 Atlantic Ave (Bond)
Tel. (718) 797 5667; Daily 11am (11.30am Sun)–6.30pm
Unusual gifts, rugs, antique model ships, board games and more. Also at 148 and 352 Seventh Ave.

Diane T (B3) **22**
→ 174 Court St (Bergen)
Tel. (718) 923 5777; Tue-Sat 11am–7.30pm (6.30pm Sat); Sun 1–5.30pm
Well-edited selection of women's clothes and accessories.

Consignment Brooklyn (C3) **23**
→ 371 Atlantic Ave (Bond)
Tel. (718) 522 3522
Daily 11am–7pm (6pm Sun)
Vintage womenswear and accessories.

Saipua (A4) **24**
→ 177 Dwight St (Van Dyke St); Tel. (718) 624 2929
Wed-Sun noon–7pm
Flowers, hand-made soap, and other items that make the perfect gift.

BROOKLYN ACADEMY OF MUSIC

NEW YORK TRANSIT MUSEUM

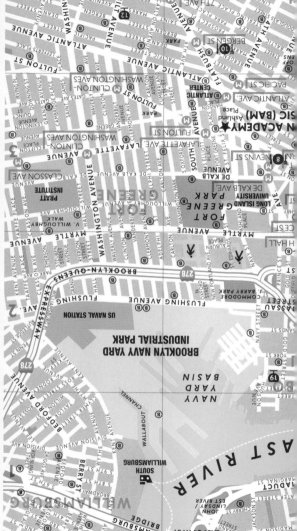

▶ Map J

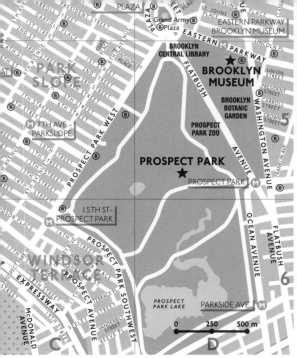

PROSPECT PARK

BROOKLYN BOTANIC GARDEN

llations (children can at being guards or rs). One platform every type of car used e 1904, complete old ads of the period.

rooklyn eum (D5)
o Eastern Parkway
718) 638 5000; Wed-Sun
–6pm (10pm Thu, 11pm
Sat of each month)
2 departments
de collections
yptian, Asiatic,
essionist and American
Retrospectives of
rtant contemporary
s have included
uiat and Murakami, as
as Gilbert & George. In

2004, the glass and metal Rubin pavilion was built in front of the 19th-century Beaux Arts façade as the museum's new entrance and lobby. See also page 11.

★ **Prospect Park** (D5)
→ Entrance on Grand Army Plaza; Tel. (718) 965 8951 Daily 5am–1am
Laid out in 1867 by the designers of Central Park, Olmsted and Vaux, this park (585 acres) contains the only area of natural woodland in Brooklyn. In the northwest corner is a large field where concerts are given in summer, and in the east is a leafy ravine and a zoo. To the south

is a 60-acre lake, great for boating in fine weather. It is a more rustic park than its Manhattan rival, and popular among the locals for Sunday outings.

★ **Brooklyn Botanic Garden** (D5)
→ 900 Washington Ave Tel. (718) 623 7200; Tue-Sun 8am (Sat-Sun 10am)–6pm (10am–4.30pm Nov-Feb)
This 52-acre botanic garden in the northeast corner of Prospect Park was laid out in 1910, and contains more than 10,000 species of plants. There are gardens within the garden too: Cranford Rose Garden is a beautiful spot in early

summer; the Fragrance Garden has scented plants (designed with the vision-impaired in mind); and the Shakespeare Garden has flowers and herbs mentioned in the works of the English dramatist. Look out too for the Japanese Garden, whose cherry trees flower in April during the Cherry Blossom Festival.

★ **Brooklyn Academy of Music (BAM)** (C3)
→ 30 Lafayette Ave Tel. (718) 636 4100
This 1908 venue hosts important theater, opera, concerts and dance. There is also the Harvey Theater and a cinematheque.

MOMA PS1

DORSKY GALLERY

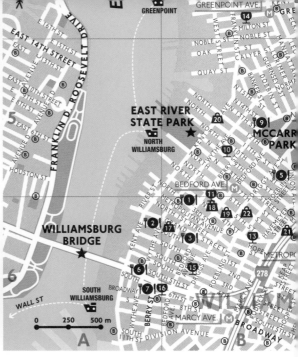

J

★ **Williamsburg Bridge** (A6)

At the time of its construction (1896–1903), the all-steel Williamsburg Bridge held the record for the longest suspension bridge in the world (7,308 ft). The jazz saxophonist Sonny Rollins used to spend hours practicing on the 'Willy B' when he lived on the Lower East Side in the 1950s and 60s.

★ **East River State Park** (B5)

→ *90 Kent Ave (Ninth)*
Tel. (718) 782 2731
Daily 9am–dusk
Opened in 2007, the park stretches along the East River for several dozen yards. It was laid out on the site of a 19th-century dock, of which several features remain: old cobblestones, a railroad track. It offers great views of Williamsburg Bridge and midtown Manhattan skyscrapers.

★ **MoMA PS1** (C3)

→ *22-25 Jackson Ave (46th)*
Tel. (718) 784 2084
Thu-Mon noon–6pm
Moved in 1976 to a former public school, this cutting-edge exhibition space became, in 2002, part of MoMA's contemporary wing. Its many exhibitions

(there are more than 50 each year) have included James Turrell and Richard Serra. On Saturdays in summer it becomes the venue for outdoor concerts known as Warm up Parties (3–9pm), showcasing new musical talent.

★ **Hunters Point Historic District** (C3)

→ *45th Ave (21st and 23rd)*
This block of elegantly proportioned brownstone houses is a reminder of the prosperity of Queens in the 19th century. The relocation of the Long Island City Railroad terminus and the nearby waterway made the area

an important urban junction in the 1860s. In the following decade developers Spencer Ro and John Rust built the houses, which were abandoned by their well-to-do inhabitants when the noisy overhe railway arrived in 1909 There are all kinds of st to be seen in the house including Italianate, Queen Anne and Frenc Second Empire.

★ **Dorsky Gallery** (C

→ *11-03 45th Ave (11th)*
Tel. (718) 937 6317
Thu-Mon 11am–6pm
This not-for-profit art space shows

EAST RIVER

HUNTERS POINT SOUTH

GANTRY PLAZA STATE PARK

QUEENS HUNTERS POINT HISTORIC MO

DORSKY GALLE

FDR FOUR FREEDOMS PARK

UNITED NATIONS HEADQUARTER

MIDTOWN TUNNEL

ROOSEVELT ISLAND

QUEENSBORO BRIDGE

ROOSEVELT ISLAND

GRAND CENTRAL (42ND ST)

42ND ST

ST. PATRICK'S CATHEDRAL

ROCKEFELLER CENTER

LEXINGTON AVE - 53RD ST

LEXINGTON AVE 59TH ST

5TH AVE 59TH ST

57TH ST

THE POND

HUNTER COLLEGE

CENTRAL PARK

PULASKI BRIDGE

KIPS BAY PLAZA

FRANKLIN ST

EAST 34TH ST

ROOSEVELT DRIVE

FRANKLIN AVENUE

EAST 72ND STREET

EAST 60TH STREET

YORK AVENUE

LEXINGTON AVENUE

MADISON AVENUE

PARK AVENUE

5TH AVENUE

McCARREN PARK

EAST RIVER STATE PARK

WILLIAMSBURG BRIDGE

Many young artists and writers have flocked to the north of Brooklyn, Williamsburg. Bedford Avenue is at the heart of this area, a street filled with lively bars and colorful boutiques. Queens, to the north, is conveniently only 15 minutes from Grand Central Station. Long Island City (LIC) is a fascinating labyrinth of avant-garde museums and artists' studios. A few stations along is Astoria, a multicultural quarter popular with the Greek and Brazilian communities.

MAISON PREMIERE

MISS FAVELA

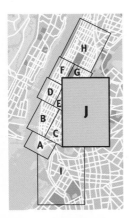

RESTAURANTS

Egg (B6)
→ 109 N 3rd St (Berry)
Tel. (718) 302 5151; Daily
7am (8am Sat-Sun)–5pm
Phenomenal sandwiches with Southern roots (pulled pork) and fried chicken, organic produce, salads and breakfasts too. Sandwiches $9–19.

Cafe de La Esquina (A6)
→ 225 Wythe Ave
Tel. (718) 393 5500
Tue-Fri noon–10pm (11pm Wed-Thu, midnight Fri); Sat-Sun 11am–midnight (10pm Sun)
An outpost of its NoLIta sister, a cantina in a colorful 50s-style diner with a breezy, take-out taqueria and a pleasant patio. Dishes $5–13 (taqueria); $10–22 (diner).

Maison Premiere (B6)
→ 298 Bedford Ave
Tel. (347) 335 0446
Mon-Fri 2pm–2am (4am Thu-Fri); Sat 11am–4am; Sun 11am–2am
Evoking the Belle Époque – a horse-shoe shaped bar, small tables inside or in the garden under an arbor. Try up to 30 kinds of oysters, crudo, vegetable soup or venison tartare. Reserve

for parties of 6 or more. Dishes $21–31.

Roberta's (off D6)
→ 261 Moore St (Bogart)
Tel. (718) 417 1118
Daily 11am (10am Sat-Sun)–midnight
Great artisanal pizza, along with salumi and duck prosciutto. Pizza $11–18. No reservations.

Lilia (B5)
→ 567 Union Ave (North 10th); Tel. (718) 576 3095
Daily 5.30–11pm
In a room of white furniture and bleached wood, try Missy Robbins' ethereal pappardelle with veal bolognese or the black bass in a salsa verde. Reserve. Dishes $20–30.

Miss Favela (A6)
→ 57 S Fifth St (Wythe)
Tel. (718) 230 4040
Daily noon–midnight (1am Fri-Sat)
Brazilian specialties such as feijoada (stewed beef and pork with beans) and moqueca (fish stew). At night, be prepared to dance the samba. Dishes $17–29; cash only.

Marlow & Sons (A6)
→ 81 Broadway (Berry)
Tel. (718) 384 1441
Daily 8am–midnight
Daily-changing menu but in winter you may find

BOTTLE COFFEE

KNITTING FACTORY

CATBIRD

duck liver pâté, rabbit leg or trout. They own 'Diner' next door. Reservations for parties of 6 or more. Dishes $26–28.

Llama Inn (B5) **8**
→ 50 Withers St (Meeker Ave); Tel. (718) 387 3434
Mon-Fri 5–10pm (1am Thu-Fri); Sat-Sun 11am-3pm, 5pm–1am (10pm Sun)
In a bright airy space, an open kitchen and delicious Peruvian/American dishes: duck sausage, or tuna *tiraditu* with ponzu, lime, cucumber and avocado. Dishes $16–19.

Leuca (B5) **9**
→ William Vale Hotel, 111 N 12th St (Wythe Ave) Tel. (718) 581 5900
Daily 7am–3pm (4pm Sat-Sun), 5.30–11pm (midnight Sat-Sun)
In an airy space, Andrew Carmellini's nod to Abruzzo and Sicily: pastas, wood-fired pizzas, fish and meats. Dishes $17–44.

ICE-CREAM PARLOR, CAFÉ, PATISSERIE

Van Leeuwen Artisan Ice Cream (B5) **10**
→ 204 Wythe Ave; Tel. (929) 337 6907; Daily 7am (9am Sat-Sun)–midnight

Artisanal classic and vegan ice cream and house-made pastries in a sleek, bright space; bold flavors like Candied Ginger, Earl Grey Tea and Sicilian Pistachio.

Blue Bottle Coffee (B6) **11**
→ 76 N Fourth St Tel. (718) 387 4160
Mon-Fri 6.30am–7pm; Sat-Sun 7am–7.30pm
Delicious locally roasted coffee, homemade *biscotti*, pastries and sandwiches.

Patisserie Tomoko (C5) **12**
→ 568 Union Ave (Richardson and Frost) Tel. (718) 388 7121
Tue-Sun noon–9pm (11pm Fri-Sat, 8pm Sun)
Exquisite French-Japanese pastries, and wine and coffee. Tomoko trained at Le Bernardin.

BARS, CONCERTS

Knitting Factory (B6) **13**
→ 361 Metropolitan Ave (Havemeyer) Tel. (347) 529 6696
Bar: Daily 6pm–3.30am
This post-rock bar and concert hall has a bold program of experimental and underground music; reasonable prices.

Ramona (B4) **14**
→ 113 Franklin St (Kent) Tel. (347) 227 8164; Daily 5pm (1pm Sat-Sun)–4am
Expertly crafted cocktails and vintage décor draws a vibrant crowd to this upscale two-level bar.

Fresh Kills (B6) **15**
→ 161 Grand St (Bedford) Tel. (718) 599 7888; Daily 5pm (1pm Sat-Sun)–2am (3am Fri-Sat)
Sleek space with pewter walls and hand-stitched leather booths. Among the carefully crafted cocktails made with fresh ingredients and hand-cut ice, some have very low proof alcohol.

Loosie Rouge (A6) **16**
→ 91 S Sixth St (Berry) Mon-Fri 6pm–2am; Sat-Sun noon–4pm, 6pm–2am
Draft cocktails in a cool but cozy bar – an upright piano for a New Orleans vibe. For oysters Bloomberg and po'boys, head next door to Loosie's Kitchen.

SHOPPING

Antoinette (B6) **17**
→ 119 Grand St (Berry) Tel. (718) 387 8664; Tue-Sun noon–7pm (6pm Sun)
Well-curated vintage and modern clothing for men and women in an

attractive space.

Swords-Smith (B6) **18**
→ 98 S Fourth St (Berry) Tel. (347) 599 2969
Daily noon (11am Sat)–8pm (7pm Sun)
Carefully edited women's clothing by up-and-coming designers.

Spoonbill & Sugartown (B6) **19**
→ 218 Bedford Ave (Fifth) Tel. (718) 387 7322
Daily 10am–10pm
A bookstore specializing in art, architecture and design.

Williamsburg Flea Market (B5) **20**
→ 50 Kent Ave (N 11th) May-Dec: Sun 10am–5pm
By the East River, vintage clothing, trinkets and gourmet food stands.

10 Ft. Single by Stella Dallas (B6) **21**
→ 185 N Sixth St (Metropolitan) Tel. (718) 486 9482
Daily noon– 7.30pm
A vintage shop with clothes for men and women: button-down shirts in 70s prints, summer dresses, boots and shoes.

Catbird (B6) **22**
→ 219 Bedford Ave (N Fifth St); Tel. 718 599 3457
Daily 11am–9pm (6pm Sun)
Jewelry, accessories and unique gifts.

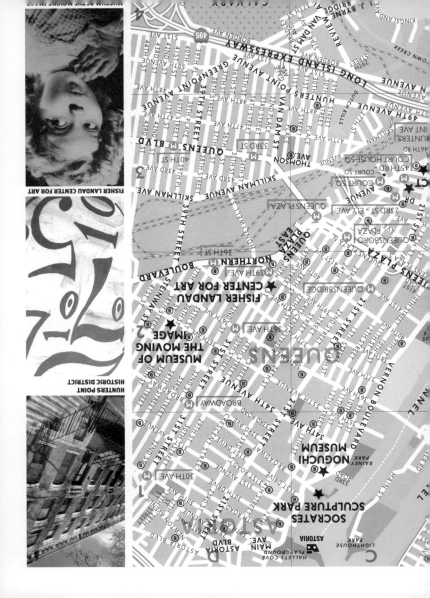

'BABY HULK', *MURAL* BY RON ENGLISH ON HOUSTON STREET

1. Downtown Art Tour

From SoHo to the Lower East Side, art can be seen in galleries and museums but also on the streets. It can even lead the way to secret bars...

→ **Start** *Leslie Lohman Museum of Gay and Lesbian Art*
→ **Finish** *Fig. 19*
→ **Distance** *2 miles*
→ **Duration** *2 hours*

✦ STEP BY STEP

In the heart of Soho

Not far from Canal Street subway station, the Leslie Lohman Museum of Gay and Lesbian Art (*see box*) is the first – and only – museum in the world devoted to LGBTQ art. It was founded in 1969 to give greater visibility to gay artists, and settled on this site in 1987. Thirty years later, it opened an extension that doubled its surface area and allows it to comfortably put on six to eight exhibitions every year. Nearby, two galleries

on Grand St are well worth a visit: the Team Gallery (*see box*), specializing in counter-culture, and the Deitch Projects Gallery (*see box*), owned by Jeffrey Deitch, an expert in 1980s street art who has represented such artists as Cecily Brown (b. 1969), Keith Haring (1958–1990) and Jeff Koons (b. 1955). On the corner of Wooster St, The Drawing Center (*see box*) is a cultural institution devoted entirely to illustration. Then, follow Broome St to West Broadway, one of the busiest streets in SoHo, lined with restaurants and big-name retail chains and home to the Broken Kilometer (*see box*), an installation made by Walter de Maria (1935–2013) for the Dia Foundation that has been on show here since 1979. It comprises a large empty room containing 500 polished brass rods arranged in five rows. A little further north, the same artist's New York Earth Room (*see box*) is hidden on the 2nd floor of a seemingly nondescript building. This 'sculpture' dating from 1977 consists of 127 tons of soil deposited in an enormous white space: an indoor desert dreamed up in the heart of Manhattan by one of the most important exponents of land art. Between

EMPIRE STATE BUILDING

2. New York in the Movies
No other city has been so completely immortalized on celluloid – every street corner in New York seems to trigger memories of a film!

→ **Start** Metropolitan Museum of Art
→ **Finish** Empire State Building
→ **Distance** 11 miles
→ **Duration** 1 day (although the walk can be adapted to the time available)

✖ STEP BY STEP

Central Park from north to south
The Temple of Dendur, visible from Central Park, provided the backdrop for one of the many conversations between Sally Albright (Meg Ryan) and Harry Burns (Billy Crystal) in the romantic comedy *When Harry Met Sally* (Rob Reiner, 1989). On the other side of the Great Lawn, on the western edge of the park, the American Museum of Natural History (**F** C3) was plunged into chaos in

Night at the Museum (Shawn Levy, 2006) when the stuffed animals and dinosaur skeletons came to life. Five blocks to the south, the neo-Renaissance Dakota Building (**F** C4) contained Tom Cruise's apartment in *Vanilla Sky* (Cameron Crowe, 2001) – and, in real life, that of John Lennon. Going back to Central Park, several scenes from *Hair* (Milos Forman, 1979) were shot here: most memorably, the hippies spent the night near the Bethesda Fountain (**G** B3). A little further south comes the Mall (**G** B3), where Billy was taught to ride a bike by his father, Ted (Dustin Hoffman) in *Kramer vs Kramer* (Robert Benton, 1979). Stop at the Loeb Boathouse (**G** B2) near 72nd and 5th and have a snack on the terrace overlooking the lake.

From 59th St to 52nd St
Ninth Avenue is the location of Saint Paul the Apostle Church, where one of the famous dance numbers from *West Side Story* (Jerome Robbins and Robert Wise, 1961) was filmed. Going eastward, it was at the corner of 6th Ave and 58th St that Dustin Hoffman and Jon Voight were almost run over by a taxi in *Midnight Cowboy* (John Schlesinger, 1969) – a legendary scene

that was later referenced in *Forrest Gump* and *Back to the Future 2*. The next stop is the jewelry store Tiffany & Co (**E** A1): Holly Golightly dreamt about its showcases in *Breakfast at Tiffany's* (Blake Edwards, 1961). On 60th St, between 2nd and 3rd Avenue, Serendipity III is the cafe in which Kate Beckinsale and John Cusack shared a scrumptious chocolate sundae in *Serendipity* (Peter Chelsom, 2001). If that memory stimulates your taste buds, head to Casa Lever (**E** B2) for delicious Milanese fare. Then, go along 58th St to the East River, where the Queensboro Bridge provided the iconic image featured in the poster for Woody Allen's black-and-white *Manhattan* (1979). Another landmark image – that of Marilyn Monroe's white dress swirling upward as she stands on a subway grate – was captured on the southwest corner of the junction of 52nd St and Lexington Ave. It took a full 14 takes to get this scene in the can, under the watchful eyes of almost 5,000 onlookers. This image's notoriety would go on to contribute to the international success of *The Seven Year Itch* (Billy Wilder, 1955).

NEW YORK IN THE MOVIES WALK

From 52nd St to 34th St

Two blocks further south, one of New York's most famous hotels, the monumental Waldorf Astoria, appeared in *The Godfather 3* (Francis Ford Coppola, 1990). To the west, at the junction of 49th St and 6th Ave, the façade and lobby of the McGraw-Hill Building were used for the job interview of Andrea Sachs (Anne Hathaway) by Miranda Priestly (Meryl Streep) in *The Devil Wears Prada* (David Frankel, 2006). On 8th Ave, between 47th and 48th Sts, Robert de Niro stopped at the sex shop Show & Tell (now a ticket office for Gray Line tours) in *Taxi Driver* (Martin Scorsese, 1976). On 46th St,

Saint Mary the Virgin Church stood in as the school for aspiring performers in *Fame* (Alan Parker, 1980). The New York Public Library (**E** A4) has played a role in countless films, including *Ghostbusters* (Ivan Reitman, 1984). And, to finish in high style (literally), go to the top of the Empire State Building (**E** A5), indelibly associated with *King Kong* (Merian C. Cooper and Ernest B. Schoedsack, 1933), although it was also the setting for Cary Grant and Deborah Kerr's heart-rending meeting in *An Affair to Remember* (Leo McCarey, 1957), one of the most beautiful love stories ever.

NOGUCHI MUSEUM

SOCRATES SCULPTURE PARK

pendently
ted exhibitions of
emporary art, from
a Maar to R. Cumming.

**Noguchi
seum** (C1)
→ 01 33rd Rd
on and Tenth)
212) 204 7088
Fri 10am–5pm;
un 11am–6pm
all museum devoted
e Japanese sculptor
u Noguchi (1904–88),
gned by the artist. The
en and ground floor
ries house the
nanent collection;
airs are temporary
bitions. The shop has
es furniture, objects

and Noguchi's famous
rice-paper light sculptures.

**★ Museum of the
Moving Image** (D2)
→ 36-01 35th Ave (37th)
Tel. (718) 777 6888
Wed-Sun 10.30am–5pm
(8pm Fri, 6pm Sat-Sun)
The museum, devoted
to the audiovisual arts,
is located next to the
Kaufman-Astoria Studios,
and gives a behind-the-
scenes glimpse of movies
and television through
interactive installations.

**★ Socrates
Sculpture Park** (C1)
→ Broadway / Vernon Blvd
Tel. (718) 956 1819
Daily 10am–sunset

This open-air sculpture
museum is set in a park
opposite Roosevelt Island;
also screens movies and
hosts cultural events.

**★ Fisher Landau
Center for Art** (D2)
→ 38-27 30th St (38th)
Tel. (718) 937 0727
Thu-Mon noon–5pm
This former parachute
factory was converted in
1991 by British architect
Max Gordon to house
the Emily Fisher Landau
Foundation, amassed
since 1960. It contains
1,500 works by such
artists as Jasper Johns,
Andy Warhol, Matthew
Barney and Cy Twombly.

**★ Franklin D. Roosevelt
Four Freedoms Park**
(B2-3)
→ East Road, Roosevelt
Island; Tel. (212) 204 8831
Wed-Mon 9am–7pm
Take the tramway at 59th
and 2nd to this beautiful
park designed by Louis I.
Kahn, with a bust of FDR
by Jo Davidson, a 'granite'
room, monumental stairs,
allées of linden trees
and lawns.

★ McCarren Park (B5)
A pool here turns into an
ice-skating rink in winter,
but its outdoor Northside
music festival and
SummerScreen series
are the big draw.

The Broken Kilometer and The New York Earth Room at 101 Spring Street, at the corner of Mercer, walk by the beautiful, grey, cast-iron building owned by the artist Donald Judd, where he lived and worked. It was here and later in Marfa, Texas, that he developed his ideas about installation. For a guided tour, book at *juddfoundation.org*. Before moving on to the Lower East Side, stop for an Italian snack or salad at Il Buco Alimentari & Vineria (**C** A4).

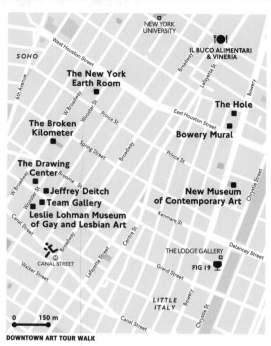

DOWNTOWN ART TOUR WALK

The Lower East Side

Cross over Houston St to take a look at NoHo ('North of Houston St'). At the junction with Bowery St, the mural painted without permission by Keith Haring in 1982 first brought him to public attention. Since 2008 the entire Bowery Wall has become an open-air exhibition space for internationally renowned artists invited by a gallery called The Hole (*see box*), one of the nerve centers of the local art scene. It puts on two shows a month, as well as various events and performances, and it forms part of the network of Lower East Side Galleries, whose members are all featured on an online map (*lesgallerymap.com*). Go back down Bowery St to visit the New Museum of Contemporary Art (**C** B5), set in a striking building (SANAA, 2007) in the form of cubes piled on top of each other. Take advantage of its roof terrace, the Sky Room Deck (weekends only), for wonderful views of Downtown. Round off the tour at 131 Christie St. At first sight this seems to be an art gallery – the Lodge Gallery – indistinguishable from so many in Manhattan, but it also provides access to a hidden cocktail bar. To get inside, just tell the attendant that you want to go to Fig. 19 (*see box*), and you will be ushered to the bar's entrance through a series of rooms.

Leslie Lohman Museum of Gay and Lesbian Art
→ 26 Wooster St
Tel. 212 431 2609
Wed-Sun noon–6pm
(8pm Thu); leslielohman.org

Team Gallery
→ 83 Grand St
Tel. (212) 279 9219
Tue-Sat 10am–6pm
teamgal.com

Jeffrey Deitch
→ 76 Grand St
Tel. (212) 343 7300
Mon-Fri noon–6pm
deitch.com

The Drawing Center
→ 35 Wooster St
Tel. (212) 219 2166
Wed-Sun noon–6pm (8pm Thu); drawingcenter.org

The Broken Kilometer
→ 393 West Broadway
Tel. (212) 925 9397
Wed-Sun noon–3pm, 3.30–6pm; diaart.org

The New York Earth Room
→ 141 2B Wooster St
Tel. (212) 989 5566
Wed-Sun noon–3pm, 3.30–6pm; diaart.org

The Hole
→ 312 Bowery St
StTel. (212) 466 1100
Wed-Sun noon–7pm
theholenyc.com

♥ Fig. 19
→ The Lodge Gallery, 131 Chrystie St; Tue-Sat 8pm–4am; Sun 6pm–2am
figurenineteen.com

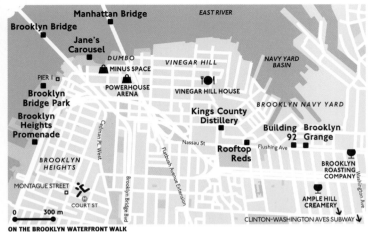

ON THE BROOKLYN WATERFRONT WALK

take a rest and enjoy the food served under the cherry tree in the garden of the Vinegar Hill House (**I** C2).

Brooklyn Navy Yard
Further east, the old Brooklyn Navy Yard once manufactured the country's largest warships. One of the first buildings to come into view is the Kings County Distillery (*see box*), which produces whiskey and is open for tasting sessions. Wine connoisseurs will prefer the Rooftop Reds (*see box*), a vineyard planted on a roof terrace, first harvested in the fall of 2017. A further incentive to linger is provided by the hammocks that have been hung here, affording fine views of Brooklyn. Nearby, Building 92 (*see box*) contains a museum commemorating the Brooklyn Navy Yard, which was one of the most active in America over the course of 165 years. Themed guided tours (booking essential) focus on specific aspects of the site, from its industrial history to its great photographic potential. On the way out, do not miss the Brooklyn Grange (*see box*), the world's largest rooftop farm, spread over some 6,000 sq. m. Organic tomatoes, lettuces, peppers and other vegetables grow here completely out of sight of the

street below – and out of reach of its pollution. The farm can be visited. Equally demanding with respect to the quality of its produce, the Brooklyn Roasting Company coffee shop (*see box*) serves some of the best coffee in town. The walk's endpoint, Clinton-Washington Avenues subway station, is only 500 yards away.

Jane's Carousel
→ Brooklyn Bridge Park
Thu-Sun 11am–6pm
Powerhouse Arena
→ 28 Adams St
Tel. (718) 666 3049
Daily 11am–7pm
(6pm Sat-Sun)
Kings County Distillery
→ 299 Sands St
Tel. (347) 689 4211
Mon-Fri 10am–10pm
(6pm Mon), Sat-Sun
noon–10pm (8pm Sun)
Guided tours: Tue-Sun
3pm, 5pm, Sun 1–4pm
(every 30 mins)
kingscountydistillery.com
Rooftop Reds
→ 63 Flushing Ave,

Bldg 275
Tel. (571) 327 3578
Hours vary, see
rooftopreds.com
Building 92
→ 63 Flushing Ave
Tel. (718) 907 5932
Wed-Sun noon–6pm
bldg92.org
Brooklyn Grange
→ 63 Flushing Ave,
Bldg 3
Tel. (347) 670 3660
Hours vary, see
brooklyngrangefarm.
com
🍷 **Brooklyn Roasting Company**
→ 200 Flushing Ave
Tel. (718) 858 5500
Daily 7am–7pm

JANE'S CAROUSEL

3. On the Brooklyn Waterfront

How to escape from the city... without actually leaving it? By exploring the old dockyards alongside the East River, where vineyards and market gardens have now taken over the rooftops.

→ **Start** *Court Street subway station*
→ **Finish** *Clinton-Washington Avenues subway station*
→ **Distance** *4 miles*
→ **Duration** *Half a day*

 STEP BY STEP

Brooklyn Heights

Court Street station leads up to Brooklyn Heights, one of the oldest neighborhoods in the borough, distinguished by its stylish brownstones (sandstone rowhouses built in the mid-19th century). Over the years the area has played host to several non-conformist creative spirits, such as the painter Salvador Dalí and the novelists Richard Wright, Norman Mailer and Truman Capote. Montague Street, a lively thoroughfare with many shops and restaurants, ends at the East River, and

further up the bank the Brooklyn Heights Promenade (❶ B2) offers constantly shifting views of the Statue of Liberty, the Manhattan skyline and Brooklyn Bridge. Further north, the promenade extends to Brooklyn Bridge Park (❶ B2), which runs along the waterfront. Pier 1 has appeared in many films, and it is also a popular spot for wedding photos. Don't miss the organic, homemade ice cream of Ample Hill Creamery (❶ D4).

DUMBO / Vinegar Hill

Just after Brooklyn Bridge (❶ B1), the 48 horses of Jane's Carousel (*see box*) come into view. This exquisitely restored fairground attraction, dating from 1922, is now protected from the elements by a glass box designed by the architect Jean Nouvel. In the approach to Manhattan Bridge (❶ B1), DUMBO (Down Under the Manhattan Bridge Overpass) beckons. This former industrial hub has now been taken over by luxurious lofts and artists' studios. For a cultural break, visit the Powerhouse Arena (*see box*), a publishing house specializing in art books, but also a gallery and bookstore that organizes events with such celebrated writers as Paul Auster and Jennifer Egan. Continuing eastward, the next port of call is Vinegar Heights (popularly known as Irishtown in the 19th century), with its charming alleyways and stunning views of Manhattan. In fine weather,

THE CLOISTERS

Day trips within 1–2 hours of the city

STATEN ISLAND

→ *Staten Island Ferry (free), approx. 25 mins Departure every 30 mins from Battery Park*
This peaceful Italian-American enclave, reached via ferry, offers unrivaled views of Downtown. The enormous Freshkills Park, popular beaches and the old Wadsworth Fort, in the shadow of the Verrazano-Narrows Bridge, are open every day from sunrise to sunset.

¶●¶ Enoteca Maria

→ *27 Hyatt St*
Tel. (718) 447 2777
Wed-Sun noon (3pm weekend)–10.30pm
Traditional home cooking from all over the world, with supremely fresh ingredients. Dishes $10–28.

FLUSHING MEADOWS-CORONA PARK

→ *Subway to Mets-Willets Point (line 7), approx. 30 mins* **Queens Museum** *New York City Building*
Tel. (718) 592 9700; Wed-Sun 11am–5pm
New York Hall of Science *47-01 111th St/47th Ave*
Tel. (718) 699 0005
Mon-Fri 9.30am–5pm; Sat-Sun 10am–6pm
The vast site of the 1939 Universal Exhibition, housing the Queens Museum (with an extraordinary model of the city), the New York Hall of Science (interactive exhibits, including two NASA rocket heads) and a zoo. The park also plays host to the US Open.

¶●¶ Park Side Restaurant

→ *107-1 Corona Ave*
Tel. (718) 271 9274
Mon-Sat noon–11.30pm; Sun 12.30–10pm
An Italian restaurant specializing in seafood and grilled meat; with a good pasta selection. Dishes $16–40.

THE CLOISTERS

→ *Fort Tryon Park; subway to 190th St (line A), approx. 45 mins*
Tel. (212) 923 3700
Daily 10am–5.15pm (4.45pm in winter)
In this museum celebrating the art and architecture of the Middle Ages, elements imported from churches, chapels and cloisters in Europe were reconstituted between 1934 and 1938. The galleries present John D. Rockefeller Jr.'s collection of medieval objects, including the *Hunt of the Unicorn* (ca. 1500). Nearby, the banks of the Hudson are largely unspoiled.

¶●¶ New Leaf

→ *1 Margaret Corbin Drive, Fort Tryon Park*
Tel. (212) 568 5323

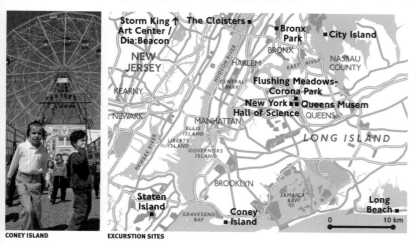

CONEY ISLAND

EXCURSION SITES

Mon–Fri noon–7pm (8pm Fri); Sat–Sun 11am–3.30pm, 4–8pm (7pm Sun)
A charming stone cottage serving mostly local organic food (salad, cheese from Vermont). Large terrace in summer. Dishes $16–28.

BRONX PARK

→ *New York Botanical Garden 2900 Southern Blvd, subway to Bedford Park Blvd (lines B, D, 4), approx. 50 mins*
Tel. (718) 817 8700; Tue–Sun 10am–6pm
Bronx Zoo Bronx River Parkway, subway to Pelham Parkway (lines 2, 5)
Tel. (718) 367 1010; Daily 10am–5pm (5.30pm Sat–Sun, 4.30pm in winter)
A beautiful park dissected by the Bronx River, its banks lined with maple trees. Two major attractions: one of the world's biggest botanical gardens, with over 50 themed areas and an imposing early-20th-century greenhouse; and the Bronx Zoo, similarly one of the finest in existence. More than 650 species are represented here by 4,000 animals.

¶●¶ Pine Tree Cafe

→ *2900 Southern Blvd*
Tel. 718 817 8700; Same opening hours as the gardens
In the heart of the botanical garden, an informal café with an extensive terrace. Salads, freshly made sandwiches and pizzas from a log-fired oven. Dishes $11–34.

CITY ISLAND

→ *Pelham Bay Park subway (line 6), approx. 1hr, then bus Bx29, Orchard Beach stop (10 min journey)*
This island, measuring two by 1/2 miles can be reached via a bridge and explored on foot. The only legacy of its dockyards, which constructed first warships and then yachts, is one small marina, as elegant as the white wooden houses nearby. At weekends these picture-postcard scenes attract New Yorkers in search of fresh air – and fresh seafood.

¶●¶ Johnny's Reef Restaurant

→ *2 City Island Ave; Tel. (718) 885 2086*
March–Nov: Daily 11am–11pm (midnight Fri–Sat)
For 60 years this restaurant's enormous waterside terrace has attracted countless customers from the Big Apple. Seafood, fried or steamed, with French fries or Italian bread: lobsters, clams, shrimps, oysters – all with the backdrop of the city lights at night time. Dishes $13–30.

CONEY ISLAND

→ *Subway to Coney Island (lines D, F, Q), approx. 1hr*
Fairly deserted during the week but comes alive at the weekend. See the famous Luna Park funfair and the famous 3-mile boardwalk linking Coney Island with Brighton Beach (also known as Little Odessa). Ukranian and Russian Jews settled here in the 1970s, hence the store and restaurant signs written in the Cyrillic alphabet.

STORM KING ART CENTER

❙●❙ Skovorodka

→ *615 Brighton Beach Ave*
Tel. (718) 615 3096
Daily 11am–10pm (11pm Sat)
A taste of Russia: eggplant caviar, Borscht, blinis and a fine selection of vodkas. Live music at the weekend. Dishes $10–24.

LONG BEACH

→ *LIRR train from Penn Station; approx 1 hour*
Daily pass for the beach $15 (free for under 13s)
In summer, the white sandy beaches lining this long, thin island provide a refreshing escape from the stifling heat of the city.

❙●❙ Atlantica

→ *Allegria Hotel,*
80 W Broadway, Long Beach
Tel. (516) 992 3730
Mon–Fri 6.30am–10pm; Sat–Sun
6.30am–10am, 5–10pm
Fresh fish and seafood by the edge of the ocean. Dishes $10–37.

STORM KING ART CENTER

→ *Old Pleasant Hill Road, Mountainville, Cornwall*
Coach USA (Short Line Bus) from Port Authority
Bus Terminal, 8.30am and 10am, approx 1½ hrs
Tel. (845) 534 3115; coachusa.com
Wed–Sun 10am–4.30pm/5.30pm/8pm
depending on the season
This sculpture park of more than 500 acres,

has large-scale pieces and land art. See Maya Lin's *Wave Field*, Andy Galsworthy's 750-ft-long dry stone wall, and works by Mark di Suvero, Alexander Calder and Richard Serra, set amidst magnificent landscape.

❙●❙ Storm King Café

→ *Same opening hours as the park, from 11am*
Local, organic produce in this café inside the park. Dishes $6–10.

DIA:BEACON

→ *Metro North train from Grand Central Station*
to Beekman St, approx 1½ hrs
Tel. (845) 440 0100; mta.info
Jan–Mar: Fri–Mon 11am–4pm; April–Dec:
Thu–Mon 11am–6pm (4pm Nov–Dec)
A former Nabisco box-printing factory plays host to works by Joseph Beuys, Louise Bourgeois, Dan Flavin, Sol LeWitt and Andy Warhol. Don't miss *North, East, South, West* (1967), the gigantic 'negative' sculptures hollowed out of the ground by Michael Heizer, or Richard Serra's dizzying *Ellipses* (2000).

❙●❙ Café du Dia:Beacon

→ *Same opening hours as the museum*
(from 10.30am)
Salads, quiches, burgers and sandwiches. Dishes $6–12.

PRACTICALITIES

All the essentials for your stay in New York

CITY PROFILE

■ 8.5 million inhabitants (1.6 million live in Manhattan)
■ Approx. 50 million visitors each year
■ Five boroughs: Queens Manhattan, Brooklyn, Bronx and Staten Island
■ Spread over three islands: **Manhattan, Staten Island** and part of **Long Island** (Queens and Brooklyn). The Bronx is the only borough built on the mainland itself

9/11 MEMORIAL

New York is subject to a humid, continental climate and experiences great extremes of temperature: up to 40°C (104°F) in July and Aug, and around 0°C (32°F) from Dec-Feb. Nevertheless, the joyous New Year's Eve celebrations attract huge crowds. The most temperate months are May, June, Sep and Oct.

WWW.

→ *nycgo.com*
Official website of the NYC tourism organization.
→ *nyc-architecture.com*
New York's most famous buildings; plus themed walking tours.
→ *timeout.com/newyork*
Cultural events listing.

TOURIST INFORMATION

Official NYC Information Center
(**D** E4)
→ *Macy's Herald Square, 151 W 34th St (Broadway)*
Tel. (212) 484 1222
Daily 9am (Sat 10am, Sun 11am)–7pm
Brooklyn (**I** B3)
→ *Brooklyn Borough Hall, Joralemon St (Court)*
Mon-Fri 10am–6pm
South Street Seaport (**A** E3)
→ *South Street Seaport, Horn Blower Cruises, Pier 15; Daily 9am–7pm (5pm Sep-April)*
City Hall (**A** C2)
→ *Broadway / Park Row*
Mon-Fri 9am–6pm;
Sat-Sun 10am–5pm
Times Square (**D** E3)
→ *Broadway Plaza (44th and 45th Sts); Daily 9am–6pm*

TELEPHONE

212, 917 and 646 are the area codes for Manhattan; 718 and 929 are the codes for New York's four other boroughs; 347 is the code for part of Manhattan as well as the outer boroughs.
To call NY from abroad
→ *00 + 1 (USA) + area code + the seven-digit number*
To call abroad from NY
→ *Dial 011 + country code + area code + local number*
Emergency numbers
Police, fire brigade
→ Tel. 911
Useful numbers
Directory enquiries (national)
→ Tel. 1 + area code + 555 1212
Collect calls
→ Tel. 1-800-COLLECT
Lost and Found
→ Tel. 511
For subway and bus lost property.

DIARY OF EVENTS

New Year's Day; Martin Luther King Jr Day (third Mon in Jan); Presidents Day (third Mon in Feb); *Memorial Day (last Mon in May); Independence Day (July 4); Labor Day (first Mon in Sep); Columbus Day (second Mon in Oct); Veterans Day (Nov 11); Thanksgiving (fourth Thu in Nov); Christmas Day*
January-February
Martin Luther King Jr Day
→ Third Mon in Jan
To mark the birthday of the civil rights activist; there is also a parade along Fifth Ave at the end of Jan.
Restaurant Week
→ One or more weekend Feb-beg March
Cheaper set menus in high-end restaurants.
Chinese New Year Festival
→ Jan or Feb (varies)
Carnival and fireworks in Chinatown.
March-April
St Patrick's Day
→ March 17
Parade along Fifth

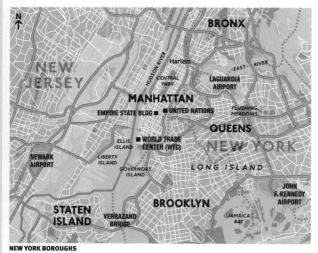

NEW YORK BOROUGHS

Avenue.

Armory Show
→ *Half a week in March*
Contemporary art fair at Piers 92, 94 (**D** B1).

Easter Parade
→ *Easter Sunday*
Procession along Fifth Avenue.

TriBeCa Film Festival
→ *10 days, mid-late April*
International film festival.

May-June

Memorial Day
→ *Last Mon in May*

Shakespeare in the Park
→ *Usually June-Aug*
Free theater in Central Park.

Museum Mile Festival
→ *2nd Tue (variable) in June*
Live music and entertainment along Fifth Ave (82nd to 104th Sts), and free entry to the seven participating museums (from 6–9pm).

July-August

Independence Day
→ *July 4*
Fireworks display

over the East River.

Mostly Mozart Festival
→ *End July-end Aug*
Concerts and shows at Lincoln Center (**F** B5).

Summer Streets
→ *First three Saturdays in Aug (7am–1pm)*
7 miles of pedestrian-only streets in the middle of Manhattan: walks, races, games, music.

Tennis US Open
→ *End Aug-mid Sep*
In Flushing Meadows (Queens).

Restaurant Week
→ *Two weeks or more during July-Aug*
See January-February.

September

Labor Day weekend
→ *Weekend prior to the first Mon in Sep (public holiday)*
Caribbean Carnival in Brooklyn.

Feast of St Gennaro
→ *Ten days mid Sep*
Celebrations all around Little Italy.

October

Hispanic Day Parade
→ *Sun before Columbus Day*
Festive parade along Fifth Ave to mark the end of National Hispanic Heritage Month (Sep–Oct).

Columbus Day
→ *Second Mon of the month*
Parade along Fifth Avenue.

Halloween Parade
→ *Oct 31*
Parade on Sixth Avenue, starting from West Village.

November

New York Marathon
→ *One Sun in early Nov*
Staten Island to Central Park, via the five boroughs.

Thanksgiving Day
→ *Last Thu of the month*
Huge parade on Broadway, between Central Park and Macy's.

December

Christmas lights
→ *The whole month*
Don't miss the Rockefeller Center Christmas tree (**D** E2).

ARCHITECTURE

Federal style (1780–1830)
Introduction of English neoclassical style: **City Hall** interiors (**A** D2).

Greek Revival style (1820–50) Inspired by Greek architecture: **Federal Hall** (**A** D3).

Gothic Revival (1840–80) Inspired by European Gothic style (end of 12th–15th c.): **Trinity Church** (**A** C3).

Italianate / Second Empire (1880–1900) Mixture of Haussmann and Italian Renaissance styles; **brownstones** (made of rich brown sandstone): **Washington Square Row** (**B** C4).

Beaux-Arts (1890–1920) Mixture of neo-Baroque and classical styles: **Public Library** (**E** A3), **Little Singer Building** (**B** D5).

Skyscrapers (20th–21st c.)
The Chicago School designed the first skyscrapers in the late 19th century. A variety of styles since then: Gothic – **Woolworth Building** (**A** C2); neo Renaissance – **Flatiron Building** (**B** D1); Art Deco – **Chrysler Building** (**E** B4); International – **United Nations** (**E** D3); Post-modern – **432 Park Ave** by Rafael Viñoly (**E** B1); **220 Central Park South** by Robert A. M. Stern (**F** D6); Late Modern – **NY Times Building** (**D** D3), **New York** by Frank Gehry (**A** D2), **1 WTC** (**A** C2) by Skidmore, Owings and Merrill.

THE MANHATTAN SKYLINE SEEN FROM BROOKLYN HEIGHTS PROMENADE

BROWNSTONES IN BROOKLYN

MANNAHATTA TO MANHATTAN

Around 3000 BC
First Native American settlement
1524 Discovered by Giovanni da Verrazano
1624 A colony is founded in the south of Manhattan island: New Amsterdam
1664 Captured by the English; the colony is renamed New York
1820 The most populated city in the US
1900 The world's main port; immigrants flow into Ellis Island
1919–1933 Prohibition
2001 Attacks of September 11

New Year's Eve
ball drop countdown
in Times Square (**D** E3);
fireworks in Central Park.

MONEY MATTERS

State taxes
A state and city tax of 8.875% is added to restaurant food and most music, clothing and electronic goods. Clothing and footwear less than $110 are taxed at a reduced rate of 4.375%.

Budget
A standard room: $220–320
A meal: $20–50
A coffee: $4–5
A glass of wine: $10–15
Museum entry: $15–25
Ticket to a Broadway show: $120–220.

Discounts in museums
Discounts are available to students and those over 60; they vary depending on the museum.

Free / reduced entry to museums

Pay-What-You-Wish
→ *Suggested donation at Museo del Barrio, Brooklyn Museum, MoMA PS1, Cloisters, American Museum of Natural History, the Museum of the City of New York and others.*

Free entry or Pay-What-You-Wish
→ **Tue:** *Brooklyn Botanic Garden 9am–6pm* **Wed:** *Bronx Zoo 10am–5pm; Frick Collection 2–6pm; NY Botanical Garden (grounds only) 10am–6pm; Museum of Jewish Heritage 4–8pm* **Thu:** *New Museum of Contemporary Art 7–9pm; Museum of Arts and Design (MAD) 6–9pm;* **Fri:** *Frick Collection (1st Fri of month): The New York Historical Society 6–8pm; MoMA 4–8pm; Whitney Museum 7–9.30pm; Asia Society 6–9pm (Sep- June); Noguchi Museum 10am–5pm*

(1st Fri of month); *Morgan Library 7–9pm; Rubin Museum of Art 7–10pm; Neue Galerie 6–8pm (1st Fri of month)* **Sat:** *Brooklyn Museum 5–11pm (1st Sat of month); Guggenheim 5.45–7.45pm; Brooklyn Botanic Garden 10am–noon; NY Botanical Garden (grounds) 9–10am* **Sun:** *Studio Museum in Harlem noon–6pm*

OPENING TIMES

Restaurants
→ *Generally Mon-Sat 11am–11.30pm; closed between 3–5/6pm. Often closed earlier, or the whole day on Sunday*

Stores
→ *Generally Mon-Sat 10am–7pm; Sun noon–6pm Some are closed Sat; larger stores: Mon- Sat 9am–8.30pm; Sun 11am–5pm*

Museums
→ *Usually 10am–5pm (last*

ticket 30 mins before close)
Open 24/7
Restaurants
City Diner (**H** A5)
→ *2441 Broadway (90th)*
Tel. (212) 877 2720
Pharmacy
Duane Reade (**D** D1)
→ *250 W 57th St (Broadway)*
Tel. (212) 265 2101

EATING OUT

New York City boasts over 20,000 restaurants. You almost always need to reserve. To make reservations online, use *opentable.com* or *resy.com*

Bars or restaurants?
In New York, one can have a drink in a restaurant and order a steak in a bar.

Diners
Originally restaurants in the shape of a train's dining car, they serve classic American fast-

21

KATZ'S DELI ON THE LOWER EAST SIDE

food: burgers, omelets etc.
Tips
Leave about 20 percent of
the bill – or twice the tax
amount on the bill. In
bars, allow $1 per drink.

SIGHTSEEING

City Pass card
→ *Nine-day pass;*
$116 adults, $92 youth
citypass.com
Free access to
participating monuments,
museums and attractions:
Empire State Building,
Guggenheim Museum,
American Museum of
Natural History, etc.
Guided tours
NYC.com
→ *Tel. (888) 847 4869*
nyc.com/guided_tours
By helicopter, bike,
boat, or with a theme –
shopping, gastronomy,
architecture, TV series
(*Sex and the City, The
Sopranos, Gossip Girl*)

**Lower East Side
Jewish Conservancy**
→ *Tel. (212) 374 4100*
by appt: nycjewishtours.org
The history of the Jewish
community in New York.

GOING OUT

Show reservations
Ticketmaster
→ *Tel. 800 745 3000*
ticketmaster.com
Reservations and ticket
sales for various venues
throughout the city.
**Reduced-price musical
tickets**
→ *TKTS, 47th St (Broadway
and Seventh); also at 199
Water St (corner of Front/
John) and 1 MetroTech
Center (corner Jay/Myrtle)*
Reductions of 20–50
percent + $4.50 service
charge per ticket for
same-day performances.
**Movie and show
listings**
New York Times

→ *Weekend supplement,
at newsstands and
nytimes.com*
Useful addresses, places
to go and cultural events.
New York Magazine
→ *Bi-monthly;
at newsstands and
nymag.com*
Lists events in the city.
The Village Voice
→ *Wed, in bars
and restaurants;
villagevoice.com*
Free weekly listings.
Time Out New York
→ *Free copies distributed on
Wed; timeout.com/newyork*
Weekly events.
Bars
You must be 21 years old
to drink and may be asked
for proof of identity.

VIEWS OF THE CITY

Battery Park (A C4)
Public park at the
southern tip of Manhattan
with views of the harbor.

**Empire State
Building (E** A5)
Exceptional views of
downtown Manhattan
and Central Park.
**Rockefeller
Plaza (D** F2)
A fantastic panorama
with the Sky Shuttle
Elevators to the Top of
the Rock (floors 67, 69
and 70). Children under
6 go free.
The Tram (G D4)
Cable car ride to
Roosevelt Island: a
birds-eye view of the
Upper East Side.
**Brooklyn Heights
Promenade (I** B2)
Magnificent views
over Brooklyn,
Manhattan and the
East River.
**One World
Observatory (A** C2)
→ *oneworldobservatory.com*
Views of the city from
floors 100–102; café with
snacks and drinks on 101.

TAXI

AIRPORTS

→ panynj.com
**John F. Kennedy
International Airport**
→ Tel. (718) 244 4444
**Newark International
Airport**
→ Tel. (973) 961 6000
LaGuardia Airport
→ Tel. (718) 533 3400

AIRPORT ACCESS

ACCOMMODATION

Prices given are for a double room en suite excluding hotel tax (14.75% of the price of the room + $3.50 surcharge). Advance reservations are recommended, especially in the fall and at Christmas.

FROM $100

Gatsby Hotel (C B4)
→ 135 E Houston St (Forsythe)
Tel. (212) 358 8844
A hotel with 45 small, modern rooms; HD TV. From $152.
Chelsea Inn (B C2)
→ 46 W 17th St (Fifth and Sixth); Tel. (212) 645 8989
chelseainn.com
A beautiful red-brick building with bow windows. Tasteful rooms from $89; one-bedroom suite with kitchenette from $189.

Chelsea Lodge (B B2)
→ 318 W 20th St (Eighth)
Tel. (212) 243 4499
chelsealodge.com
22 basic, clean rooms with shared bathrooms. Great location and value. $129–189.
The Jane (B A3)
→ 113 Jane St (West St)
Tel. (212) 924 6700
thejanenyc.com
This 1908 building held the survivors of the Titanic in 1912. Try Old Rose café. Rooms are: Bunk Bed Cabin, Standard Cabin and Captain's Cabin. $100 (shared bathroom)–225.
Pod 51 (E C2)
→ 230 E 51st St (Second and Third); Tel. (212) 355 0300; thepodhotel.com
Compact but smartly designed rooms ('pods') with free WiFi and flat-screen TVs. Also see **Pod 39** (145 E 39th St). $165–289.

Ace Hotel (E A6)
→ 20 W 29th St (Fifth and Broadway); Tel. (212) 679 2222; acehotel.com
A funky hotel with 269 rooms and two restaurants by the Spotted Pig owners: The Breslin Bar for terrines and charcuterie, and the John Dory for seafood; No. 7 Sub for submarine sandwiches. From $159.
**The Hotel
Wolcott (E** A6)
→ 4 W 31st St (Fifth); Tel. (212) 268 2900; wolcott.com
The lobby, with its gilded moldings, chandeliers and columns has an air of Versailles kitsch. Spacious, well-equipped rooms. From $190.
Roger Smith (E C3)
→ 501 Lexington Ave (47th and 48th); Tel. (212) 755 1400; rogersmith.com
130 rooms and suites, all individually decorated. Free for children; rooftop bar. $160–510.

**Washington Jefferson
Hotel (D** D2)
→ 318 W 51st St (Ninth)
Tel. (212) 246 7550
wjhotel.com
Near the theater district, these comfortable rooms are all black and white. From $160.
The Evelyn (B D1)
→ 7 E 27th St (Fifth)
Tel. (212) 545 8000
theevelyn.com
Italian sheets, flat-screen TVs, modern furniture; 150 rooms. From $194.
Hudson (D D1)
→ 356 W 58th St (Eighth and Ninth)
Tel. (212) 554 6000
hudsonhotel.com
Ian Schrager and designer Philippe Starck mix styles: the dining room with refectory tables and oak benches, the bar with a glowing glass floor that illuminates the Francesco Clemente ceiling painting. From $120.

AIRPORTS TO MANHATTAN

By bus
→ $18 (JFK), $17 (EWR), $13 (LGA); every 15-30 mins

By minibus
Super Shuttle
→ Tel. (800) 258 3826
To Penn Station: JFK ($20), EWR ($21), LGA ($16). Stops on request.

By subway
→ From JFK only: Air Train ($7.75) to Howard Beach then Line A; or to Jamaica Center then line E ($2.75)

By taxi
→ $55-60 (JFK, 1 hr), metered fare from LGA (approx. 1 hr) and EWR (approx. 1/2 hr and $17.50 surcharge); plus $4-12 toll

GRAND CENTRAL TERMINAL

$200-300

Eventi Hotel (D F4)
→ 851 Sixth Ave (29th and 30th); Tel. (212) 564 4567
Has 292 modern rooms and suites with floor-to-ceiling windows. Laurent Tourondel's Italian restaurant (L'Amico); The Vine bar; and George Mendes' Lupulo with rustic Portuguese food. From $238.

Washington Square Hotel (B C3)
→ 103 Waverly Place (MacDougal)
Tel. (212) 777 9515
washingtonsquarehotel.com
On Washington Square Park, 150 well-equipped rooms from $238 (breakfast included). Restaurant: the North Square.

414 (D D2)
→ 414 W 46th St (Ninth)
Tel. (212) 399 0006
hotel414.com

A boutique hotel with 22 stylish rooms and large bathrooms; continental breakfast. $249-309.

The Frederick (A C2)
→ 95 W Broadway (Chambers); Tel. (212) 566 1900; frederickhotelnyc.com
The 131 spacious rooms are comfortable and modern. From $250.

Hotel Wales (H C5)
→ 1295 Madison Ave (92nd and 93rd)
Tel. (212) 876 6000
hotelwalesnyc.com
This boutique hotel on the upper east side is quiet; restaurant and pleasant roof terrace. From $200.

Chambers Hotel (E A1)
→ 15 W 56th St (Fifth)
Tel. (212) 974 5656
chambershotel.com
This small hotel has large windows and flat-screen TVs. From $250.

Bryant Park

Hotel (D E3)
→ 40 W 40th St (Bryant Park); Tel. (877) 640 9300
bryantparkhotel.com
Luxury in the 128 rooms of this 1924 midtown landmark with a celebrated Japanese restaurant: Koi. From $250.

Public (D F3)
→ 215 Chrystie St
Tel. (212) 735 6000
publichotels.com
Ian Schrager's 367 stylish, sleek rooms have big windows; Jean-George restaurant, the more informal Louis with take-out, and two bars: Diego and The Roof. From $235.

The Standard, New York (B A3)
→ 848 Washington St (13th)
Tel. (212) 645 4646
standardhotels.com
André Balazs' 337 sleek modern rooms straddle the High Line; eat at The Standard Grill or

BOATS

Water Taxi
→ Tel. (212) 742 1969
Daily; hop-on/hop-off pass: $37 / $31 for children; nywatertaxi.com
Cruises with commentary.

Liberty & Ellis Islands
→ Circle Line
Tel. (212) 563 3200
Castle Clinton (A C4)

Staten Island (A D4)
→ Free ferries; Tel. 311; siferry.com; Whitehall Terminal Battery Park

TAXI

Yellow cabs
→ $2.50, then 50¢ for each 1/5 mile (50¢ night charge from 8pm-6am)
→ Tip: 15% of the fare

ALTERNATIVE TRANSPORTATION

By bike
Citibike
Self-service bikes for hire around most of Manhattan, Brooklyn, Queens and New Jersey
→ See 'B' symbols on maps
Rates
→ Day pass (24hrs): $12; 3-day pass (72hrs): $24
→ Usage fees: free for first 30 mins then $4 for each additional 15 mins
By uber
Instant car service with base fee of $2.55-14, thereafter $1.75-4.50 per mile.
→ Use app or website
By helicopter
Liberty Helicopter Tours
→ Tel. 1 800 542 9933
libertyhelicopter.com
Three flight options: $214-$1,950/pers.

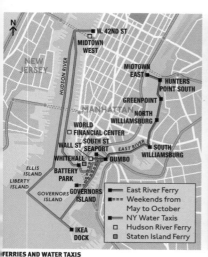

FERRIES AND WATER TAXIS

- ■ East River Ferry
- ■ ■ ■ Weekends from May to October
- NY Water Taxis
- ▢ Hudson River Ferry
- ▣ Staten Island Ferry

WATER TAXI

TRAINS AND STATIONS

New York has two main stations:
Grand Central Terminal (GCT) (E B4)
→ 42nd St (Park Ave)
Tel. (212) 340 2583
Serves the suburbs (Metro-North) in the states of New York and Connecticut.
Penn Station (PS) (D E4)
→ Eighth Ave (31st St)
Tel. (212) 630 6401
Links Manhattan to Long Island (Long Island Railroad – LIRR), New Jersey, Boston, Washington DC, Chicago, other US cities and Canada (Amtrak).

Biergarten and have a drink at the Top of the Standard. From $265.
The James Hotel (B C5)
→ 27 Grand St (Sixth Ave and Thompson St)
Tel. (212) 465 2000
This stylish hotel of 114 rooms has a rooftop pool and bar, Jimmy's, and a David Burke restaurant. From $269.
Marlton Hotel (B C3)
→ 5 W Eighth St; Tel. (212) 321 0100; marltonhotel.com
This nine-story, 107-room hotel feels like Left Bank Paris. Downstairs, Margaux serves breakfast, lunch and dinner; there is a wood paneled bar and espresso bar. From $255.
Wythe Hotel (J B5)
→ 80 Wythe Ave (11th and 12th); Tel. (718) 460 8000
wythehotel.com
The 72 rooms in this eight-story hotel have wallpaper, bare floors with radiant heating and

large windows; Reynard's restaurant and Ides rooftop bar. $250–900 for loft rooms.
The Ludlow (C B4)
→ 180 Ludlow St (E Houston); Tel. (212) 432 1818; ludlowhotel.com
A cozy 184-room, 20-suite hotel from the owners of the Bowery, Jane and Marlton. Restaurant: Dirty French. From $255.
Hotel 48LEX (E B3)
→ 517 Lexington Ave (48th St); Tel. (212) 888 3500
Boutique hotel with stylish rooms, mid-town local and a restaurant: Lexington Brass. From $246

OVER $300

11 Howard (C A5)
→ 11 Howard (Lafayette)
Tel. (212) 253 1111
Danish-style modern hotel with French restaurant Le Coucou and The Blond Bar, a nightclub and

lounge. From $400.
The Algonquin (D E3)
→ 59 W 44th St (Fifth and Sixth); Tel. (212) 840 6800
algonquinhotel.com
A classic building with old-fashioned decor (wood paneling, leather, velvet); quiet rooms and pretty tiled bathrooms. From $329.
Hotel on Rivington (C B5)
→ 107 Rivington St (Essex and Ludlow); Tel. (212) 475 2600; hotelonrivington.com
There are 110 rooms, all with floor-to-ceiling glass walls, in this 21-story tower; ask for a shower with a view. From $300.
The Lombardy Hotel (E B1)
→ 111 E 56th St (Park Ave)
Tel. (212) 753 8600
lombardyhotel.com
This hotel has 40 rooms and 75 suites and is perfect for museums and shopping. From $304.

SIXTY Lower East Side (C B4)
→ 190 Allen St (Houston and Stanton)
Tel. (212) 460 5300
An industrial chic hotel of 83 rooms and 58 suites with a rooftop pool, terrace lounge and the luxurious Blue Ribbon Sushi Izakaya restaurant. From $300.
The NoMad Hotel (B C1)
→ 1170 Broadway (28th)
Tel. (212) 796 1500
thenomadhotel.com
Experience Jacques Garcia's haute Boho style in this 168-room hotel; great restaurant as well as the beautiful Elephant Bar, NoMad bar and the Library. From $295.
SIXTY SoHo (B C4)
→ 60 Thompson St (Broome and Spring); Tel. (877) 431 0400; sixtyhotels.com
This 97-room hotel has a rooftop bar, open in late spring and summer.

LOWER EAST SIDE / 2ND AVE.

CROSSING WILLIAMSBURG BRIDGE

TAXI IN TIMES SQUARE

BUS

French restaurant: Bistro Leo. From $300.

Smyth (A C2)
→ *85 W Broadway (Chambers St); Tel. (212) 587 7000; thompsonhotels.com*
A 1960s look in the 100 modern, stylish rooms; Little Park restaurant and Evening Bar. From $375.

Gramercy Park Hotel (B D2)
→ *2 Lexington Ave (21st) Tel. (212) 920 3300 gramercyparkhotel.com*
Julian Schnabel designed the interior. Two bars: The Rose and Jade, and Maialino, a Roman-style trattoria. 185 rooms and suites. From $399.

The Carlyle Hotel (G C2)
→ *35 E 76th St (Madison) Tel. (212) 744 1600 thecarlyle.com*
Luxurious and discreet; have a drink at Bemelmans Bar or listen to cabaret in the Café. From $675.

The Bowery Hotel (C B4)
→ *335 Bowery (Second and Third); Tel. (212) 505 9100 theboweryhotel.com*
Boho chic: velvet upholstery, threadbare carpets and floor-to-ceiling views from the rooms. Italian restaurant: Gemma. From $325.

Langham Place Fifth Avenue (E A5)
→ *400 Fifth Ave (36th and 37th); Tel. (212) 695 4005 capellahotels.com/newyork*
With 157 rooms and suites; Ai Fiori restaurant by chef Michael White. From $550.

The Mercer (B D5)
→ *147 Mercer St (Prince and W Houston); Tel. (212) 966 6060; mercerhotel.com*
Decor of the 75 rooms by Christian Liaigre, and the Mercer kitchen is popular for lunch. From $625.

Four Seasons (E B1)
→ *57 E 57th St (Madison)*

Tel. (212) 758 5700
fourseasons.com
The height of luxury: great rooms, a fitness center. Restaurant: The Garden. From $745. Also at 27 Barclay St (downtown).

The New York EDITION (B D1)
→ *5 Madison Ave (24th) Tel (212) 413 4200 editionhotels.com*
From Ian Schrager, 273 rooms in the clock tower of the 1909 Metropolitan Life Insurance building; clock tower restaurant. From $495.

The Whitby Hotel (E A1)
→ *18 W 56th St (5th Ave) Tel. (212) 586 5656*
Kit Kemp's colorful patterns abound in this hotel of 86 rooms and suites with floor to ceiling windows; The Whitby bar, restaurant, and Orangery serve breakfast, brunch, lunch and dinner. From $625.

PUBLIC TRANSPORTATION

Bus and subway information
→ *Tel. 511 mta.info*
Most lines run 24 hours.
Fares
Single ticket
→ *$2.75 each ride (bus and subway)*
→ *$6.50 each ride (express bus)*
Metrocard
Rechargeable magnetic card (load $5.50 or more on the card and get an 11 percent bonus)
→ *$1 new card fee*
→ *Unlimited number of journeys by bus and subway: $32 for a week; $121 for 30 days*
Free
Free travel for children under 44 inches (1.1 m).
Subway
Fast and economical service, practical for north-south journeys.
Stations
Stations are normally marked with the street names and signaled by green globes (ticket vending machines open 24/7) or red globes (no ticket machines or restricted opening hours).
Train types
'Local' stop at all stations, 'Express' only stop at main stations.
Bus
Handy for east-west journeys. The letter preceding the number of the bus indicates the destination borough.
→ *Every 3–20 mins depending on the line and the time of day/night.*

Art galleries: best picks

Petzel Gallery (B A2)
→ *456 W 18 St (10th Ave);
Tue-Sat 10am–6pm*
This always-interesting gallery shows artists like Wade Guyton and Adam McEwan; bookstore too.

David Zwirner (B A2)
→ *519, 525 and 533 W 19th St; 537 W 20th St (11th Ave) Mon-Sat 10am–6pm*
Shows of important 20th- and 21st-century artists: Donald Judd and Giorgio Morandi to Chris Ofili, Sigmar Polke and Yayoi Kusama.

Paula Cooper Gallery (B A2)
→ *521 and 534 W 21st St (11th Ave); Tue-Sat 10am–6pm*
This maverick gallerist shows icons of 20th- and 21st-century art; don't miss 192 Books, her book store on 10th Ave (21st & 22nd).

Hauser & Wirth (B A2)
548 W 22nd St (11th Ave) Tue-Sat 10am–6pm
While a new space is finished next door, this four-story building is the venue of a wide-ranging collection of important art; its café, The Roth Bar, is amusing-looking; bookstore too.

Matthew Marks Gallery (B A2)
→ *523 W 24th St; 502, 522 and 526 W 22nd St (10th Ave); Tue-Sat 10am–6pm*
Three galleries showing European and American artists including Jasper Johns and Robert Gober.

Gagosian Gallery (B A1)
→ *555 W 24th St and 522 W 21st St (11th Ave) Tue-Sat 10am–6pm*
Two vast spaces that have museum-quality shows and handle many artists

including Richard Serra, Brice Marden and Anselm Kiefer.

Pace Gallery (B A1)
→ *537 W 24th St; 510 W 25th St (10th & 11th Ave) Tue-Sat 10am–6pm*
Exciting shows, from David Hockney, Louise Nevelson, Julian Schnabel and Elizabeth Murray etc.

Gladstone Gallery (B A1)
→ *515 W 24th St; 530 W 21st St (10th Ave) Tue-Sat 10am–6pm*
Always worth a look, since the artists include Matthew Barney, Sol Lewitt and Elizabeth Peyton among others.

Cheim & Read (B A1)
→ *547 W 25th St (11th Ave) Tue-Sat 10am–6pm*
Diane Arbus, Jenny Holzer and Louise Bourgeois are among their artists.

Paul Kasmin Galleries (B A1)
→ *293 and 297 10th Ave; 509–511 and 515 W 27th St*
Original shows on Post-War and Modernism; plus emerging and established contemporary artists.

Edwynn Houk (E A1)
→ *745 5th Ave (57th & 58th); Tue-Sat 11am–6pm*
Spectacular photography shows specializing in the 1920s and 1930s but also many contemporary photographers, from Lynn Davis to Annie Leibowitz and Stephen Shore.

Pace Gallery (E A1)
→ *32 E 57th St (Madison & Park); Tue-Sat 10am–6pm*
Well-curated shows of giants of the 20th century (Miro, Picasso); also African and contemporary art.

Marian Goodman Gallery (D E1)

→ *24 W 57th St, 4th floor (5th & 6th); Tue-Sat 10am–6pm*
An important gallery for more than 30 years; among their artists are John Baldessari, Pierre Huyghe, Julie Mehretu and William Kentridge.

Gladstone 64 (D D5)
→ *130 E 64th Street (Lexington Ave) Tue-Sat 10am–6pm*
In a 1956 townhouse redone by architect Edward Durrell Stone, imaginative group and solo shows.

Di Donna Galleries (G C4)
→ *744 Madison Ave (65th St) Mon-Fri 10am–6pm*
Specializing in surrealism, their show of Alaskan Yup'ik masks mixed with the work of Breton, Ernst, Miro, Carrington and Brauner among others, was groundbreaking.

Hauser & Wirth (G D3)
→ *32 E 69th St (Madison Ave); Tue-Sat 10am–6pm*
A townhouse gallery with shows of Paul McCarthy and Phillip Guston among others.

David Zwirner Gallery (G D3)
→ *34 E 69th St (Madison Ave); Tue-Sat 10am–6pm*
A gallery with shows of artists like Joseph Albers and Alice Neel; upstairs the Alder Beatty gallery has old masters and the estate of Ray Johnson.

Craig F. Starr Gallery (G C3)
→ *5 E 73rd St (5th Ave) Mon-Sat 11am–5.30pm*
Expect the unexpected in this tiny gallery; imaginative 19th- and 20th-century American and European shows.

Lévy Gorvy Gallery (G C3)
→ *909 Madison Ave (73rd St); Tue-Sat 10am–6pm*
20th- and 21st-century contemporary American and European shows on three Floors.

Nahmad Contemporary (G C2)
→ *980 Madison Ave (77th St); Mon-Sat 10am (11am Sat)–6pm*
Contemporary group shows worth visiting.

Michael Werner Gallery (G C2)
→ *4 E 77th St (5th Ave) Tue-Sat 10am–6pm*
In a modern space in a townhouse, exquisite watercolor and drawing shows of artists such as Sigmar Polke.

Almine Rech Gallery (G C2)
→ *39 E 78th St (Madison Ave); Tue-Sat 10am–6pm*
Imaginative shows comparing 20th- and 21st-century art.

The Mnuchin Gallery (G C2)
→ *45 E 78th St (Madison Ave); Tue-Sat 10am–6pm*
Brilliantly curated group and solo shows of contemporary artists. The Reds and minimalism shows are recent stand-outs.

Pioneer Works
→ *159 Pioneer St Wed-Sun noon–7pm*
This renovated 19th-century iron factory houses artist Dustin Yellin's non-profit gallery, which aims to meld art and science. Hosts dances, musical performances, film screenings, lectures and seminars.

Entries are followed by a letter in bold (**A, B, C...**) which refers to the corresponding area and map. Entries followed by ✪ are featured in *Unmissable Sights* (pages 2–11).

GOING OUT

Bars, clubs

Theaters

Concert venues

Jazz clubs

PLACES TO VISIT

Libraries

Religious buildings

Sites, monuments and places of interest

Museums, galleries

Parks and gardens

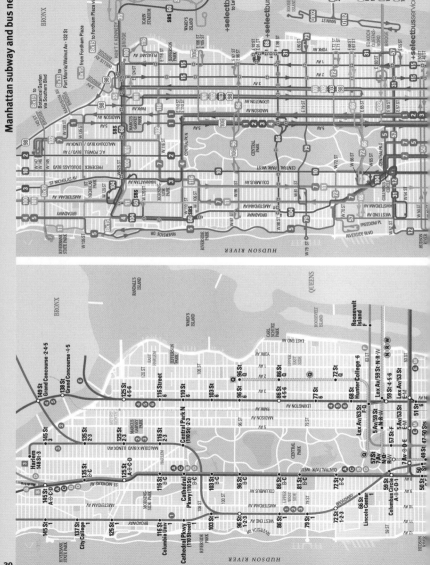

Nickie Roberts was b
She left grammar sch
jobs, including waitre
With a similarly ad
London, where she
years. Ms Roberts h
Italy and Tunisia, where she became an accomplished
belly-dancer. *The Front Line* is her first book.

NICKIE ROBERTS

The Front Line

GRAFTON BOOKS

A Division of the Collins Publishing Group

LONDON GLASGOW
TORONTO SYDNEY AUCKLAND

Grafton Books
A Division of the Collins Publishing Group
8 Grafton Street, London W1X 3LA

A Grafton Paperback Original 1986

ISBN 0-586-06828-7

Printed and bound in Great Britain by
Collins, Glasgow

Set in Times

To my parents and to all the Girls and Boys –
everywhere

To all my friends who contributed their stories and spoke from the heart; my agent Barbara Levy, for believing in me from the outset; my editor Judith Kendra, for her encouragement and advice; to Nina Lopez-Jones, Selma James and all the women at the King's Cross Centre, for blazing the trail; above all, to my husband, Steve, for his patience in helping me find my own voice, and also for doing *all* the housework (not just his half) whilst I worked on this book. I would also like to thank my parents, George and Lily Greenwood, and my parents-in-law, Geoff and Helen Roberts, for their loving support. Finally, thanks to my faithful little friend, Moustique, for putting up with me – and Soho – all these years.

Contents

Out of Soho

I've had it with the Soho sex industry; I'm out of it for good now. Not because I'm a reformed character, or because I got religion, or anything like that. It isn't that easy. No, the only route out is by finding another way of making a living, and that's hard for women like me, with no education, no qualifications, no real prospects. In other words nothing to sell except ourselves.

My way is becoming a writer. It's much more difficult than being a stripper, in some respects, but once you know exactly what you want to say, it can be very gratifying.

For years I've wanted to write about working in Soho; how it is for a woman. I wanted to tell the world about my experiences there, but every time I tried to put it down on paper, it all came out wrong and I just got more and more depressed and confused. I had very little confidence in my writing at first; again, that's lack of education for you. I was certainly glad that I'd taken every opportunity I could, throughout my stripping years, to read as much as I could lay my hands on. I wanted to learn so badly . . . still do, in fact.

It was during the last three or four years that I started reading feminist books, and learned a whole new way of seeing things: the world, my life, everything. But even there, within the women's movement I found there was nothing coming from women like me – everything that was said or written about the sex industry was coming from outside it, as usual. We weren't included in any of the debates and arguments, although it seemed that just about everyone else *was*.

I read lots of books that were written by academics, sociologists, psychologists, sexologists, and all the other 'experts'. These were educated people who were addressing only each other; we were being excluded as always. They wrote *about*, not *for* us.

Nobody seemed to know the truth about us; everywhere I looked I found prejudice and ignorance, and, often, guilt, thinly disguised as animosity. It was all a pain in the arse, and the fact that I was getting nowhere with my own writing didn't help matters. What did I want to say? I've always been able to think straight, talk straight: why shouldn't I just *write* straight? So that was how I got started. I thought of all the times I've been asked questions about my life as a stripper; always the same old questions:

'What's it like?'

'What do you think about when you're taking your clothes off?'

'Does it turn you on?'

'Do you make a packet?'

'Do you hate men?'

'How could you do it?'

'What does your husband think?'

'What's a girl like you . . . ?'

– and so on. You just wouldn't believe how often I hear that stuff, from all quarters, too, including so-called 'educated' types. It makes you realize that straight society is mostly ignorant about women like me, which is hardly surprising since few of us have had the opportunity to speak up for ourselves about our own lives. We're simply dismissed as 'pathetic victims' or 'hard-hearted sluts'; either way we're considered to be too thick to have anything of value or relevance to say. And yet the arguments rage all around us, from feminists, from (usually male) sexual libertarians, from Whitehouse & Co. . . . *Everybody* it seems has an opinion about the sex industry and what should or should not be done about it; everybody except us, that is. Yet we are the ones most closely involved. It's amazing.

It all came to a head, for me at any rate, when a group of anti-porn feminists started doing actions in Soho, where I was working as a stripper. There were 'Reclaim the Night' marches, with women slapping stickers all over the place: 'This degrades women'. Then came the big May 1983 march, where thirty thousand women 'reclaimed' Soho. Fine, except that the only women who were excluded from these actions were those of us who actually worked in the sex industry. Nobody even bothered to ask us what we thought. We were overlooked by our 'sisters', almost as if we didn't exist.

I particularly remember one of the earlier 'Reclaim the Nights', back in the mid-70s. I was working at the Doll's House, and we were sitting in the dressing-room one night when another stripper came flying in shouting that 'women's libbers' were on the rampage, sticking labels on the doors and windows of clubs – and on some of the girls. Now I don't know if that was an exaggeration, and I don't care; all I know is that for the rest of the night we strippers were frightened to run between our clubs, because we didn't want any aggravation from hostile feminists. In other words, we were being intimidated. I heard later that some of the feminists involved got badly knocked about by coppers who arrested them outside one of the sex-film clubs. Maybe if they'd consulted some of us beforehand, we could've told them what to expect. After all, everybody in the West End knows that the police will side with club bosses any day, rather than with a bunch of women.

But the women of Soho weren't consulted. We were just strippers, or just prostitutes, even as far as those feminists were concerned. Even *they* couldn't see beyond our jobs to the people we were. If that's not objectification, I don't know what is. I don't want to knock feminism on the head; there's plenty of others eager to do just that. But there's no escaping the fact that the anti-porn campaigners didn't exactly endear themselves to sex industry women from the start and things haven't improved since those early days, what with the New Puritanism rearing its vindictive head, in this country as well as the USA. Feminist anti-porn campaigners or the Whitehouse brigade: it makes no difference to us. Both factions clamour for more repression and censorship at the hands of the state; both divert attention from the real issue of women's poverty in this society; and both are responsible for the increased hounding and vilification of women who work in the sex industry. When the forces of law and order have already decreed that you are an outlaw, 'an outcast first of all, among other women';[1] when you are denied basic civil liberties on account of the job that you do, it does not come as a vote of confidence to have thousands of women marching through Soho proclaiming that the sex industry (and us too, by implication) is responsible for men's violence towards women.

Don't get me wrong: I'm not trying to defend the sex industry. God knows it's an ugly, pathetic business, but that doesn't mean to say that those of us who work in it should be classified as trash. The work sometimes is, and so are the bosses; but *we* aren't. And so far the anti-porn campaigners have neglected to make a distinction between us workers and the work we do. Otherwise they would be more responsible in their actions. They are silent, too, on the issue of the sexist, misogynist laws that criminalize prostitute women. There has been little support for women who work in the sex industry, even from feminists. I'm hoping this book will go some way towards remedying that situation.

I had many problems in working out my approach to this book at the beginning. I wanted more than anything to get across to people that women who work as strippers or prostitutes are not sluts and weirdos, but human beings. I got sick of hearing (from feminists as well as men): 'Oh but, you don't *look* like a stripper . . .'

What does 'a stripper' look like? One of Tom Sharpe's ladies, presumably, a cross between Mae West and Bet Lynch. I was incredulous at people's ignorance. I thought, you stupid sods; you don't even know that we come in all shapes and sizes, as do all women. Sometimes I would say, 'That's funny; you don't look like a student/brain surgeon/librarian . . .' and then I'd get really crazy looks. But I know that it's because people have these fixed stereotypes in their heads when they think of a stripper or a pro; not real people.

This made me decide to write about my own past, the time before I was a stripper; I just thought I'd like to show that women like me have histories; we weren't always strippers. All too often sex industry women are visible only in our working environments – a smoky Soho club, or on a street in some sleazy inner-city red light area. And then it's as if we're the same as that environment, nothing more . . . we become the sleaze and the seediness, in straight people's eyes. As if we'd always existed like that. It's all so wrong.

The only time I can think of when strippers were portrayed as something other than the work they do was in Peter Terson's play *Strippers*, which concentrated on the girls working up North, on Tyneside. His play wasn't wonderful, but he at least made an attempt to show the women in a sympathetic light, as real people with thoughts, feelings, families. Which made it all the more frustrating when I found out that Women Against Violence Against Women, the anti-porn group, were planning to picket the play's West End opening night. I could hardly believe it, with so much else to demonstrate against in this country: Thatcher's 'Wild Bunch' economic policies, the ones that are responsible for so many women going into the sex industry in the first place, for instance. It seemed ridiculous to me that a national demo was being organized against something as innocuous as Terson's play. I decided to organize a counter demo, or, as I told my Soho pals: 'Let's picket the picket!'

It was a rushed affair, but everybody I spoke to was enthusiastic and wanted to join in; girls jumped at the opportunity to get a word in edgeways about what was after all our way of making a living, supporting ourselves and our families. After a few quick phone calls, the Alliance of Strippers against Prohibition (ASP) was formed. Girls even missed their shows to come along. A couple of women from the English Collective of Prostitutes turned up at short notice to demonstrate their solidarity with Soho strippers who were fed up with being held responsible for rape and violence towards women.

The media turned out in droves, hoping to see a big catfight. Well, they were disappointed, even though there were a couple of ugly moments. A big strapping WAVAW woman glared over my shoulder at one of the ECP girls and asked her what she thought she was staring at . . . I was instantly reminded of the time I was asked the same question, in exactly the same manner, by a big woman copper from West End Central . . .

A twerp of about nineteen shrieked in my face that I was 'exploited' as a stripper, but she really needn't have bothered; I already knew that. Just as I knew that *all* workers in *all* industries are exploited. The sex industry isn't an exception. I told the child that I considered myself less exploited as a stripper than as a machinist in a factory. That didn't go down too well.

'I was going to be a stripper myself, but I didn't because the wages were so bad,' another woman told me. I should have asked her what she did instead, maybe she's an airline pilot, but I didn't, because to tell the truth, I was damned annoyed by this time. I thought, these women call themselves *pro-woman* but they don't want to listen to us. And as for their 'consciousness' – as far as working-class women were concerned, they hadn't a clue!

By this time I was raring to go. Soon after that picket I sat down and began writing my story. I thought if people read about what I left behind to go to London and become a stripper, then maybe they would begin to understand more, and stop asking me '*Why* did you do it?' It was whilst I was writing that part of the book that something began to niggle me. I couldn't think what it was at first. Then it dawned – it wasn't enough just to tell my own story; other voices needed to be heard, too. Otherwise what I said could be dismissed as the experience of one individual, a token stripper. Why shouldn't some of my friends get the chance to speak up too? After all, they were people whose words and thoughts were no less valid than my own. They had their own stories to tell, and I was in a good position to help them get heard. So I talked to eight of my friends, strippers and prostitutes, and asked them if they were interested. What they had to say forms the second half of this book. I transcribed their stories word-for-word: three female strippers, one male stage manager, one male stripper/ prostitute, and three female prostitutes. They are here, in this book. Those women and men come alive and speak to you through these pages. They have not been specially chosen because I thought their stories would make a more interesting book. From my own experience, I know that what they say is typical.

We have a lot of prejudice to overcome before we can reach people; so many myths and lies have obscured the reality of our lives. What we want is for you to listen to what we say, and to understand that, first and foremost, what follows is the truth.

Notes.

1. Selma James, 'Hookers in the House of the Lord' (*Feminist Action 1*) Battle Axe Books.

My Story

When I was young my prime concern was to escape from the Northern mill-town I was born and brought up in; that miserable grey world. I can remember very well the deep oppressiveness of the place: the huddled-together streets of terraced houses, row after row of them all the same; too many, in too small an area. Everyone living on top of everyone else. It seems funny now, seventeen years after I left, because the memory of those narrow streets and cobbled ginnels fills me with nostalgia, and I feel a great deal of affection for Burnley nowadays. But these emotions I recognize as really belonging to the days of my early childhood, when the little backstreets represented my freedom; the place where I and my friends had all our adventures. It seems a long time ago.

With the onset of adolescence, my outlook changed, and my environment seemed to me restrictive and grim. I could feel a hunger inside. It was in my blood, my bones; a great yearning to get out and experience life, to have adventures and, above all, to become a *person*. It had a lot to do with the whole sixties thing: the feeling, especially amongst young people, that it was all happening, and that it was *our* time. For some of us working-class kids, too, it seemed that we could get caught up in the whirlwind. We could make things happen for us. The Beatles, the whole Northern sound scene had proved that. Some of us really believed that *anything* was possible. Nothing would be the same again, we were rejecting the tired old lives of our parents and all the generations before them. I'm talking about the endless struggle to 'manage'; the old familiar cycle of work work worry work.

'A man mun work from sun till sun, but a woman's work is never done,' my Grandma Kainey used to say, in a weary voice.

It was true. All around me I saw the worn-down faces of Lancashire women. It seemed as soon as they got married, that was it; they started to look old. The ones I mostly knew were mill-workers like my mother, who worked horrible shifts in the cotton-sheds, six-to-two one week, two-to-ten the next. Then they came home and did the housework shift. As for the men, you hardly saw them. They were always on overtime. One of my strongest and most vivid memories is of my Dad sitting, exhausted, at ten o'clock at night, watching the news on TV and eating his kept-warm tea from a tray balanced on his lap. Whilst depending on what shift she was on, Mum would be either in the kitchen, putting her bait up, or just arriving home after the lates.

It seemed I hardly saw my parents when I was a kid. And yet in spite of all their work, we never seemed to be free of the monster: worry. Even so, Mum kept the house spotless, and we took great pride in the fact that everything we bought was brand-new – Mum wouldn't be seen dead at a jumble. And if we got a bargain, so much the better. Even today I balk at the idea of buying from second-hand shops and jumble sales; it's that old question of pride/shame, bred into me by my mother. Although nowadays my middle-class friends tend to see it as an eccentricity on my part.

I hated the cotton-sheds where Mum worked. Sometimes I had to go in to see her, on an errand or something, and when I did, I felt somehow torn in two. On the one hand, I liked talking with Mum and her workmates in the canteen; they always made a fuss of you and said things like 'She's right bonny, your lass,' which was the sort of thing I could stay and listen to till the cows came home.

On the other hand, the mill itself gave me the creeps, and for that reason I couldn't get away from there fast enough. The ear-battering noise was the worst thing about it; it felt like you were being run over by a train. The air was filled with hot raw cotton fibres, you breathed them in all the time and they tasted sickly-sweet. As for the cotton-looms themselves – 'loom' was the exact word for them. They were like big, skulking traps, waiting for you to fall into them. There were terrible accidents Mum told me about, and I was afraid for her. She told me about her friend, a reacher-in, who got his hair caught in the loom-belt and was *scalped*, and of somebody who got snared up and pulled right round the shafting: killed.

Mum was determined that I should never work in the mill.

'Don't worry,' I told her. 'I've no intention of doing that.'

But at the same time I had no intention of stopping on at school; I hated the place. It was a prison, in my view. I'd passed the eleven-plus, to my parents' delight, but I was never happy at grammar school. I was always in trouble, and so were my pals.

The school's motto was 'Vincit Qui Se Vincit' (He conquers, who conquers himself). They made us wear dark brown uniforms, ugly things that made us look like serried ranks of turds in assembly. The teachers were very much into discipline – the kind of discipline I would now describe as arbitrary and neurotic; like being made to walk the entire length of a corridor twice because previously you'd been three inches out of line, that sort of thing. There were one or two teachers I could get on with but in general my relationship with authority operated in a very straightforward way. It went like this:

everything I said or did was wrong, and if I questioned why this was so, I merely compounded the evil deed by being 'insolent'.

School was the subject of endless and sometimes violent rows in our house. It's easy to see why now, with the benefit of hindsight. The conflicts that were taking place at home came about largely as a result of my parents' resentment of the fact that they had both passed the eleven-plus in their day, but neither had been able to take up their place at grammar school, because their families needed wage packets at the earliest opportunity. Both started work at the age of fourteen.

It was a classic example of the parents wanting for their child all the chances they had had stolen from them as a result of the barbaric British class system. They saw my determination to leave school as a washing down the drain of all their own frustrated hopes and ambitions, whereas I saw it as my first step towards independence and freedom. We were continually at loggerheads.

'There's no telling you anything, lady,' my Mum would say to me with great bitterness, and it was true. I thought I knew it all, you do at that age. To me, 'going to university' was a prospect to be dreaded. Apart from me, nobody in our huge family, none of the cousins, had even got as far as grammar school, so we didn't know any eggheads. They were another species. As far as I could see, university would be just another school, where they jumped on your head all day long. I was as ignorant as hell.

So I left at the age of fifteen, with one Grade A O-level under my belt. They'd let me take it a year early, because I was so good at languages (I'd started teaching myself French at the age of seven or eight, I loved the sound of it).

My first job was a junior at a photographer's studio.

The man who owned it had one other female assistant besides me. He was the bloke who'd taken portraits of me from when I was a baby right up to my thirteenth birthday (after that I dug my heels in and refused to go any more; I thought I was too old for such childishness). I was genuinely interested in photography, and the idea of learning all there was to know on the subject appealed to me. Unfortunately, my boss was a dirty old bastard with roving hands. He would try to touch my boobs in the darkroom and one time he brought in some pornographic photos to show me. I was only a kid, and just couldn't handle that. And I was too scared to tell my parents, in case they thought I was making it up. I've often thought of that man since; of how his behaviour towards me stopped me from getting on in photography. For working class boys of that period, becoming a photographer was a trendy way of getting on, but then they didn't have to contend with 'sexual harassment' – a term that didn't exist when I was fifteen. Sometimes I honestly wish I'd at least kicked him in the balls. As it was, the only thing I could do at that age was to leave and get some other job, so that's what I did. In those days – twenty years ago – you could literally walk out of one place in the morning and start in another in the afternoon.

Over the next three or four years I had a steady stream of tedious jobs. From the photographer's I went to Woolie's, where some of my old school cronies worked. They put me on the sweet counter, but I kept eating the merchandise, so they moved me on to tights and nylons, which was even better for pilfering purposes. But the wages were bad and the hours worse, and vice versa. All that time on your feet – your back ached and your ankles swelled like balloons. And the way some of the customers spoke to you – as if you were scum! You had to laugh at the cheek of them. I stuck it out there for quite a while though.

One summer I worked as a waitress at Pontin's in Blackpool. It was bloody hard work, another killer on the feet, but I made lots of friends there and it got me out of Burnley for a while. I got friendly with the girl I shared a chalet with; her name was Cathleen and she came from Belfast. She worked there every season. I remember she had the habit of banging two empty soup tureens together in the kitchens – they made a tremendous racket – and roaring: 'UP THE IRA!' at the top of her voice. I hadn't a clue who the IRA were, but I thought that if Cath liked them, they must be okay.

Cath and I got on well together. After work we used to catch the bus into town and have fun in the pubs. One night we met a US airman who was in the process of cleaning out Blackpool with his poker-playing activities. He told us he was due back in West Germany the next day. I got a bit drunk, and gave him my knickers in response to a bet from Cath. I didn't fancy him, though.

A few days later he sent me a card saying that my pale blue keks had been hauled up the flagpole and were fluttering merrily in the breeze above the base. All the men were cheering. Cath and I had a good laugh at the time, but now when I look back and think about it – knickers off and men applauding – it seems to have been almost a portent of what was to come.

At the end of June the students turned up at Pontin's for their taste of life amongst the masses. They were posh kids on their 'vacs'.

'Just wait while you see this lot,' Cath told me. 'They're as thick as a workhouse butty.'

She was right; I couldn't get over how gormless these supposedly brainy types were. They were useless as waiters and waitresses. I remember one of them, a girl, fell flat on her face coming out of the hatch, smack into a bowl of trifle. She sat there wiping 'Dream-Topping' from her glasses. I felt sorry for her, but I couldn't help laughing my head off. It was the students who were always last to finish their tables. They went through the wrong hatch and collided with each other, and dropped plates and cutlery all over the place. They were like poor babies who hadn't any practical sense at all. They'd got no gumption, as Mum would say.

After Pontin's I came back to Burnley and worked for a year as an office junior. This was in order to 'better myself', or so I thought. The reality was quite different from the way office work was portrayed in magazines like *Honey*, *Petticoat*, and the rest. There were no gorgeous bosses with red Aston Martins, just a bunch of boring drips with dandruff, who sat around with their feet up whilst their secretaries and mugs like me did everything for them. It was the usual story: the women did all the work and the men took all the credit for it. All the reps were men too, and they weren't stuck in dreary little offices the whole day long. The pay was worse than Woolie's, so I left and decided to try factory work.

I started at a place where they made cute pottery rabbits. I lasted less than a month. My job was to paint the whites of their eyes as the little buggers passed me on a conveyor belt; it sounded nice and cushy, for factory work but, my God! it was like Chinese water-torture. After the first two days I could hardly get to sleep at night. Every time I shut my eyes I saw legions of rabbits marching towards me just like they did at work, in that annoying, steady, conveyor-belt rhythm. Then they began to actually infiltrate my dreams; that's when I gave in my notice.

My parents were hopping mad about me switching jobs all the time, and there were more big rows. With my teenager's, know-it-all arrogance I told them, in all seriousness, that I didn't think I was cut out to be a member of the working class.

'*Who the hell is?*' Dad shouted in my face.

My last straight job was at Diana Cowpe's in Burnley, where they made the world-famous candlewick bedspreads. I was put on cot-covers the day I started, which meant I had to machine little yellow ducks all day long. I couldn't believe it; I'd escaped the rabbits only to get landed with ducks. I thought it must have something to do with the way I looked: people were always going on about me having a 'baby-face'.

Factory work was hard, but better paid than office or shop work, and the girls and women I worked with were great; you could have a laugh together. At Cowpe's there were certain similarities with the cotton-sheds, although there wasn't the terrible volume of noise. The air was stifling and choked with candlewick fibres; they got in your throat and up your nose so that you suffered from constant irritation. It was worse for those women who had been there years; they were practically addicted to 'Strepsils' and 'Fisherman's Friends'. A girl who started the same day as me brought some disposable white masks into work, the kind surgeons wear. She got them from her mum, who cleaned at Victoria Hospital, so for a few days we all wore them. It looked dead comical, everybody sitting at their machines looking like extras from *Doctor Kildare*. But the management didn't think so, and our surgical masks were swiftly banned.

It was while I was working at Cowpe's that I decided I wanted to be a pop singer. I had a good voice, so I started doing the working-men's clubs in Yorkshire, with a fellow I'd met in a coffee bar. He called himself 'Linton Lee' (his real name was Duncan) and he had a voice like a drain, but he did a regular gig at a club in Keighley. I

soon found out why it was regular – the custo...
so rough, nobody with any sense would work the...
I was willing to take the chance, so Duncan a...
rehearsed a few numbers, I put on my sexiest mini-dress,
drank four Bloody Marys, and 'Yorkshire's Answer to
Lulu' was born (I couldn't be 'Lancashire's Answer . . .'
because in working-men's clubs, in Yorkshire and Lancashire, the War of the Roses is still being fought and that
mob would have torn me to pieces).

I loved it there, even though I shook with terror every
single time I went on. If the audience liked you, they
were warm and wonderfully responsive, and made you
feel like you could fly; but God help you if they hated
you! They threw chairs and beer at one poor bloke, a
trumpeter. Mind you, he was pretty awful.

Dee and I sang hit songs of the time – 'Cinderella/
Rockefella', 'Something Stupid'; stuff like that. Then I
would get up and do songs I could really belt out: 'Rescue
Me' and Lulu's 'Shout!' – that was my favourite, because
you could tame the wildest audience with it. They all
wanted to outshout each other in the chorus. Some nights
they nearly took the roof off. The club gave Dee and me
a fiver between us, plus all the drinks we wanted and a
meal that was fit for cockroaches. One night the resident
compère, Ray Smith, of the 'Ray Smith Trio', pulled me
to one side and said: 'You've got talent, little girl, but
you need voice coaching and you haven't a clue about
breath control. When you've been on the club circuit for
another five years, you'll be ready to hit the Big Time.'

I could've hit him, never mind the 'Big Time'. In five
years I would be twenty-three – ancient – and I had no
intention of hanging around Burnley that long. I was
eighteen, and raring to go.

It was all through this period, of course, that the so-called 'Sexual Revolution' was going on, and even backward old Burnley had latched on. The keywords were 'promiscuity' and 'liberation', and the Great God was 'the Pill'. Nevertheless, my female friends were going down like ninepins; getting fucked, getting pregnant, then getting married, or not. I was still a virgin, not so much because I believed in being 'good'; it was more a question of being scared of ending up with a bun in the oven. Also, I didn't make much of the boys round our way. To me they were mouthy, puerile yobs who spent most of their time loafing round the bus station and bragging to each other about which of us girls they'd 'shagged'. In the end, I lost my cherry to a busker in Manchester; he was the first hippy I'd ever seen and he told me that my eyes were like 'green forest pools'. That got him the goods! But he wasn't like the Burnley mods; he was calm and gentle, with a lovely warm smile (this was largely because he was permanently stoned). His name was 'Thatch'. I never saw him again, but that didn't matter; I was rid of my innocence, or so I thought.

My closest friend at the time was a girl called Greta. We'd played together when we were kids, then grown apart during the adolescent years, only to gravitate towards each other again at eighteen. Greta had been in some trouble with her family recently because she had a 'no-good' boyfriend, a lad called Dave, who was the drummer in a group. He was also a thief, and had absolutely no scruples about anything, but you couldn't help liking him for his personality. He seemed so much more alive than all those dopey local lads. I think it was because he'd been shoved from pillar to post in his childhood; that made him more resourceful and independent.

My last summer in Burnley Dave and Greta filled my

head with tales about their recent adventures in London, particularly round the the clubs of Soho. It sounded like the streets were paved with cash. Greta certainly seemed to have blossomed during her weeks in the 'Smoke'. Her clothes were fantastic, all the latest gear – nicked, no doubt, by the crafty Dave. They told me about the strip-clubs, where a girl could earn up to a hundred pounds a week, running from club to club. It was an amazing sum, but all the same . . .

'You should come and see for yourself,' Greta said.

I thought about it. The gigs with Dee were becoming less frequent and more hassle-ridden. It was the usual story: he thought our professional relationship should extend into our personal lives; I thought he was crazy.

'That'd be like incest,' I told him. So we argued a lot and, you know how it is when you turn a boy down; he started to actively dislike me. As for Cowpe's, that place was bad enough at any time, but in the hot weather it was unbearable. One day there was a big leaving-do. May, one of the women who had worked there for about a hundred years, was retiring. She was kind and well-liked by everybody, so we all clubbed together to buy her a mint-green bath set and twenty-four-piece dinner-service. We were given sherry in the canteen, and Mr Ross, the overseer, gave a speech thanking May for her dedicated-service-all-these-years-on-behalf-of-the-company. Suddenly, he presented her with a Cowpe bedspread. I could not believe my eyes. All around me people were clapping and going 'Aaaah . . .' To cap it all, May looked pleased.

I went out of the canteen and into the toilet; it felt like my stomach was boiling and made of steel at the same time. I told Greta that night 'The poor sod's worked there all that time making their bedspreads and now, when she finally drops they give her one as a leaving gift. That's an insult.'

I thought, if it had been me I would have torn the bloody thing to shreds in front of their faces; or set it on fire right under Ross's nose. I couldn't get over it.

My social life at that time consisted of the occasional Keighley gig plus the odd night out at either the Burnley Mecca, where all the mods hung out, or the Nelson Imp., which was a dump but which got all the good groups – the Beatles had played there, also the Stones, Spencer Davis, and my own favourites, the Small Faces. As a matter of fact it was when I first saw little cat-faced Stevie Marriott, the lead singer with the Faces, that I realized small people could be successful. If he can do it, I thought, so can I . . .

I'd started going out with a lad called Mick, who worked as a local DJ. He was gorgeous, but didn't he know it. You couldn't kiss him properly because he said things like 'Mind my suit, it's hand-tailored', and he was always watching himself in mirrors. My Mum used to kill herself laughing at his vanity. Once when he came to pick me up she told him: 'Mick, you look that grand I could fancy you myself.'

'I don't blame you, Mrs Greenwood,' he said.

Mum fell about, but Mick was being perfectly serious.

I wouldn't sleep with Mick, and I think that pleased him. He could 'respect' me, he said. On the other hand, it meant that he often two-timed me and went with girls who *would* 'go'. This confused me. I thought, why do boys pester you to have sex with them then announce that the girls who did were sluts and whores? *I* didn't feel I was any the worse a person since I'd lost my virginity, but I knew that if I told Mick, I'd become an instant 'fallen woman' in his eyes. It did not make sense – the boys wanted 'it' so much and yet doing 'it' made a girl really bad. This seemed to me to be the height of masculine illogic. Mick drove me mad.

Everything drove me mad, though – above all, working at Cowpe's. I was almost nineteen years old, and nothing was happening. I couldn't bear the thought of reaching twenty and still being stuck in grey old Burnley. I became increasingly depressed and lethargic, and stopped going out altogether, apart from work and occasionally to meet Greta and Dave at the Wimpy Bar in town where he was working.

I told Dee to fuck off when he rang me. I never saw him again after that. Mick was going out with a girl from Bacup whom I didn't know personally. But I had my suspicions about her. The arguments in our house were endless. My parents were worried sick about me but I didn't think of them. I had withdrawn into a shell, with the ugly, lumpish feelings of a young person who had no idea what to make of her life and who seemed to have no hope whatsoever of getting anywhere. God, was I feeling sorry for myself.

Then one morning I got the sack from Cowpe's. Eileen McKillop and I were cutting each other's hair behind a mountain of cot-covers and the overlooker caught us: instant dismissal. We gave him a mouthful, collected our wages, and skipped out of there, laughing. I couldn't believe my luck; now I *had* to do something with my life.

Greta was usheretting at a local fleapit; it was 'bent' work, that is no P45; cash-in-hand. She said they always needed staff, why didn't I try it for a little while? She and Dave were planning to go back to London any minute; I could go with them.

I worked at the cinema for two weeks, and saw *Sands of the Kalahari* twenty-four times: I knew the script backwards. I thought if I saw Stanley Baker crawl across the desert once more, my brain would burst. A local

prostitute used the cinema during the matinée performance. She would pay to see the film, then pull punters
from the audience. Apparently, it was a well-known ploy,
doing the flicks. What happened was this: the woman
would give some fellow the eye, then leave the theatre.
She'd be gone for about five minutes. This happened
every twenty minutes or so; I thought at first that the
lady had a weak bladder, then I noticed that every time
she left her seat, a different bloke followed her. It turned
out she was doing hand-jobs in the men's bogs.

'Worth the price of a ticket,' Greta remarked. I had to
admit it was a pretty ingenious method of working. You
live and learn.

My Burnley days were coming to an end. After work,
Greta would come round to our house and we would
sneak up to my bedroom, light joss-sticks, play records
and sit huddled on my bed, discussing our plans in frantic
whispers. I couldn't honestly see myself as a stripper –
that was too way-out – but Greta said no problem, we
could get jobs as barmaids or doorgirls. We'd get massive
tips, she said. Not like up here.

One Sunday afternoon, at the beginning of September,
I was sitting on the settee in our living-room, staring out
of the front window. Everybody was washing their bloody
car. Mum was reading the *News of the World*; Dad had
the *Sunday Express*, and *Family Favourites* was blaring
from the radio. Outside, the sky was grey as only a
Burnley sky can be; it looked like it weighed a ton.
Inside, the house smelled of boiled cauliflower and roast
lamb. It was a typical, stagnant Lancashire Sunday, in
other words.

'I'm going to London,' I announced.

And that was that.

It was agreed that I could go for a week, and if I hadn't
found a job in that time, I was to come back. Apart from

my parents, everyone I knew seemed to share my Uncle Harry's attitude: 'She'll be back in no time with her tail between her legs and a bun in the oven.'

But they were all wrong; I never went back.

We left the following Friday evening. Greta and I got the coach to Preston, from where we intended to hitch down the M1 overnight. Dave was to travel down separately. We would go with the lorries, Greta said; they were safer than cars, and so were the drivers.

'They respect travellers,' she said.

From the coach, climbing out of Burnley, my home town and the countryside around it had never looked so beautiful, especially those wonderful, mauve-green hills that surround our valley. It was incredible; as if I were seeing it all for the very first time, through the eyes of a stranger. Maybe I was. I felt like crying when I saw dear old Pendle Hill for the last time. I'd had so many adventures there as a child, when we used to go and see Jack Moore's monkey and the old woman everyone said was a witch (because she lived alone in a derelict old cottage and had warts and a giant tabby cat). Even the stinking factory chimneys somehow achieved a sorrowful and picturesque look as we whizzed by. I have to admit it; my heart was in my throat, until we hit Blackburn. That place is enough to pull anyone up sharp; there's just no getting sentimental over a dump like Blackburn.

What a strange night that was; the strangest in my life up till then (I've had plenty of stranger ones since). It passed like a dream. In fact, I've had dreams that were more real than that night on the motorway with Greta.

We were picked up at the Preston Services with no trouble, by a nice lorry-driver called Bert, from Hartle-pool. I'd never been in one of those gigantic vehicles before; it was bad enough climbing up into the cab without a pair of stilts, especially if you were five foot two; but once you were up there, it was fantastic. It felt like you were practically airborne, hurtling down the motorway so high up off the road. The little ordinary cars looked like tempting Dinky-toys; they made me want to mow them down.

'Perverted little bugger aren't you?' Bert said when I mentioned this.

The cab was extremely comfortable, with deep, cushioned seats that you could really sink your bum into. We sang along to the radio and exchanged corny jokes, and Greta and I swigged from a quarter bottle of brandy.

Bert dropped us at Birmingham. It was the middle of the night by then, and it seemed strange to be down on the ground again. I felt scared and cold, after the lovely warm lorry. We were about to wander into the Services for a coffee when a man parked in a car nearby called across to us. We went over, and he opened the passenger door.

'Looking for a lift?' he said, in a pleasant voice. He was youngish, with a smiling face. Greta and I looked at each other with our eyebrows raised. We'd planned to stick to the lorries, but then, you could hardly turn a lift down.

'How far are you going?' we asked him.

'London.'

Great! I was just about to get in beside him when Greta suddenly gave a yelp and yanked me back by the elbow. The bloke looked annoyed. What was going on?

'Go on, piss off, you wanker,' Greta snarled at him. I thought she'd flipped.

The driver slammed the door and said 'Cunts!' and drove off like a maniac.

'Didn't you *see*?' Greta was saying. 'You blind, or what?'

I hadn't seen a thing.

'He had it out,' said Greta.

'What? *Oh*!' I was shocked. 'Well, I wasn't looking down there . . .'

'That's the first place you look,' said Greta, sounding exactly like one of my old school-teachers.

After that we stuck with the lorries. One warm, comfy cab after another; dozing and waking up to the dark night and the loud purring engines. The last leg of our journey was the worst, coming into the city suburbs at dawn. We were dropped somewhere horrible in North London. I felt like something the dog had dug up, and if Greta's appearance was anything to go by, we looked like a pair of escaped mental patients.

'We can catch the tube into the West End,' Greta said. Her breath was like a blowtorch.

I don't want to dwell on my first spell in Soho; not here, in this book, at any rate. This isn't the place for it. The reason for this is that neither Greta nor I got directly involved with the sex industry during this time; we were at best peripheral to the scene, We hovered on the sidelines; two green North Country kids who couldn't get over what was happening all around us. It was certainly different from anything I'd seen in Burnley! The lights, the music blaring into the street, and the neon signs everywhere you looked – 'GIRLS! GIRLS! GIRLS!' and 'THEY'RE NAKED AND THEY DANCE!' Above all, the people – the working girls, strutting about so self-assured and contemptuous of the men who wandered up and down with a certain look on their faces – devouring, obsessive . . . ugh! They terrified me at first, but then I got used to them; you can get used to anything.

There was laughter, too, in those streets, and freedom. In Soho, nobody pestered you with nosy questions, or wanted to know your business, unless they were Old Bill.

It was alive, and real. No factories – except of course that the entire area is one massive sex-factory, but that's not how it seemed. Really, I thought Soho was more like one of those crazy Southern European villages than a place in England. There was dancing and music and lots of noise all the time, and sometimes, there were fights.

Still, as I say, I didn't start working in the sex industry this time round. But one or two incidents I feel should be recorded here, because they do concern the politics of sex. One was when I got arrested for 'footway' in Greek Street, and hauled off to West End Central, that Pit of Pits.

I was talking to the doorman of a Blue Film club when two plain-clothes walked in and said to me 'Get your hat and coat darlin', you're nicked'. It didn't seem to matter to them that I wasn't working there; they had their quota to fill so they might as well nick some little thing like me as anyone else. I was frightened. These big cops talked as mean and nasty as any of the real 'hard' villains. They stuck me in between them and walked me to the station, talking over my head all the way. I felt like a bag of shopping.

At West End Central I gave them a fictitious name and address. What an ugly place a copshop is. I can't remember the details, except that it was bare and depressing, and the lights made everyone look as though they were made of dripping. From the moment you walked in through that door, you felt like you had ceased to exist; that anything could happen to you in there and nobody outside would ever know. You felt like you were nothing.

I was strip-searched by a female, which was very humiliating. Then they shoved me into a cell with a filthy bed and blanket. The cell next door to mine was occupied by somebody very drunk singing 'My Way'. A couple of hours passed. Suddenly the door banged open and a big macho she-cop stood there and said, 'Do I look like I just dropped off of a Christmas tree?' There must have been something wrong with the look on my face, because she followed that up with did I want a good hiding? I said no; not that that made any difference because she still gave me a tremendous whack round the head. My left ear was ringing for hours after that, and even now, sixteen years later, I have problems with that ear – sporadic deafness and tinnitus. She said, 'Now give us your real name', which I did with alacrity.

'Date of birth.'

I told her. She got mad again and called me a lying slag.

'I want the truth,' she said. 'You're not a day over fifteen . . .'

But by then I was too scared to lie, and she knew it. They rang my parents up at 4 A.M. to check up that I wasn't a juvenile, then they let me go. I was to appear at Marlborough Street court the next morning.

That was my first lesson on how the law basically regards females in Soho: as so much trash. Although, I suppose I should mention that I knew one or two nice cops round the West End; not many though. Most of them at that time were as bent as the villains they purported to catch, and there was a great deal of truth in the old saw: 'Set a thief to catch a thief' when applied to the ladies and gentlemen of West End Central. Ditto pimps and conmen.

But I got to know one cop – this was a few years later, when I was a stripper – who was good to me. We used to go to the pub occasionally. He was a DI from the Flying Squad; he had a good sense of humour. He once told me, 'Nickie, if you get any aggro round here just you let me know and I'll sort it out for you.' He was very fatherly and protective. I suppose there are cops and cops, it's like society as a whole; people abuse the power they have over others. It's the same with all institutions: the law, schools, work, marriage . . . you name it. Having said that, I must say I think that policing attracts a certain type – the megalomaniac type. But for the record I feel I should mention my Sweeney pal, otherwise it wouldn't be fair. Even so, his kindness to me does not erase the memory of the incident with the she-cop. Nowadays I see they have TV series about the daring adventures of policewomen. I have to laugh at the title of one programme: *The Gentle Touch*. It really isn't funny, though.

Those first months round the West End Greta and I spent dossing on people's floors, in derelicts, at Euston Station, and in all the other sordid haunts mysteries like us had to resort to ('mysteries' is what West Enders call young girls like us who turn up in Soho every day of the year). We got by on stale buns and hot dogs and whatever we could scrounge. We went shoplifting in Oxford Street, but not often. I wouldn't do that at all now, my bottle's gone, but I don't feel ashamed of myself for doing it in the past, and I didn't then. How else were we to get a few of the lovely things we saw all around us? I thought, when you're poor, it's only logical to steal from the wealthy.

There was a young man called George, from Liverpool, who wheeled his hot-dog barrow up and down Greek Street. He had long black ringlets, like Charles the First, and he was an anarchist.

'Eat the rich,' he used to say, when he gave Greta and me food. That was the first time I ever came across the expression.

The other incident that stands out in my memory occurred one night soon after Greta and I arrived in the West End. We were on our way to the all-night cartoon cinema for a warm kip when a big wealthy-looking man with a vicious smile stopped us and said, 'I'll give you two fifty pounds if one of you shits into the other's mouth.'

I could have thrown up on the spot, except that would have probably turned him on. We turned and walked away. We couldn't even call him a name, because there wasn't one horrible enough. There still isn't. There are plenty of bad names for women – scrubber slag slut brass tart whore to name but a few. Vile words. But that man was vile, what he wanted was vile. What can you say? The language just does not exist.

My first spell in Soho was exciting, sickening, magical and dangerous. It was certainly different from Burnley. I lost my innocence quite quickly. You do, in the West End. Nowadays, I would call it *ignorance*. I can't say exactly when it happened. It just seems to me now that one day I was a bit of a kid, and then I wasn't any more; and it had nothing to do with my own sexuality. In a way, it seemed to have little to do with me at all.

After three years of travelling round Europe and North Africa, I went back to London and found Greta living in a squat in West Kensington. She was four months pregnant and on the verge of being thrown out. Dave was nowhere to be found. We were both skint.

I took her to the DHSS to get some money to buy her food. That was a terrible experience. We sat for hours in a smoky waiting-room filled with men. We had to wait till last, and then they refused to give us anything because we had no cards. The bloke over the counter kept shaking his head; he wouldn't give us a cent. He looked really pleased about this. Poor Greta was getting hysterical. I knew it was all the anger and tension she'd been bottling up inside her. The jerk said he was going to call the police if we didn't leave soon. I felt sick with anger at the humiliation he was trying to inflict on Greta. She was in tears now, saying 'Well, will *you* in that case give me ten pence for a bottle of milk . . . from your own pocket, you won't?'

I said, 'Let's get out of here.' I wanted to rip his flabby white face off with my fingernails, just to see what lay underneath.

We walked to a little working-man's café in Fulham Road; we had enough money between us for one cup of hot chocolate. When you are hungry, hot chocolate is much better than tea or coffee; it makes you feel fuller, and it doesn't give you palpitations if your stomach is empty.

It smelt wonderful inside the café. At another table a bunch of Irish workmen were tucking into beans, sausages, eggs, toast . . . Our eyes were like saucers. We were practically drooling, but the blokes didn't seem to notice. When they finished, I felt like crying, it had almost seemed that we were enjoying their meal as they ate it. Daft . . .

We couldn't speak to each other; we were so low. The truth was at that point we had hit rock-bottom. The workmen were taking ages paying up at the counter; they kept nudging each other and glancing back at us. I didn't have the energy to tell them to piss off. Suddenly, out of the blue, the waitress appeared at our table with a pile of hot toast and some knives and forks. Greta and I looked at her, then at each other, then at the toast. The fellows were filing out of the café.

'We didn't order this,' Greta croaked.

'The lads had a whip-round,' said the woman. And gave us two pounds in change.

There they were, smiling and waving through the window. We stared back.

Then: 'Thank you! Thank you!' We were laughing and

crying. The men looked sheepish; they ducked their heads and disappeared. This was like a miracle to Greta and me. It was a minute or two before we could eat, hungry as we were.

I was worried about Greta; she looked so ill and drawn; thin, even though she was pregnant. I thought having a baby might kill her, in that state. We had to do something.

'Don't worry,' I told her. 'We'll get out of this crap.'

We caught the tube to Piccadilly, and walked up through the familiar streets: Great Windmill Street into Brewer Street. It was late afternoon, already getting dark; miserable November. We saw a strip-club called *El Paradiso*; a woman was standing on the door, talking to someone. She had a Maltese accent. We went up to her and said 'Excuse me, are you a stripper?'

'You looking for work?' she said. 'Come with me.'

An hour later, we were strippers too.

If I just close my eyes now and think about it, I can relive the moment we walked into that club and had to go right the way down through the theatre, past all those men sitting with their eyes glued to the girl on-stage. She was little and thin, stark naked except for two tassels on her tits. She was sending them flying in all directions.

I couldn't get over the size of the place; it looked like a downbeat Palladium. We didn't realize at the time, but we'd only gone and picked the biggest strip-joint in London in which to make our debuts. It was like a vast, dark hangar, except for the stage, which was very brightly lit. The men didn't even see us as we went by; they were absorbed in the tassel-dancer's act. I noted the expressions on a couple of their faces; they looked much the same as the ones Greta and I were wearing when we watched our workmen eat their breakfasts.

The Maltese stripper, Marlene, led us backstage to a dressing-room the size of an airing cupboard. It was incredible! There must've been half a dozen girls in there, all shapes and shades, chattering away. Knees, breasts, arses all over the place. In one corner was a clothes-rail, like the ones they have in shops, only this one was dripping with exotic-looking costumes, glittery with feathers and sequins and trailing long negligées. Beside it was a battered wreck of a dressing-table that was covered in debris, mostly of the make-up variety. Plus there were bottles . . . Cinzano, Bacardi, Bells; and a half-eaten shish-kebab, congealed and drowned in red chili sauce; it looked like something wounded.

What a dump!

A tiny bloke appeared as if by magic and told us he was the choreographer. Another Malt (at that time most of the clubs were Maltese-run; the 'Maltese Mafia' they called the bosses. This was before the big clean-up of 1973, under the auspices of Commander Robert Mark: Mister Clean himself!).

'You can start straight away,' he told us.

In those days they threw you on-stage before you had time to get scared or change your mind. Greta was given a ramshackle negligée.

'No G?' said the 'choreographer'. 'Wear your knickers, *allah*.'

'First record – you dance with the costume on. Second record: take off the negligée and dance in the knickers and bra. Third record: take off the bra and dance with the knickers. Use the bed. Three records, got it? At the end of the third record, you take off the knickers and *stand still*. Raise your arms like this . . . that's the "flash-chord". Then it's finished, innit?'

'What? What?' Greta was still babbling when they opened the curtains, or 'tabs' as the choreographer called them. Her first record always sticks in my mind: 'I Still Get The Same Old Feeling', by 'Pickety Witch'. Poor

Greta! She was shitting herself. She'd had a couple of good slugs of Cinzano before she went on; the other girls were very kind to us. They obviously all remembered *their* first time.

'Don't worry,' said one who introduced herself as Cherry Tart. 'It's like losing your virginity; once you've done that first spot, you're laughing.'

Greta came off in tears. It was my turn next. This was like a living nightmare.

'Gimme some more Cinzano,' I was shouting. I was already light-headed, thanks to a combination of booze and terror.

They put me in a double-act. It's better with somebody else on-stage, you don't feel so alone out there. But I was still scared stiff; you always are. What scared me more was that it was meant to be a lesbian routine – disgusting! Worse still, with a complete stranger. I was mortified. But lesbian acts are always popular with the punters. They think 'Those sweet little girls, what they need is a man . . .'

My partner was a girl called 'Kitten' – 'Kitten Jones, from Tiger Bay' – but she came from Middlesbrough really, of Polish origin. She was eighteen and extremely beautiful. I thought, what the hell is she doing here, with a face like hers? They asked me my name, so I said 'Nickie', and it's stuck to me ever since. The choreographer told me what I had to do; it sounded terrible. It was billed as the 'Cleanest Act in Soho', because it was a bath-number. A voyeur's dream scenario:

'The Countess Bathing, With the Help of her Maid'.

I listened to the introduction, which consisted of the Maltese choreographer going on and on about two women who fell for each other; one 'High Born' the other 'A Lowly Maidservant' (guess who). He was trying to make it sound sexy and dramatic, but it just sounded bloody daft. I thought, how can those men out there take any of this seriously? (I'm wiser now, and know that logic and reason have little to do with the man-as-punter phenomenon.) This is what we had to do:

Curtains open on naked woman in bath-tub, splashing away with her back to the audience, to the accompaniment of dreamy, 'Milk Tray' advert music. After a minute or so, the maid totters on carrying a jug of water, which she empties into the tub. She washes the Countess then wraps her in a bath towel, dries her, and leads her over to a chair set right at the front of the stage. The Countess kneels on the chair whilst her maid rubs Baby Lotion over her back. Then she turns round and rips off the maid's costume, which is held together by a spit and a prayer. Then on to the rug for the lezzie bit.

I was waiting to go on. Peeping through a slit in the backdrop, I could see Kitten splashing away in the tub. Lots of bright yellow lights. For a split second I almost wished I were back at my machine in Cowpe's.

'Go ON . . .'

They had to prise the bottle of Cinzano from me.

I wobbled on-stage on my two jelly-legs, in that stupid maid's outfit. I was so scared of dropping the water-jug, that gave me something to concentrate on. I tried to stop the water from slopping over the top; I didn't want to get electrocuted.

'Mind you don't fry on the footlights,' a black girl had said, moments before I went on.

I poured the water into the tub. So far, so good. Kitten was pulling faces at me, trying to make me relax. I looked up . . . Christ! That was when I nearly ran off the stage. All those men! The heat . . . I wasn't sure where it was coming from, the lights, me, or the packed audience. Yes, mostly the latter. It rose like a mist, thick and clogged, smelling of men; a hundred, two hundred white blobs of faces were raised towards us. Fishy eyes watched our every move. I felt sort of transfixed, staring back at them.

'Wrap the towel round me,' Kitten was saying. 'Ignore *them* . . .'

Ignore them!

'They're looking at me!'

The lights were scorching hot colours – yellow, pink, magenta, amber. I went through the first spot feeling that it wasn't really happening; it was too absurd and surreal. Yet at the same time, there was something so ordinary and everyday about all the props – tub, sponge, towel, soap – that it almost felt reasonable to be taking your clothes off, people took their clothes off to have a bath. My thoughts babbled on like that . . .

The men in the front row were so near, they could have tickled my feet.

My Big Moment arrived. Kitten took off my costume and chucked it to the back of the stage; I felt like running after it. I thought of all those bastards staring at my backside. This couldn't be real. It was time for the naughty bit. Kitten was on the rug; I dropped down beside her, like a plank. We had to stroke each other 'erotically'. I pretended she was my dog. I was surprised at how soft her skin felt. All-in-all, that part was a cinch. A brilliant white spotlight fell on us; Kitten jumped up and pulled me to my feet. It was the flash-chord; the moment when you stood there stark-naked and in a manner of speaking, took your bow. You had to stand dead still; it was illegal to move with no G-string on.

The men clapped, the tabs closed, the lights went out.

That was my first time on-stage; I was in a state of minor shock, I know that now. I think we all put up our psychological defence barriers, so that when we were on-stage, we responded to what was going on with only the surface emotions; the ones with which you take on immediate sensory impressions. We each in our different way tried to block off the deeper knowledge of what was happening. It was much easier – and safer – to shrug it off, or laugh at the absurdity of it all.

Beneath the surface, the core of me, the one I am, was tight like a knot, untouched, or so I believed. All I thought at the time was that all those men out there were crazy, and so was I, for that matter. But under the circumstances, there was nothing I could do about it.

Time functions differently in Soho; it's just not the same as in the straight world. It is regulated, and it moves on, but it seems to do so in a curiously static way. You get carried along with it, without seeming to be aware of it. Well, that's the impression you get. You inhabit this crazy world where strange things happen all the time, whether it's day or night makes no difference. The illusion is strong: time doesn't move on, and still you work, live, sleep. That's why when I look back at this long period of my life, everything seems a great tangle, and it's difficult to straighten it out. It really does seem that one day I was twenty-two and a stripper; the next I was thirty, and a stripper. That wasn't what was supposed to happen, but it had; it was as if an infinity had passed in the blink of an eyelid.

Seasons, of course, mean nothing in the wankers' city jungle. I think that had a lot to do with it.

We worked a seventy-two-hour week. Non-stop from noon till midnight, that's what the clubs boasted, and it was true. You had to run from club to club, depending on how many you were prepared to do. Most girls did five or six clubs; the ones with ponces did even more. This was the famous 'Circuit'.

At first I did three clubs, and was considered by many

to be lazy, but I didn't care about that. To me, three
decent wage packets were a vast improvement on the
pittance I'd earned at Cowpe's. You got fifty pence a
spot, doing six spots a day at each of the clubs you
worked at; with my three clubs that meant I was doing
eighteen strips a day. It was enough. We worked in two-
hourly shows called 'rounds', starting at noon. It went
like this: 12–2 P.M. was the first round; 2–4 P.M. the
second; 4–6 P.M. the third, and so on until the sixth and
final round, from ten till midnight. Just like boxing. Mind
you, it felt a bit like that; by the end of the working day
you were feeling pretty roughed up. Each spot, or
number, you did lasted around nine minutes, and you
had thirty seconds either side of your tape in which the
stage manager had to get you and your props on and off
the stage in time for the next girl. Props were mostly of
the red satin-covered bed, or the high stool or the fluffy
white rug variety, although a couple of the clubs were a
bit flash; they liked to be ambitious and theatrical, and
then you got the whole production number routine.

I did my first single act, going on alone, at a club in
Wardour Street called the Playboy. It was a real dive,
one of the smallest joints in the West End, but I was still
bloody nervous to be up there on my own, with no Kitten
for moral support. They gave me a tape of really fast
African drumming music, the bastards, then all the girls
went out front for a good laugh. But I handled it well,
considering; I did a belly-dance, which I'd learned on my
travels in North Africa. All the same, when I came off
that stage I was dripping with sweat and gasping like a
landed fish.

'You did okay,' the other girls said. 'But keep that up
and you'll be dead in a week.'

You knackered yourself anyway, from what I could
see. Stripping was hard physical work, and dashing the

length and breadth of Soho in between spots didn't make it any easier. Plenty of pill-popping went on, how could you expect to keep going otherwise?

Kitten showed Greta and me to a third club; the Oriental, another little fleapit at the top end of Frith Street. This was the place where I was so preoccupied with when the tape was going to finish, I completely forgot to remove my bra. I come off-stage wondering why all the punters were looking at me strangely.

'Are you mental or what, *allah*?' the fat Maltese choreographer spat in my face 'They want to see your tits; you have tit-men out there, you know.' I was mortified.

The Oriental girls played a rotten trick on Greta. They got the stage manager to play a tape of the *Pink Panther* theme music then went and stood at the back of the audience, laughing at poor Greta, who was slinking about the stage with a helpless look on her face. I felt sorry for her, but she did look comical.

'It's because she's so long and lanky,' one of the girls explained to me, 'just like the cartoon character. Whereas you're a little squit.'

'Thank you.'

But though the girls liked to take the piss out of you, there was no malice intended. They reminded me of my first week at grammar school, when all the marauding second years came up to us first years and flicked our ties and ragged us. Actually, the Soho girls weren't as bad as those schoolgirls; they didn't try to shove your head down the toilet, which is what happened to some unfortunates at my school.

I hardly seemed to notice my first few weeks as a stripper. I was in a complete spin, trying to remember where I was on next and at what time, then having to negotiate all those labyrinthine streets and alleyways. It's funny; during my first short spell in Soho, in 1969, I believed I'd got to know the streets and their people well, but now, seeing the place through the eyes of a stripper, it was almost as if I were new to it all again. It seemed different somehow. My life was no longer centred around the streets, I think that's what it was. They were no longer my world; my habitat was now the Soho strip-club scene: 'The Circuit'. That meant a certain loss of the freedom and wildness I'd come to enjoy when I was knocking about the streets, but I didn't miss it. I didn't have time to. My head was a whirl of coloured lights and loud music, and all the shadowy faceless men *out there*, away from me (but not far enough). And in between times there were the dressing-rooms; cluttered-up caves that smelt of clashing perfumes, takeaway meals, make-up, and female bodies. At night the dressing-room could be the craziest place. Sometimes it felt like you were at a witches' sabbat that was going on in Aladdin's cave.

But I was still frightened every time I went on-stage alone. In those few seconds before the stage manager opened the tabs on me, it was agony. I stood in the dark, listening to the low mumble of the audience out front and wishing myself nine minutes into the future, when I would be back in the safety of the dressing-room. I was as tense as a soldier, waiting for action. The punters scared me, but I never let them see I was afraid. If they knew that, they could eat you up alive; they'd be the ones in control of the situation. You could guarantee there'd be one smartarsed clown out there who'd try and make your torment worse if he thought you were at all nervous. You had to brazen it out, and not show them that you were in any way vulnerable. *That*'s where your hardness came in; that's why people say 'hard-as-nails' about strippers. They don't realize that it's just a shell, a coat of varnish, over the real, feeling you. You can't get up on a stage and just be naked, all soft skin and unprotected; you need *some* psychological defence against those buggers out there. Of course, it would be different if the audience were naked, too – then you'd all be equal. But since you're not, you have to devise your own method of dealing with the situation. Mine was to send up the numbers I was doing. If I could get the audience laughing along with me – and I could – that was fine; it humanized the whole business, and took it out of the realms of pure objectification of my body. Because, it must be said, I hated *that*; we all did. Nobody likes to be reduced to a thing, and strippers are no exception.

It was difficult for me at first, though. It was hard enough keeping myself from shaking like a jelly. Sometimes my bloody mouth used to tremble, never mind the rest of me.

'Just pretend they aren't there,' Big Linda told me. 'I always look over their stupid heads, at the lights. And all the time I'm thinking, what colour shall I do the bedroom? What shall we eat this Sunday? . . . I smile, do it, and ignore the pigs.'

Big Linda was something else, the last sort of person I would've imagined in this job. Because she was – well, a *housewife*; her talk was all Rotary washing-machines and Allied carpets. And she did her knitting in the dressing-room! At first I was really shocked, but then I got used to finding her in there, waiting to go on for her next spot, her needles going click click click all the while. What made it funnier was the fact that as she was so big, and well-built, most of the choreographers gave her a whip number, so she'd be sitting there in all the black leather gear, with her cat o'nine tails propped up against the dressing-table, right next to her bag of wool. Weird. Big Linda was married to a Maltese minicab driver; they were plotting and scheming for the day when they would pack up and go, leave the West End and Britain for good, and move out to Malta where they'd buy a bar, settle down, procreate . . .

A few of the girls thought like that.

'House prices are falling, in Valetta,' they said to each other. 'In another two years, we'll have so-much' . . . To tell you the truth, they got on my tits with their dreams of domestic bliss. I couldn't get over how *normal* they were. Where was all the glamour? I truly believed I'd left all that boring shit behind me, in Lancashire, in the works canteens. I was slow to realize that so-called 'glamour' does not exist, it's merely an illusion. Behind the façade – the make-up, the glittery costumes, the coloured lights – we were all women and girls together; not a wild, exotic species apart. There we were, a bunch of females; we came in a variety of sizes, shapes and colours and, once you got down to it, you saw that we were all in the business for the same reason: to make a living. Thrown together in our workplace in exactly the same way as we would be in any other; it just so happened that this was the glamour-puss factory. But still a factory.

Another thing that took me by surprise was the degree of solidarity among the girls – well, most of them, anyway. There were one or two head-cases. But I'd prepared myself for a lot of bitchiness, girls clawing each other in the competition for jobs, that sort of thing. Nothing was further from the truth – there was always help, co-operation and support from those women. To this day I'm convinced that being naked in the dressing-room together had a lot to do with it. When you're yourself, without clothes and without the defences you use on-stage, you're bound to be more honest and straightforward with each other. You can't get away from the fact that fundamentally, you're all the same – human, and vulnerable – and that I believe cuts through any bullshit. Sometimes we girls talked among ourselves, and we all agreed that if the world's governments were forced to sit and debate and argue policies in the nude, then maybe the world would be a better place. It certainly couldn't help but improve matters, that's for sure.

A lot of the girls were Northerners who, like me, had hitched down to London with lots of high hopes, big dreams and fuck-all else. One or two had escaped from children's homes and crazy fathers who beat or raped them. These were the ones the media and all the 'experts' call 'sick victims'. They were nothing of the sort – they were kids who had the guts to do something about their bad 'home' situation: they ran away, and found sanctuary in the sex industry. That may sound absurd, but it isn't. Those young runaways, some as young as fourteen, fifteen, were independent; they had control over their lives, whereas back where they came from they had none.

Some of the girls were would-be 'straight' actresses, dancers, singers. Kitten was one of these; she wanted to be a star. She should've made it, with her looks and talent, but she didn't; she got lost in the ghetto.

The pair of us hit it off from the start. Greta stayed around the clubs for less than a month, then she went back up North to have her baby. She got married and disappeared into the ranks of Lancashire working-class women.

But Kitten and I became very close. We were given lots of double-acts round the clubs because the wankers liked us together, we contrasted well: her dark, me blonde. Kitten was a bit of a comedian, too; she was brilliant at impersonating somebody being sick. One of her favourite tricks was to start licking and sucking her fingers *erotically*, really turning the punters on, then she'd start heaving as if she were about to vomit. She was a good little mimic, as well; sometimes she would do a whole number pulling her face to look like old Steptoe. That used to really crease me up. We did all sorts of routines: 'Couple of Swells'; football numbers (they confiscated our footballs and gave us balloons because we kept bouncing the balls off the punters' bald heads, and they didn't like that); schoolgirl numbers (they confiscated the hockey-sticks because we 'bullied off' on the punters' laps, and they didn't like that either; it made the poor dears nervous); Red Indian numbers; Charlestons – you name it. We got plenty of laughs.

After we'd got to know and trust each other, we told each other our real names. It was like an exchange of vows; a sign of true friendship, each letting the other one know the name of the person inside the stripper. We spent hours after work down Ronnie Scott's, listening to the jazz, then talking downstairs, and smoking a couple of joints in the bog. Kitten told me all she could remember of her very early childhood, before her family left Poland. It wasn't much.

'There was a hot summer day and we were out in the countryside near Warsaw with my grandmother. We were picking mushrooms and laughing. I must've been about three. That's all I can remember.'

Kitten's Dad died soon after that, and she and her sister came with their mother to England. Kitten left home when she was fifteen, hitched to London and got stripping right away. She'd been at it four years when I started. At one point, when I'd been stripping a couple of years, Kitten moved into my flat above one of the clubs in Old Compton Street. It had been a particularly lousy time for both of us: I'd just split up with my boyfriend, who went off with somebody else, and Kitten had finished with her old man, the beast she eventually married. We spent about three months living together, and had a fine old time. The boss called us a pair of dykes, but so what? Lots of girls round the clubs had relationships with women from time to time; there was nothing wrong with that. Sometimes a girl got tired of men's shit, and it was as another stripper once said to me: 'With a woman you can get the tenderness a man can't or won't give'.

It was like that between Kitten and me; we weren't exactly lesbians, in that ours wasn't a sexual relationship, but we were close and trusting; we could relax with one another and enjoy ourselves. There was no tension between us. But her old man was a pain in the arse. He kept showing up in the dead of night; he would stand right smack in the middle of Old Compton Street bellowing for Kitten. He rang her at work and sobbed her name down the phone. Then came the acres of bloody flowers, the solid gold bracelet; the whole caboodle. It was a war of attrition, all right. He wanted to 'start afresh'; he was 'a changed man'; it would be 'different' . . . All this from a bastard who'd twice put her in hospital.

She went back to him in the end. Sometimes women are gluttons for punishment, only we call it 'love'. But that's the same story everywhere, not just in Soho. Women just take so much crap from their men. I saw it outside the sex business as well as inside, and I still see it today, in the straight world. If anything it's worse than in Soho, because a woman in Soho is at least financially better off than most outside women – she can literally afford to get away from a violent guy if she wants to. (I'm talking about the ones independent of ponces.) Let's face it, if you're making shitty wages, or if you're a housewife who depends on the old man, it's not easy to leave an abusive situation. Whereas if you're earning a hundred or two a week, it's less of a problem.

It was the girls with pimps I really felt sorry for – they hadn't a chance. Most of the pimps were Maltese – which isn't the same as saying that *all* Maltese were pimps (the women certainly weren't), nor that you didn't get English blokes poncing. What I'm saying is that at that particular historical moment in Soho – the late 60s to mid-70s – Soho was more or less organized by the Maltese 'Mafia', along with their English pals from Vine Street and West End Central copshops. So that made it difficult, damnnear impossible, for a girl who was with a West End Malt to leave him and still hang on to her clubs. Really, she had no choice whatsoever, if she wanted to stay in work. I'm thinking now about one girl in particular: a Scottish girl called Pat, who was a fine person, intelligent, humorous, caring. Her problem was her sleazeball husband, who ponced all her money and gave her plenty of good hidings to 'show her who's boss'. Pat tried to leave him, but she couldn't; he was in with all the Maltese club bosses. She went back to him again and again. One time he beat her so badly that there was not one inch of her body that wasn't bruised. I'll never forget it, because I was one of the girls who tried to cover up the bruises with Leichner body-paint before she went on-stage. It took ages, as we were being as gentle as we possibly could; Pat was in such pain.

'*Give her dim lights*,' we told the stage manager. That's what we always said when a beaten girl went on-stage. *Dim lights*, to hide the marks. Those words used to choke me; I felt so much rage and sadness.

Pat came into work one day with her eyes shining and happy, full of hope.

'He's taking me on holiday, to Malta,' she told the rest of us. 'It'll be different when we're out there. I'll send you a card, Nick,' she told me. She didn't, though. Two months later they were back, and Pat was a wreck. He'd had her committed to a mental hospital out there, and they'd burned bits of her brain out; ECT, they call it. She wasn't Pat any more. She was like a zombie, and she didn't remember half of the girls; we had to introduce ourselves to her.

Poor Pat. She worked again, but not for long. She just wasn't together enough to do the clubs. One night another stripper dashed into the Carousel dressing-room and told us that Pat was round the corner in Greek Street, in a right state. I went out to see for myself, and there she was, taking her clothes off and screaming at people in the middle of the street, like a madwoman. They were all laughing at her. I tried to get her out of the road, and she went for me with her stiletto-heeled shoe. Then somebody rang the police, and they rolled up in half a dozen squad cars and nicked Pat for disorderly conduct. She finished up in Tooting Bec Mental Hospital. When she came out, a few months later, she left the West End altogether, and none of us ever saw or heard from her again. Her old man was later deported, along with a load of other Maltese West Enders.

It's all a kind of haze in my mind as to when different incidents actually happened. Soho has that effect on you; it's like I said earlier: time acts strangely. I know that I slipped into the strip-club routine incredibly quickly. I worked at the three dives – Paradise, Playboy, and Oriental – for just a few months before 'graduating' to places like the Bijou, the Carousel, the Sunset, the Doll's House. The Bijou was one of the 'better' places, with a bar and a catwalk (yes, I fell off it one night; we all did at some time or other), and sophisticated lighting. I'll never

forget the introduction to my tape; it was puerile. It went
like this, in a man's slimy voice: 'Cindy Delmar could be
a *very good girl* if she really tried . . . but first, she'll have
to change her *evil ways*! . . .' then the music started; the
Santana track of that name. It was also at the Bijou that I
worked with my first male partner – a big brawny bugger
who looked a lot like Burt Reynolds. Because I was so
tiny, I was a 'natch' for being thrown around the stage
and turned inside out by this hulk. He had a sense of
humour, but sometimes he would go too far, and start
tying me up in knots the way Tom does to Jerry. Years
later, this guy was to become a Soho VIP; he made a
packet and now lives in Miami, Florida. But in *those*
days, he was my prop!

I liked working at the Bijou; it had a great atmosphere,
and the dressing-room wasn't a subterranean cave like
most of the other places. We were at the top of the
building, overlooking Old Compton Street and Charing
Cross Road.

It was whilst I was at the Bijou that I saw one of the
rare fights between strippers. There wasn't that much
aggravation among us. It *did* happen, of course, but
far less frequently than you would imagine, given the
conditions of our lives; the tensions and pressures of
working in that business. Because in spite of the freedom,
Soho could be a terrible place for a woman, the worst
kind of hell. And sometimes, all the laughter and camaraderie in the world wasn't enough; you went under, you
couldn't help it. The tension and bitterness you thought
was buried so deep would surface anyway. It might leak
out in the dressing-room, disguised as an argument with
the stage manager, poor beleaguered sod, about the
lights: 'too bright!' or the music: 'too low!' But sometimes
it resulted in a ruck with another girl, whether or not
there was a reason. It could be a wrong word, a 'funny'

look – or nothing at all. Once that pressure builds up inside you, you're like a powder-keg and you just have to go off. A fight was a good way of letting go the tensions – or so it seemed at the time. Usually *everybody* would get involved, but it would be over fast, and we'd all be pals again. The fight I remember at the Bijou was quite funny really. Preposterous.

It happened round about the time a lot of clubs were getting shut down, mid-1973. Everybody was whispering about which club would be going next; it was frightening. There were rumours that the Bijou was about to get the chop, and that scared the girls who worked exclusive to that club: the 'residents'. They didn't run round the other clubs like the rest of us. They earned less, but considered themselves better off as they didn't have all the schlepping to do. One of these residents was an Italian girl, Lucia, who had the makings of a maniac. She would fly off into a temper if something annoyed her. Once she threw a plate of chilli-con-carne right across the dressing-room because it wasn't 'piquant' enough. Then one day one of the runaround strippers, Jacquie 'Ding-Dong' Belle, introduced a new act into the club: a vampire number. You know the sort of thing – ghoulish green and blue lights; spooky music; dry ice, and then Jacquie herself, emerging from her coffin, centre-stage. I must say she looked the part, in her ankle-length white nightdress with her black hair hanging down and her lips painted crimson. Kitten and I thought she looked great; she even frightened the wankers. But Lucia hated the whole idea of there being a coffin on the premises; even a mock-up light-weight object like Jacquie's.

'It's no good,' said Lucia. 'It's *evil* . . .'

And she crossed herself every time the stage manager dragged the damned thing out of the props room. Jacquie ignored her at first, until one day she came in and Lucia started sticking brown paper all over her dressing-table mirror, so that she didn't have to see the coffin's reflection.

'Are you trying to wind me up, or what?' Jacquie fumed. 'You'll be wanting to run a stake through my heart next.'

'Maybe!' Lucia agreed.

The rest of us were on pins, but nothing happened that day. We knew it would, sooner or later, though. Kitten said 'There's gonna be trouble' and she was right. The following Saturday morning we arrived at the club only to find a notice in the dressing-room: the Bijou was closing down that night. We had twelve hours' notice.

That was bad enough for us circuit girls – nobody liked to lose a wage-packet – but for the residents, it was a disaster. They were going spare. We all went across the road to the 'Spice of Life' in Cambridge Circus. The residents sat in a huddle with the stage manager and sobbed into their drinks. Then Lucia let out a howl.

'It's that coffin; I said it from the start, *porca miseria*, it's the bastard coffin that's brought the bad luck.'

Nobody could convince her that it was the council who were responsible, not Dracula. But then nobody tried very hard. Tension was high; the girls needed a scapegoat. Jacquie 'Ding-Dong' Belle, or rather, her coffin, would do nicely. We all trooped back over the road, Lucia marching up front swearing her head off. Jacquie hadn't showed up yet, but that didn't deter Lucia. She made straight for the props room, dragged the coffin out – the stage manager didn't dare stop her – and kicked it all the way down the stairs, through reception and out into the street. The crowds queuing outside the Palace Theatre to see *Jesus Christ Superstar* were delighted, but Jacquie took a very dim view when she turned up for the first spot and found her precious prop all broken up and being rained on in the gutter. She ran straight up to the dressing-room, grabbed somebody's wig-stand and hit Lucia over the head with it, and then all hell was let loose. Chairs, tables, make-up, costumes – everything went flying, including the stage manager when he tried to intervene. Me and Kitten ran and hid on the stairs, and laughed at the commotion; it was nerves made us laugh, though, not vindictiveness.

The place was a tip by the time they'd all calmed down (it was a tip anyway) but as usual, I marvelled at the fact that nobody had got badly hurt. There were the scratches and bruises, and a big chunk of somebody's hair wafting about on the floor, but it wasn't like when the men fought – knives and all the other heavy stuff. And it ended the same way all the other rucks did, with tears, cigarettes, drinks, shrugs . . . Nowadays when I remember the fights among us girls, I'm reminded of something I read not long ago about battery hens – how, in their intolerable conditions, they tend to peck and tear at each other; sometimes at themselves. There were times when it was just like that round the strip-clubs; it's true; what amazes me is that they were so few and far between.

Mostly, the dressing-room was a kind of sanctuary, a haven, for us lot. It had a very special atmosphere, a warmth and openness I've not experienced since. When you're stuck in there together, in and out for twelve hours a day, you grow close, and you develop trust and friendship amongst yourselves. You could talk about anything and everything in the dressing-room, and we did – sex, life, death, people's homes . . . There was a lot of hilarity, and some sadness, some serious moments, too. You could say what you really felt. Nobody froze you or guilt-tripped you the way they did in the straight world. Girls just talked and listened, laughed or sympathized. Sometimes one of us might disagree with another, but that was okay, too; nobody was going to force you to change your view, or even make you feel bad about it. It was honest.

I'm not saying that a Soho strip-club dressing-room is an idyllic place for a woman to be, but there's no denying that I enjoyed myself in there; we all did. Sometimes now when I look back on those times I feel a sharp longing to be back there again with my pals. It isn't simply nostalgia; I truly miss the relaxed atmosphere and the frankness, and most of all, the humour. It's just not the same in the outside world; people police themselves all the time; it amazes me. I find people fraught with tension *all the time*, they live their lives like that, really stiff and repressed. It's a very British thing: 'stiff upper lip', and all that crap. In fact, it's their whole bodies that are tense and rigid. The first time I realized there was a different way to be was after my first spell in the West End, when I travelled to North Africa. I watched the way the Arab women moved, it was lovely: fluid, languorous and strong. The way they walked and, especially, the way they danced; they were so *there*, happy in their bodies, not like us lot. A South Tunisian dancer called Ahlem taught me to dance, how to really move and feel at home in my body. I found it an incredible experience, that dancing. So sensuous and proud, and powerful. And I liked the way the Arab men did it too; they didn't just sit back and watch women dance, they would leap to their feet and shimmy away to their hearts' content. It was wonderful.

Then when I came back to England I was struck by the way people moved here. All stiff and jerky, like a bunch of sticks. It was only round the clubs that I found that same relaxed, flowing harmony with the body. I saw it in the women I worked with – the really good strippers, I mean. I saw it in the way we moved and sat around the dressing-room, at ease with each other and ourselves. Sometimes, I saw it on-stage; often, in fact. Because you *could* get up there and take pride in your performance; the skill and rhythm – not the objectification – of your body and its movements. Then you could feel something happening, almost the way it did in those Arab places. But what was sad about it was the way in which here in the West, it was all reduced to this: to a Soho strip-club, a kind of desperate frenzy, where men paid to watch women take their clothes off. There was nothing reciprocal; no shared delight in the experience of being *at ease* with the body. That's Western repression for you. If you ask me, I think it's a big part of the problem.

I got a reputation for being good and reliable; just as well, since the Clean-Up Soho Campaign had taken off with a vengeance, and the clubs were losing their licences, closing down, right left and centre. Competition for jobs became cut-throat, there was a real panic on. You couldn't take a day off work for being sick or anything; you just didn't have any clubs to come back to. Nothing personal; that's politics, kid! (Politics are fine so long as they *include* you.) Thanks to the GLC Cutler & Co., and Westminster Council, the number of prostitutes working the West End streets more than doubled practically overnight. As far as I'm concerned it's those mealy-mouthed politicians and fat councillors who should get done for pimping and 'procuring for the purpose of prostitution'. After all, weren't they the ones directly responsible for pushing my friends and colleagues into 'the life' in the first place?

I was slowly beginning to understand how society operates. There was no justice. That was my first lesson, and it came across loud and clear. But what to do about it? Don't ask me, I thought; just let me get on with this mess of a life, and then we'll see. Something would happen. In any case, what were my alternatives? I'd already tried them, and they were worse. Go back to Burnley, find a 'nice bloke', get a straight job, have kids, settle into the drudge's life without a word of complaint? That's what we were supposed to do, working-class women. And if you were unhappy, no problem! There was always the kind doctor with his magic pills to blank out the misery, anger and frustration.

I had a letter from my mother around that time. She told me that all my aunties, and most of the female cousins of my age group, were on tranx and moggies, bloody sleeping pills (non-addictive, of course, unless you tried to get off them). Call that a life? I thought. They must be desperate. No, I was better off as a stripper, even if I did hate the punters, the bosses, the flash cops. I was earning good money; I had my friends, my independence. But at the same time I knew something bad was happening to me; I was growing bitter and resentful, and I hurt inside. I didn't really understand why. It wasn't just the work, the hours, the shit you had to put up with at times. It was more than that – there was a sort of emptiness in my life. I had a boyfriend, Rob, who worked as stage manager at one of my clubs, and he was intelligent and in many ways sensitive, but he didn't make up for the *something* that was lacking in me. I hadn't a clue what it was, except that it was a lack; something missing. I felt like I was groping towards . . . what?

I knew that being in Soho, living the life I led, had changed me beyond recall; there was no going back now. My Lancashire past was left behind. Something happened to you when you came to the sex industry; it opened your eyes but at the same time it somehow denied you your existence, at least as far as the straight world was concerned. You became 'tainted'; not even working-class any more; a moral untouchable. You were not a person;

society regarded you as a *stripper*, or a *prostitute*, and that was it: nothing more. I realized I had become one of the women I'd been taught to abhor: a Bad Girl. It didn't make any sense to me; just as the attitude of the lads back home hadn't made sense, when they went on about girls who were 'scrubbers' and girls who were 'useless'. What was 'Good'? What was 'Bad'? Why were we, the strippers and prostitutes, tarnished and regarded as trash, whilst our clients, the punters – men – remained untainted? Because it was obvious to me that the majority of those punters who roamed the streets and frequented the clubs of Soho were outwardly 'respectable' men. Not, as I'd been led to believe, pathetic 'sick' creatures in scruffy wankers' macs. Oh no. That was one myth working round the clubs quickly dispelled for me. True, there were the odd dirty-raincoat-brigade types, but most of the men were Mr Norman Normals. It occurred to me that the whole ethos of what was good/bad, right/wrong, was perverse and hypocritical. It was based on myths and lies and, above all, on the enforced silencing of 'baddies' like me.

I decided I was ignorant; what I needed was education. Night school was out, so my only alternative was to try and learn as much as possible off my own bat. Books! I thought; books are the answer. I started spending all my daytime breaks in Foyles, buying anything and everything, whatever took my fancy. Talk about eclectic! I thought: choosing books is much more fun than choosing make-up. I took to reading in between spots in a corner of the Carousel dressing-room, which was comfortable and relatively spacious. This earned me the nickname of 'The Professor', for a time, until the other girls got used to the sight of me curled up beneath the costume-rail with my nose buried in a book. I even took them on-stage with me in my schoolgirl acts. One time I was so absorbed in what I was reading, I almost forgot to strip!

The other girls smiled at me indulgently; they thought I was a bit daft, but so what? – if it kept me happy.

'Education's like sex,' Cherry Tart warned me. 'You can have too much of it, you know . . .'

Dear funny faithful Kitten declared that she was 'too thick' to read 'proper books' *yet*, but one break she flew to Foyles and bought a 'really good dictionary', so that she could increase her vocabulary. Before too long the pair of us were spending most of our breaks reading in 'our' corner. Bernie the doorman, another Maltese, used to take the piss out of us in his laconic way, whenever he found us like that:

'It's the *ha'allah*, university in here, innit?'

Kitten wasn't exactly systematic in her approach to learning new words. What happened was, she would flick the pages of her dictionary, and then pick a word at random; the longer, the better. She would choose her word on the Monday morning, then drive everybody mad by using it incessantly throughout the remainder of that week. I remember one week the chosen word was 'inconsequential', and that was it; for the next five days you couldn't get anything sensible out of her.

'As far as I'm concerned, it's perfectly *inconsequential*,' she would say in response to just about anything. The baffled faces of men in the bar who'd maybe asked her if she wanted a drink were a treat to behold. But by the end of the week I was about ready to hit her over the head with the dictionary. The following week she moved on to 'indifferent':

'It's a matter of total indifference to me . . .' etc.

One day I discovered the Patisserie Valerie, in Old Compton Street. It was on my route to the Sunset Strip, a club in Dean Street that I did after the Carousel. I had a thirty-minute break in between these two clubs, so I started spending my mid-afternoons in the patisserie. I would sit there drinking coffee and reading my latest treasure. I read Hardy in there, and Kurt Vonnegut Jnr, and wonderful Tolstoy.I also got on to Colette; all those tales of her childhood. They made me long for the countryside.

I loved the atmosphere in that tasteful little teashop; it was such a contrast to the club scene. It was another world, where posh types, men and women, sat and read their *Guardians* and *Telegraphs*, and discussed with each other their lovely homes or their holidays, or their pampered brats. Sometimes, they spoke about their *work*. I always thought of their *work* like that, in italics, because to me it was different; a career. I think I was unconsciously trying to absorb some of their lives in the same way I was soaking up the patisserie atmosphere, hoping some of it would rub off on me. I was certainly envious of their world. I saw it as a world of light, and plants, and French windows and gardens – all that Laura Ashley stuff. I daydreamed of what it must feel like to be one of those privileged creatures; to wake up every morning in beautiful surroundings; to talk posh and have people listen, and to have the space in which to develop, be a real person . . .

I must have looked kind of pathetic, I think; sitting there in all my bloody stage make-up: my armour. I stood out like a frigging sore thumb. In a diary I kept around that time (I was 'going to be a writer') I wrote:

'To be calm and self-assured, a *nice person*: that's what I want for myself. Not a shrieking mess, like I am now.'

One afternoon I watched a couple, middle-aged, well-dressed; *that type*, as I now referred to them in my head. They looked as though everything in their life was just as perfect as pie; they smiled and chatted, mostly about their kids. After a bit the wife got up and left; her old man stayed behind. Two minutes later, he tipped me the wink. At first I wasn't sure; maybe he'd just blinked. Then came that look: the look I knew so well, the one that spells p-u-n-t-e-r. The eyes glaze and harden; the entire face changes and becomes haggard and greedy. That fucking obsessed look. That man never came closer to getting a coffee shampoo.

You wanker, I thought. I was livid. It sickened me; it was like watching the transformation from Dr Jekyll into Mr Hyde, only this bastard didn't need any potion to trigger him off, just the presence of a *Soho woman*.

After that I stopped going into the Patisserie Valerie. I dismissed the episode from my mind, but I knew underneath that I was disillusioned with those nice, posh people. They might inhabit a lovelier world most of the time, but they could creep into *my* world whenever they felt like it. Privileged they might be, but they were no less crazy than the rest of us, and these were punters to boot.

'Punters drive me round the bend,' I told my pals at the Sunset. 'Maybe I'll write a book about the bastards one day; if I do, I'll call it "One Flew Over Dean Street".'

Punters!

Like all the other girls, I despised the men who used our clubs. We despised them; they exasperated us – but one thing we never did was *judge* them, the way straight people were forever judging us (and finding us guilty). We strippers took it for granted that men were 'like that' to some degree or other. Since we couldn't change their attitudes, we may as well make a living out of them. And a good living, too. Even back then, before I knew what the word 'feminist' meant, I was aware that there weren't too many jobs around where women earned *more* than men.

'Men are *thick*, Nick,' a prostitute friend told me.

'Once they get pussy in here' – and she tapped the side of her head – 'the rest just flies out of the window.'

I could hardly disagree with her; not after working round the clubs. Punters were stupid, period. They might be bloody geniuses back in the straight world, but in our little ghetto they all shared the same basic mentality, or lack of it. In that sense I suppose you could say that being a punter is a great equalizer, for a man. No matter what your background, whether you're a Duke, an MP or a navvy; you're all the same to us girls, once you're in that audience. All punters; there for one reason only – to watch us take our clothes off. Now when you think about that, it's rather weird.

Some of the guys were 'regulars': a species of mankind that is almost completely obsessed with 'sex'. A sad and sorry lot, really. Not that we felt particularly sad or sorry for them; why should we? They were the ones you saw queuing outside a club as early as ten in the morning; two hours before the first show started. The sight of them sometimes made my stomach heave.

The 'crack o' dawn wankers', we used to call these. They were mostly old crocks who hadn't a cat-in-hell's chance of seeing young female flesh in any other circumstances. There was something that was horrible and seeping about them. Some of them looked older than God; decrepit. It seemed all they had left was their obsession with *cunt*. It was as if their tattered spirits clung to life through their obsession. But what sort of life? Apart from that, they were empty husks. Some of them stank to high heaven; the girls used to crack jokes about it – 'The one in "A" seat's decomposing' – but it was pretty disgusting. And they'd sit for hours on end, staring, staring at your crotch; never raising their eyes, as if the rest of you didn't exist. Mind you, there were plenty of young and middle-aged guys who were like that as well;

we girls called them 'twat gazers'. From the moment you went on-stage and the tabs opened, that was it: it was eyes-down, look-in. And that was *before* you took the clothes off. You could perform an entire ballet; turn cartwheels; do the splits – *anything* – and those creatures would not bat an eyelid. They wanted to see *it*.

Sometimes it happened that you had a whole crowd in like that, and then it was terrible. Even before the tabs opened, you could sense the atmosphere, so clammy and funereal. It made you feel cold and dank and sticky. It was the ugliest, most depressing scene. Those types never clapped, or responded to jokes; they didn't want to have fun. You might get a damp and feeble handclap at the end of your number, but that was all.

'Clap, you bastards!' I used to roar. They infuriated me. 'Get your hands out of your pockets!'

But no; they still sat and stared, even if you were wearing fifty layers of costume, they stared at *it*. Maybe they had X-ray eyes.

Those punters really got on your nerves. One time I remember a pal of mine, Annie Arsehole, went on-stage with a brown paper bag over her head, with just the two holes punched out for her eyes.

'Those tossers never look at your face,' she said later, when we were laughing in the dressing-room. 'They didn't even notice.' And I don't believe they did.

Sometimes we went on 'Pussy Strike', by way of retaliation, which meant we didn't remove our G-strings until the tabs were practically shut. That used to wind the wankers up no end! By this time – the mid 70s – you were supposed to work the whole of the last record completely naked; you did all your floor or bed work like that. Gone were the old days, the days when you removed your G on the flash-chord and not before. Now, the strip-club was more like a gynaecology ward (as a matter of fact we did have a regular punter who was actually a Harley Street gynaecologist – we called him 'the Bum Doctor', because he tried to shine a pencil torch at your arse, then he'd chuck a pound at you). Punters expected to see your tonsils from down under, and some of the pests would complain to the boss if girls didn't 'flash' it. That didn't exactly endear them to us, either.

'So-and-so isn't *working*,' they would moan, and the girl would get a bollocking, or even sacked, if there were too many complaints. So when we hit them with our Pussy Strikes, we had to watch out for the moaners, and we didn't push it. And the girls with ponces broke the strikes anyway; you couldn't win.

Basically we regarded the regulars as a bloody nuisance; most of them, at any rate, because they liked to complain; it made them feel important. It was incredible. Because they bought a ticket once or twice a week, the wallies thought they owned shares in the building, the business, the girls. They moaned about the lights: 'Not bright enough; I can't see anything.' Never mind that they were blinding us on-stage.

'Maybe if they didn't wank so much, they'd be able to see better', we told the boss. One of my own little pleasures was to tilt the huge mirror at the back of the stage so that it reflected all the hot harsh lights back into the punters' eyes. You should have seen them wince, and try to shield themselves.

'How do you lot like it, then?' I'd shout, if I were in a bad mood. Being dazzled didn't make you feel on top of the world.

Then you got the ones who complained about us girls. They were never satisfied.

'Not enough big knockers in this show,' one pillock wrote to the boss. Another bloke said he wanted to see 'hairier privates'. Melissa, one of the more tempestuous strippers, hit the roof about that. She had this little Yorkshire terrier named Albèrt.

'Just you wait,' she fumed. 'Next time that punter's in, I'll go on with Albèrt strapped to my fanny.'

We laughed our heads off, but that Melissa was quite capable of it. It was the doorman who took most of the flak from our customers. The one at the Carousel, Bernie, was an okay sort; he really took the piss out of some of the creeps.

'What do you want; Wimpy and chips?' he would say scathingly if a guy said it cost too much to get in. One time this fellow says to him 'I wish the girls wouldn't shave their armpits', and Bernie strung him along for a good ten minutes, getting out a notebook and pen, and pretending to listen seriously to the punter's suggestions.

'Oh yes, sir, and was there anything else?' Bernie let the bloke ramble on before finally telling him to fuck off. He was like that; he would take so much then let fly – like the rest of us.

One Christmas at the Carousel this regular pain-in-the-arse Arthur came trudging upstairs into reception. He was one of those people who carry their own personal dreary aura with them everywhere they go: a sort of psychic Scrooge. I was sitting next to the desk, watching Bernie's portable TV, but I could see Arthur out of the corner of my eye, standing there, looking round for something to moan about. Bernie was being his usual ignorant self; he detested the punters more than us lot, if anything. Still old Arthur stood and looked around, like some stupid blinking owl. Suddenly his face lit up and he pointed to the display window, which was dripping with Christmas decorations. He looked triumphant.

'There's a letter "R" missing in "MERRY",' he crowed.

Bernie was in a foulish mood, having lost on the gee-gees. He turned to Arthur and gave him a look that was like a hail of bullets.

'What, *ha'il'ostia*, do you want me to do, *fush'umbook*? You want me to stand there and make the shape out of myself? I'm to be the letter "R" in the window? On your way, *allah* . . . out out out out!!'

That made my night, because that old Arthur was forever complaining about me. He told the boss I gave him dirty looks, which was true enough. He even complained that Kitten farted in his face once. She probably did, but that was his own fault, wasn't it, for leaning too close? Those punters were something else!

A few of the old regulars weren't so bad, though. The lonely old-age pensioners who saw us as their only friends; it was sad. They were okay. We didn't hate them at all. They treated us like human beings, when all's said and done. When people do that, there's no call for disliking them.

We had one old boy, 'Poppa', we called him, who was practically the strippers' mascot. He got a discount on the desk. He was such a skinny little thing, we were afraid a puff of wind might blow him away.

'Wrap up warm and put your scarf on before you go out there,' we'd yell from the stage when he was getting up to leave. 'Button your coat up.' We were like a bunch of mother hens. Pop celebrated his eightieth birthday at the Carousel, and we bought him a fantastic cake from the best gâteau-shop in the West End; I'd never seen anything like it. We got the SM to stop the tape for a minute whilst we scrambled on-stage with the cake all lit with tiny candles, and sang 'Happy Birthday dear Poppa'. That was the only time I ever saw any of us blush; I couldn't get over how shy we all were. Maybe it's because we had our clothes on.

Saturday round the clubs was 'Crazy-Day'. We got paid; we knew that Sunday was the official day of rest, so we let our hair down a bit more than usual and had wild fun in the dressing-rooms. It was also 'Saturday Club' day for the weekly regulars. Just like the kids' matinée back home in Burnley. Even now, I have only to close my eyes and I can see the entire front row of the Carousel before me. It never changed one week whilst I was there, not until old Mr Woods dropped dead, that is.

He sat plonk in the middle of the front row, looking exactly like a bedraggled old walrus. He stayed from noon until six P.M. every week, and during every second round he sat and ate his blasted lunch, still watching the show. Sandwiches, tea and a big fat doughnut. He used to knock you sick, chomping away with sugar and plum jam smeared all over his face. Even when the IRA started blowing up bits of the West End, and all the punters were asked to leave their bags at home, that old Woodsie kept on coming in with his bloody doughnuts. We had quite a few bomb scares round the clubs, so we used to joke to hide our fears: 'There's old Seamus O'Woods and his incendiary doughnuts' we would shriek from the stage.

Next to Woodsie sat a bald thing called Ken, but the girls nicknamed him 'Alan Whicker', because he had the annoying habit of giving a running commentary on the show. You could hear him when you were waiting for the tabs to open, in the seconds before your number. One Saturday I stubbed my toe on the bed whilst I was waiting for the show to start; I swore at the top of my voice.

'Nickie's on next,' I heard Ken announce. I had to laugh. Sometimes he rolled oranges and sweets under the tabs after your spot. He must have thought we were monkeys.

By Ken was a punter called 'Hoppy'. He was a sturdy little fellow with a lozenge-shaped body, one leg and one waggly tooth. Hoppy's days of punterdom stretched way back to during the Second World War; he remembered the Windmill Girls. He was a cheeky bugger, but you could at least have a laugh with him. Hoppy died a few years ago, in the front row of the Doll's House. Nobody noticed for ages; they were used to him sitting there all day, everyone thought he'd dropped off. Two girls who were doing a football number bounced balls off his head and all-sorts, because it's the height of bad manners for punters to sleep during your act. But it wasn't until the SM went round to try and wake Hoppy up that they realized the poor old sod had snuffed it. We were all pretty shocked, but we consoled ourselves with the fact that he'd died happy:

'He died as he lived; wanking', was Hoppy's epitaph, as far as we were concerned.

Another Saturday regular was this well-dressed fellow who was a dead ringer for Spencer Tracy. He made me feel weird, sitting there in the front row, looking exactly like the Hollywood star. Every time I went on-stage when he was in I would tease him: 'Hiya, Spence; how's Katharine?' and he would sit and grin at me. I think he enjoyed the fuss.

On the other side of Old Mr Woods sat a bloke with a long grizzly grey beard. He looked like a gnarled old tree, all dry and furrowed, and he smelled terrible. The girls nicknamed him 'The Hobbit'. You often saw him in the daytime, rummaging through rubbish skips up the top end of Dean Street. There were rumours that he was an 'eccentric' who really had pots of money; a Howard Hughes type, who was frightened to death of women. I personally didn't believe this, but then again, I supposed it could be true.

The punter who sat at the end of the front row was

Charlie-the-Deaf-Man: he who switched off his hearing-aid and sat with his back to the stage if he didn't like a particular act. He used to bring his favourite strippers little presents of perfume, ciggies, chocolates . . . With me, it was packages of meat or a pile of old bones for my dog, Moustique (Mous was banned from the Carousel stage for crapping on it). It was funny to see the expressions of those punters who weren't regulars when old Charlie staggered up halfway through my act to present me with a half-eaten joint or a bag of giblets! He sometimes brought nuts and raisins for Annie Arsehole's pet monkey, too.

That Charlie went spare if another punter nicked 'his' seat whilst he was in the toilet or up at the bar. He set about them with his walking stick, and believe me, he could be vicious. He was well into his seventies but he could still raise a laugh among the girls, if nothing else. One day a tall black stripper called Josetta came into the dressing-room laughing her head off. She told us that Charlie had propositioned her; not only that, he'd boasted of his prowess. He reckoned he could 'still give a girl a couple of hours of thrills'. Josetta couldn't keep a straight face every time he came in after that.

'Is it for murder or manslaughter that I would be done?' she would bellow at him from the stage.

It's true that some of the punters were characters, but you've got to bear in mind that for every one of them that sticks out in your memory, there are a dozen others who were just boring faceless nothings that got on your nerves simply by existing. I'm referring to the ones who didn't want to know or care that you were a person; there could never be any rapport between you; you were just tits 'n' ass, a *thing*, to them. And that's how they saw *all* women, not just us. Sometimes I think all that's changing now; that men are beginning to question their attitudes towards women throughout society generally. But most of the time I think it's just a surface job, because the clubs are still full of punters.

All the same, it could be very depressing when you thought about the whole man/woman business. It made you question everything in your life; your personal relationships with men. No matter how well these seemed to be going, there was always the niggly feeling underneath that something was *wrong*. You couldn't trust men. After my relationship with the stage manager broke up, I had no real love affairs with men; a few casual things, lots of laughs, but to tell the truth I was deeply suspicious of men and I felt I wasn't ready to trust another one for quite a while.

Looking back I'm convinced that it was the girls' sense of humour, above all else, that kept us sane. Without it, we wouldn't have stood a chance. We may have detested the punters as a rule, but they did give us plenty of laughs, and I can honestly say that we used to enjoy ourselves often. It gets to me nowadays whenever I come across the 'poor-thing' syndrome – usually from well-meaning feminists. Their sceptical faces when I tell them about the *fun* we had in Soho. I'm not saying it was roses all the way, far from it, but it's just not true to say that women in the sex industry are all hapless little victims. That's insulting. We have brains, and we use them – but that doesn't mean we have all the answers, especially when it comes to men's violence.

'Why are men such bastards?' we asked each other sometimes, when one of our friends showed up for work with a swollen face or a broken nose, courtesy of her old man; or when some unknown dolloper hassled you in the street.

One night when I was walking up Charing Cross Road with a friend, a guy came by and called me a 'cunt' and socked me in the face. Why? I'd never set eyes on him before in my life. It was as if the sight of me triggered off some warped impulse in his head: 'There's a woman; why don't I bop her one?'

And there was hatred in his face.

A similar sort of thing went on during the big electricity strikes in the winter of 1973–4. When the lights went out, it was incredible: every woman for herself. Men in the streets went crazy, in the pitch dark. A couple of strippers were raped, dragged into deserted car parks or on to waste ground. As for me, I bought myself one of those police whistles; I wore it on a chain round my neck. I wore lots of heavy leather gear, all black, like a bloody cat-burglar. Any bastard who came near me got his eardrums blasted.

I also carried a dirty great knife. I never knew at the time that I could get done for that; for having an 'offensive weapon'. Even if I had known it wouldn't have made any difference. As far as I was concerned, my knife was a DEfensive weapon. What are women supposed to do? Get raped and murdered, so it would seem, in the eyes of the law. They've got to be kidding.

One night I'd just finished my last show at the Sunset Strip and was trotting up Dean Street to meet Kitten at the Pizza Express. Suddenly, this bloke grabbed me and started pulling me into the alleyway. I yelled at him to let go, but he took no notice so I punched him in the face, knocking his specs off. He hit me back and I was in the gutter. Two cops were strolling down the other side of the street; they saw everything. I thought, right: that's you nicked, you creep, but no, it didn't work that way.

'You hit him first,' they said.

'But he attacked me, he was dragging me into the alley – '

'She's broken my glasses,' the creep was complaining.

It was a farce – but the best part was to come. I was informed that I could take out a *civil action* against my attacker – and vice versa.

'If you wish to proceed with this,' the cops told us, in their cops' deadpan way, 'you must first of all exchange names and addresses . . .'

I didn't hear any more. This was amazing! I was supposed to write down my name and address and hand it over to the weirdo.

'Why don't I give him my front door keys whilst I'm at it?'

'That's the law,' came the inevitable reply, 'and if you get stroppy with us, we'll nick you for obstruction.'

It seemed I couldn't go wrong.

Don't misunderstand me; I'm not saying that *all* men are no-good brutes; what I am saying is that too many of them are, and too many more are quite happy to let the vicious ones get away with it all the time. Men's violence is a *women*'s issue, appears to be the general attitude. Wrong. Men's violence is *their* problem, too. That became truly apparent to me on the nights when we had the football crowds in.

You've got to try and picture a strip-club jam packed with stomping drunken slobs all howling in unison: 'WE WANT TO SEE *PUSSY*' to get an idea of what I'm talking about. It's more than terrifying. And there's us lot backstage, shaking in our silver shoes, waiting, waiting to do our spots. It felt like hell in the dressing-room, listening to the roars up front. Sometimes I used to wonder why the boss didn't go the whole hog, and have us wheeled out there in tumbrels. That's how bad it felt. On those occasions I really did feel I was crazy to be in this job.

Even the stage managers were scared, and no wonder. At one club the SM was under instructions from the boss to lock the backstage door behind each of us when we went on-stage. This was in order to protect the precious tape decks from violent drunken marauders. More than one club had been torn apart on Cup Final nights. The girls on-stage were of course dispensable; tough on us. In retaliation we would smash the bloody lock ourselves. The boss would have it fixed, then we'd break it again, and it went on like that, a grim psychological tussle, right up to the day I left.

We never got any extra wages for working to football crowds, let alone danger money. The parasite-bosses creamed it all off; that's what bosses are for, when all's said and done. All we got was the fear, the abuse.

'GERREMOFF!' 'SLAG!' 'SHOW US WHAT YOU'VE GOT!' 'SLAG!'

Real imaginative stuff.

The worst part was waiting up there in the dark for the tabs to open; the tape to start. That's when you prayed. *Out there*, you heard them; they sounded like one gigantic monster; they stank like wolves, you could *breathe* them. Wolves would've been kinder. Then when the tabs opened, my God; there was this wall of sweaty white faces, open-mouthed, glistening with booze, hate and fear. Yes – *fear*. I used to feel almost detached, sometimes, going through my routine, and – I couldn't help myself – looking into the punters' eyes (the part of me that wasn't scared shitless, that is). And they bewildered me, more than anything else. I felt like stopping the show and saying 'Listen: what's happening here?'

Because I could not fathom it out at all; nothing made sense. If they hate women so much, if they hate our bodies, our breasts, our cunts, then *why* are they here? Why? It upset me when that tiny voice in my head spoke to me and said 'They hate us'. I thought, these men are some woman's son, father, lover, husband, brother, back in the straight world yet look at them here; they're nothing more than a yowling pack, like wild dogs. That's when I saw the relationship between men and women as a war; and here we were, strippers facing the football yobs. This was the front line, where it all went on, where these forces met head-on: sex, money, power . . .

Something in those nights showed me the way it worked: men's fascination with/abomination of women and our bodies. It was as if I were witnessing something so deep and entrenched; centuries of men's associating women with guilt and degradation. I saw how sexuality had been twisted and repressed to such an extent that this was the end result: a battle-ground; men heaping their guilty shit on to our nude bodies. It was terrible. I tried not to think about it. If they were too far gone, if the booze-aggro level was sky-high, I just walked through the number and made myself *not there*. Get on-stage; get through the routine, then get off in one piece, that was our motto. But there were also times when I thought, I can win this shower over, and I would. I'd send up my number something rotten, and more often than not I got them all laughing along *with* me. I reckoned that was the safest bet; if they were too busy enjoying themselves, having a laugh, they'd maybe forget about trying to pull you off-stage or getting up there with you, as sometimes happened.

Basically, you had to gauge your audience, the same way a 'straight' comedian or actor does, and it was fantastic when you succeeded. Amazing. Because you could feel the whole atmosphere change; it lightened, lifted, and the tension would leave both you and the punters. It would cease to be ugly and threatening; it would be *fun*. Mind you, it was also damned hard work. And at the end of your number, those guys would raise the roof with their cheers and applause and good humour.

You'd come off-stage elated; still sweating and shaking – but elated. The adrenaline was on overtime.

'Follow *that*,' you would brag to the scowling next girl.

On those occasions I really felt like I'd achieved something special, even if it was only a stay of execution, until the next show.

The other breed of punter that used to make me question men's sanity was the bowler-hat-and-brolly brigade. They more or less took over the clubs during the first couple of rounds – talk to me about late lunches! These office-types came to our clubs for a post-prandial wank. From about 2 P.M. onwards, the seats would start filling up with them, briefcases or bowler hats plonked on their laps to conceal what was going on underneath. If you looked at them you thought 'English city gent' but, my God, you should've seen the way they carried on if a seat became vacant in the front row. We called it 'The Grand National'; it was quite incredible. First they were under starters' orders, gathering up their paraphernalia, then all hell was let loose. Seats flew back and they were off; pinstriped arms and legs flaying as they climbed across the seats, each other, in the grim battle for that front row seat. Brollies and rolled-up copies of the *Financial Times* were wielded like clubs – they really did bash the shit out of each other – and their briefcases became shields. Those paragons could be violent bastards when it came to the battle of the front row. You had to see it to believe it – and we saw it a hundred times. I'll never forget one time, during a particularly vicious carry-on, two of them stopped the show when they both reached the seat at the same moment. They started slugging it out right there, in front of our noses (there were three of us on-stage at the time; it was the Finale). We moved to the back of the stage and had a smoke. We watched *them*, for once. It was quite comical; the music was still belting out, funnily enough it was 'Let me entertain you', and those two most certainly did. One was a fat pink-faced Bristow-type; the other was a scrawny bugger with a receding hairline; a real chinless wonder. But they were going at it hammer-and-tongs! In the end the doorman and the SM had to sling them out, and they were fighting all the way. We could hear them right from the back:

'I was there first' and 'You *bit* me . . .'

We said, 'If their loved ones could see them now.'

Even now when I look back I find it hard to believe I actually witnessed that sort of thing, not once, but many times. City gents galloping over the backs of seats like so many Errol Flynns. Those punters fought just as desperate and mean as any street villains, in their itsy-bitsy way. How do you like that? And they're the ones who are always screaming about Law & Order; all that stuff: 'Bring back the birch!'

One of my deepest regrets is that I never took a camera backstage and got some real action shots of 'The Grand National'.

Sometimes we got women in the audience, but not often. During the late afternoon you had the young students – girls and boys – from St Martin's College in Charing Cross Road. They came in to look at our costumes and make-up; to get ideas for their fashion designs. Punk came straight out of the strip-clubs – all the black leather and bondage gear, fishnet tights and all the rest. But the female punters we hated most were those girls who came in at night with their boyfriends. There was usually a gang together, and they would all sit at the back of the theatre, squawking and braying, pissed out of their heads. Sloane Rangers: 'Ew fack me, look et thet', that kind of thing. They drove you mad. It was bad enough having to put up with mouthy men in the audience, but getting barracked by *women* was just too much. It adds insult to injury, when your own sex tries to demean you. So, once or twice I was driven to jumping off the stage and bopping one of those bitches. There's only so much you can take. I remember once this Alaskan stripper, Tanya, damn-near scalped a 'Hoorah Henrietta'. We had enough to put up with as it was; why should we take crap from rich bitches who thought we were stupid animals, there to be laughed at? Not a chance.

I liked Tanya, she was an interesting person; quite a character, as it happened. She was Russian-American – I'd never come across that pedigree before – and she used to be a hooker back in the States. We had 'creative writing' sessions in the Carousel dressing-room together. As a matter of fact it was Tanya who showed me what a Thesaurus was (I thought it was an extinct creature like a dinosaur) and taught me how to use one. Tanya wasn't what you'd call 'beautiful' when you first looked at her, but she had one of those smiles that light the whole face up; really radiant. She had a wonderful jazzy voice, too, especially when she'd had a few.

Tanya hung around for a few months but then the Immigration hounds got on to her and she was forced to leave the country. I never saw her again. She was great.

Girls came and went, and came back again, and went again. We were always at it. I myself left the clubs three times. I came back three times, too; always for the same bloody reason: money.

The first time I left was one summer, I think it was 1974, with Rob. We went to his mother's lovely little old cottage in Tiverton, Devon. It was marvellous for a few weeks; all that fresh air, the green, the flowers; the whole slowed-down pace. I felt like a snake shedding its skin and getting renewed. But that didn't last long. The money went, as money tends to, and we were skint. We hung on for a few months but without an income it was terrible; we were at each other's throats all the time. Just before Christmas that year, we got set on at a local chicken slaughterhouse. Rob was in the blood 'n' guts department and I was in the 'ladies'' part, where they packaged the frozen portions of dead body. My job was to stand in this contraption that was not unlike a church pulpit and take the frozen corpses down off a revolving rack. Then I folded their wings back and chucked them down a chute to the next worker, who chopped them up. It was a real bummer. I had nightmares about that place for months after I left. I spent my breaks out in the yard trying to encourage stray chickens to escape. Even outdoors you couldn't get away from the stench of the slaughterhouse – it smelt of blood and feathers and blubber and, most of all, death. As far as I'm concerned, that place took first prize in the sleaze stakes. Give me a strip-club dressing-room any time.

The management kept the radio blaring all day long: Radio Two, with its inane, insane male deejays giving their Brave New World 'Happy Housewives' patter. The only reason they stick the radio on in factories is to stop the workers from thinking. Crafty bastards.

I worked at the chicken slaughterhouse for less than two months, then I thought, if people are content to be robots – well I'm not.

Early the next year I went back to that other chicken-factory; the one in Soho. The scene was not so good. There had been more upheavals and prohibition whilst I was away. I managed to get back in the clubs. I was lucky. I got a spot at the Carousel and two at the Doll's House; those were my favourite clubs anyway.

Many of my old friends and former colleagues had vanished; either to work abroad – Scandinavia was always the best bet for black girls; the Far East preferred white flesh – or up the bloody Lane, hustling. Kitten and Annie Arsehole and a few of my other pals were still flaunting it, however, along with the season's new crop of fresh-faced kids – the latest generation of mysteries from up North. Times were getting harder.

Kitten told me Vanessa Redgrave had been round the clubs.

'What, after a job is she?' I joked, but it turned out to be true. The famous star had tried to persuade girls to organize, form a union, or get into Equity (!!); something like that. She got the old heave-ho soon enough. West Enders are dead suspicious of the media and anybody connected with them, with good reason. We were sick to the back teeth of film-crews and documentary makers creeping round Soho in the dead of night and asking us to tell millions of people how degrading and depraved our lives were. Bloody pests. But, thinking about it afterwards, I came to the conclusion that Vanessa's heart was in the right place, and she had plenty of guts for coming into the clubs, a 'straight' woman like her; not only that, a famous one to boot. I reckon she had tremendous courage, and she at least saw us as workers, not perverts, which was a real breakthrough. But you can't really organize people if you're coming from outside; that doesn't work. It just becomes patronizing, and it isn't *real*. There are too many armchair socialists and generals in this world who try to do that.

Besides, our very status as outlaws, outcasts, among the rest of the human race worked against our organizing for unions or even basic civil rights. The bosses knew we were isolated; the law knew it, and we ourselves did too; we weren't stupid. When you're an illegal workforce; when there are 'plenty more where you come from', you have to accept the conditions the bosses decree and make the best of it. Take it or leave it. I'd heard a couple of strippers did once try to form a union, this was years before I came round, but all they succeeded in doing was to get themselves blacklisted from all the clubs.

I settled back into the old routine without too many problems; it was like I'd never been gone. The same old faces in the front rows. It was great to have the money again, not to have to fret about every last penny you spent.

The new choreographer at the Carousel was intriguing. She was a 'halfway there' sex-change from Sydney, Australia. She was over here for treatment, and she took the Carousel job in order to save the money to have her dick lopped off and rearranged. Her name was Miranda, and she was absolutely stunning to look at; a bit big, but you'd never have guessed she wasn't a 'real' woman yet. For years she'd toured Australia with a trans-sexual show; she knew all there was to know about the glitz-biz; how to do the whole stage make-up routine and so on. Mind you, it's nearly always the sex-changes and transvestites that are the most 'glamorous' in the stripping business; they put heart and soul into it. Miranda's eye make-up fascinated me more than anything. She used lots of subtle pastels, sugary colours that seemed to melt into her skin; then, close to the eye socket, she stroked fiery brilliant greens, and vivid purples. The effect was fantastic, like Impressionist painting.

She showed me how to do my eyes, and then I started experimenting with my own wild colour schemes: bright blues, greens, and yellows. One day I was finishing my number at the Carousel when I noticed this young fellow in the front row; he hadn't taken his eyes off my face. I was stark naked by this time, so it was a bit unnerving. I bawled him out.

'What are you skenning at?'

'Your eye make-up,' came the prompt reply. 'It's wonderful.'

I was at a loss for words; I didn't know whether to thank him or kick him. Secretly, I was well-pleased.

Miranda was also the person who disproved Freud's theory about 'flashers' for me. Papa Freud said that these men expose themselves 'in order to get a sight of the person's genitals in return', because they were anxious about women not having willies. But one morning Miranda was flashed at by some creep in Hyde Park.

'I flashed mine right back at him,' she told us, with great glee. 'The guy nearly dropped dead of a heart attack. I'm telling you, you couldn't see him for dust after that.'

That little episode tickled me pink. So did another one, only this time it was a dirty phone caller who pestered the Doll's House doorgirl every Saturday afternoon. Till one Saturday me and Annie Arsehole happened to be hanging around the desk when he rang. Annie said 'Let me take the call'. I was about to go downstairs to do my number, so I missed all the action, but when I came back up after my spot, everybody was rolling about the floor laughing.

'Well, what happened?' I demanded to know.

'He hung up,' Annie told me. 'He was giving all the usual stuff, you know, what he'd like to do to me . . . Then *I* started. I came out with the filthiest, crudest stuff I could think of, and he was going "Now stop that, you're disgusting; I've never heard anything like that in my life . . . you're evil, you're making me feel sick . . ." Then he hung up.'

That bugger never rang back; it was a case of fighting fire with fire. Now when I got the dirty callers, I used to say, 'Just ring this number, sir, I think you'll find what you're looking for' – then give them the number of West End Central. Because a man who does that is nothing but a minor sleaze, a coward. The one reaction he expects from women is 'Eeeeek!' The last thing he wants is some of his own treatment, or a cold manner.

Of all the clubs I ever worked, I liked the Doll's House best. This was slightly crazy on my part, since it paid the lowest wages. But it had such a good atmosphere, you were prepared to put up with that. It wasn't so much the clientèle – after all, you saw the same old faces in every club, along with the passing trade – it was the actual *feel* of the place. For a start, it was 'tastefully' decorated – a couple of discreet prints and some Toulouse Lautrec-style murals. It just didn't look as tacky as the other places, with their garish lights and 'GIRLS!' signs all over. The Doll's House interior was all plush carpets and a reception that looked like it had stepped out of the 'Naughty Nineties'. A friend of mine who came to see me there said it was like walking into a turn-of-the-century Paris brothel.

I've heard the place has just closed; the boss let it go to seed over the past few years anyway. But back in the mid- to late 70s, it prided itself on being a sort of mini-striptease-Palladium. We had spangly shows with a theme that changed every six weeks; a set designer, costumier, choreographer (a *real ex-dancer*!); even a script-writer. The guy who wrote these tongue-in-cheek scripts was a queen from Birmingham who wrote for television too. He obviously enjoyed himself hugely when it came to creating our little ditties and pastiches. We did a 'Star Wars' finale – 'Show me Uranus and I'll show you my ring' – and one time I did a Carmen Miranda number where I had to sing 'Down South American Way' with a new set of lyrics that went:

'The Venezuelians, are six times daily'uns, and with you
aliens, they'll go to town' . . .

and

'Aye-aye; aye-aye; in our ponchos so microscopic,
There's a view tremendous of bare haciendas,
Down South American way . . .'

That got the audience laughing, if nothing else.

The Doll's House really went to town at Christmas,
though. We did a yearly 'panty-mime', absolutely ridiculous stuff: 'Boobs in The Wood'; 'Jack and His Bean-
stalk'; 'Big Dick Whittington and His Insatiable Pussy'
. . . All good clean family fun! One year I played the
lead in 'Sin-derella'; I had a fine old time. My 'Prince
Charming' was a sweet-faced, lanky, gay dancer called
Paul, who kept flouncing off-stage during the ballroom
scene, because of the stick he got from some of the more
ignorant punters.

'Isn't it supposed to be the other way round, duckie?'
those idiots would then jeer.

We got a lot of 'straight' theatre people and actors in
the audience of the Doll's House at panty-mime time of
year; I think the club held an almost cult status amongst
them. You'd be surprised at some of the faces I saw in
our audience. One day dear old Alfie the doorman said,
'You'll never guess who was down there tonight – *Mickey
Rooney*. And on his way out he says to me "That's a
great little show you've got going".'

Well, we were thrilled to bits.

'Fancy that,' said the girl who was playing Dandini.
'Mickey Rooney's seen *me* on-stage!'

'You'd better make the most of it, love,' Prince Charming told her, 'because, let's face it; that's the closest you'll
ever get to Hollywood.'

That boy could be a sour bitch when he wanted to.

Also at Christmas every year our boss, 'Monsieur Emile', organized a raffle in the club bar, the proceeds of which went to the children's hospital. Celebrities like Henry Cooper rolled up to announce the winner and dole out the prize, which was a litre bottle of spirits and a doll that looked exactly like Barbara Cartland. One year there was a fancy-dress competition too, so another stripper and I wore our costume from the Carousel – Rudolph the Rednosed Stripping Reindeer – and entered it. We collected the first prize, a bottle of booze, from a young fellow from the hospital administration. He tried to chat me up. I remember thinking he must have been pretty hard up if he was reduced to trying to pull somebody wearing a red plastic nose and a set of antlers.

Looking back now I can almost say I was happy at the Doll's House. I loved the people I worked with, and the shows were good fun, innocuous, in a way; even the punters didn't seem to bug me so much. We had more women clients in there, too – usually in couples, heterosexual or lesbian. But these women weren't like the screeching aristocratic bitches I mentioned earlier; they appreciated your hard work. But, although the work was fun, it was still *hard*; we were still doing the seventy-two-hour week.

It was whilst I was a Doll's House resident that I met my 'sugar-daddy'. Strippers often found themselves the object of one man's particular obsession, and let me tell you that it was usually the girl's *personality* that drew the admirer. Mine was a high-up civil servant called Henry. He came to see me three times a week, and took me and my little dog out to dinner at an Italian restaurant in Dean Street. Moustique always had a steak on these occasions; the waiters loved him. He had his own special dish.

Henry was okay when I got to know him, and we had some good laughs. There was no physical relationship between us; he had my company and we became friends: that was it. As a matter of fact we're friends to this day; we keep in touch and meet up for days out occasionally. At the club, Henry used to give me presents, usually money, although he complained if he thought I was being greedy. But I've always been straight with people, and Henry was no exception.

'You're rich and I'm not,' I told him. 'So what's the fuss?'

He couldn't really argue with that, not if he wanted to carry on seeing me anyway.

Kitten also had a sugar-daddy, a man called Derrick Something-Double-Barrelled. He was four feet eleven, in his seventies, and had been raised in India at the time of the Raj. I'm talking about a real Gung-Ho type. We all called him 'Mister Magoo', because he was a dead ringer for the cartoon character. Theirs was an amazing relationship. Mister Magoo was absolutely besotted with Kitten; he'd do anything for her.

'I'm bored,' she said to him once, in the Toulouse Lautrec. 'Stand on your head.'

And he did; right there in front of everybody; he completed a faltering headstand. He was a game old bugger. One time he really did go over the top, though it wasn't whilst doing a headstand. He went and announced his and Kitten's engagement in *The Times*. That caused quite a stir. I've never seen Kitten so mad, but the rest of us thought it hilarious. We ribbed her about that for months.

Another stripper, a big woman called Justine, had a judge for a punter. 'Judge Jim', she called him. Jus had been up in front of him on a 'disorderly house' charge back in the early 70s, and he'd been her sugar-daddy ever since. He was a weirdo. He reminded me of a Thunderbirds puppet, with his chiselled features and unreal grin. Jus told me he liked 'a good toeing' – he was another upper-class masochist, in other words. They breed them at public schools, you know.

One of the other strippers who was nicked at the same time as Justine was a stunning black woman who now worked behind the bar. She actually married the cop who arrested her, the one who put her in the van. They fell in love at Vine Street copshop, which I find hard to believe. But I met her old man a few times, and I found him really nice: quiet, polite, and sober – not like most West End police officers.

At the Doll's House, we were basically one big, happy family.

And yet . . . the pressures were there. I was drinking far too much; I was in and out of the bar all day long. There wasn't anything else to do in our breaks. I wasn't exactly an alcoholic; it was sheer boredom in between spots that kept me on the sauce, that plus the fact that men were always there, always offering to buy you drinks. I was still keeping up with my 'education' as best I could. Nobody could prise me away from my books, no matter how much they took the mickey out of me, but I was finding it more and more difficult to concentrate, and I was still feeling frustrated with my life generally. Then one day my friend behind the bar said:

'Why don't you try college? You could apply as a mature student.'

That was something I hadn't thought of. Why not indeed? It was mid-August by this time, 1979. As it was so late in the year, I dashed off applications to several polytechnics in the hope that they could still squeeze me in that year. I told them the truth: that I was a stripper who wanted an education. I vividly remember filling in the forms: 'I left school early because I hated it', and writing down my one puny French O-Level. Before I knew it, I was on the train bound for Wolverhampton Polytechnic. I had an interview arranged with one Professor Wanklyn, of all people. I thought, with a name like his the man's bound to have a sense of humour. Although I knew that not all professors were stuffy types; I'd met one or two in the West End over the years ... still, this was a different kettle of fish, since it would be on *their* territory. I'd have to watch my behaviour, I thought frantically on the train; not come out with anything too outrageous.

I was nervous, so I had a couple of drinks on the train. By the time I found the place I was late, a bit pissed, and convinced it was all a big mistake. I got lost on the campus; I hadn't realized it would be so vast. When I eventually did find the room, I had a bad case of the giggles. I burst through the door and found myself in a lovely book-lined room a bit like a small library; it had the same hushed quality. People were sitting round a big polished table. All the heads turned to look at me.

'Sorry I'm late; I got lost,' I said.

All the heads turned back to the man sitting at the top of the table; a young, intellectual-looking person. He indicated a seat for me, then continued with what he was saying. It was all very serious and low-key. The other potential students were chubby-faced kids; I didn't seem to have much in common with them. A few years later, when I saw the film *Educating Rita*, the bit at the beginning where Julie Walters bursts in on Michael Caine, I thought 'That's me; that's how it was for me ...' Except I wasn't wearing stiletto heels and a tight skirt, and I didn't do the English and French degree and blossom out.

After the talk we were shown round the place and after that I found myself in Professor Wanklyn's study. He was a nice fellow. We had a drink and a chat, and he actually offered me a place. My mind was made up. I went back to London thinking, this is it; farewell Soho, I'm gonna be an academic. I quickly wrote off for a grant application. That's when the doubts crept in.

I balked at the forms they sent me. What the hell was I going to put? I didn't want to mention stripping. I stuck them on one side whilst I thought about it all. Then there was my dog . . . I couldn't just abandon my little Moustique. After all, he had been my closest and most faithful companion all those years, ever since I bought him from a crazy Hungarian stripper, a fire-eater I once briefly shared a flat with.

Henry, my punter, was against the whole idea.

'You'll hate it,' he said encouragingly. 'You'll loathe all those kids and as for living on a grant – don't make me laugh!'

'That doesn't bother me,' I told him, honestly. 'Wolverhampton isn't the West End; I could manage on the grant.'

To tell the truth, I was awed by the fact that the state was prepared to actually pay me to get educated; it seemed too good to be true. Something was sure to go wrong, I thought. You don't get something for nothing in this world.

'Watch out for the taxman,' a punter who happened to be one of the Inland Revenue's top inspectors warned me. That made me hesitate even more. Time was running out, for the grant; everything. But I wanted my education!

'Don't rush into it, that's the mistake you always make,' my pals told me. 'That's just running away. Not that we blame you, but you could always try again next year, there's plenty of time. And that way you can be more sure of what you want.'

I let it drop. Maybe I was wrong to; who knows? But I couldn't handle all the bureaucracy, and the girls were right; I *was* running away.

I worked what turned out to be my final Christmas at the Doll's House. I was hitting the bottle day after day. I went on-stage first thing in the morning with terrible hangovers. I slagged the audience off something rotten. To make it worse, Kitten left; she'd got a job at Paul Raymond's Revuebar. But that didn't last very long; she hated it there.

'It's worse than being back at school,' she said one day when I bumped into her in Oxford Street. 'You don't have the same freedom, the same laughs, we had in the clubs. There are so many rules and regulations.'

That was the last time I ever saw her.

Her old man 'barred' her from the clubs, and from seeing all her old mates, especially me. So that was that.

Some of my afternoons I started visiting a friend of mine who had a business flat in Frith Street. She was a lesbian virgin prostitute – I'm not kidding – and she called herself 'Maîtresse Sévèrine'. She was always good for a cup of tea and a shoulder to cry on. She made me laugh, too. Some days we'd sit in her cosy kitchen chatting away merrily for half an hour, then Sévèrine would suddenly leap up and rush into her bedroom, which was a miniature torture chamber.

'I've got old Mr So-and-so on the rack,' she would exclaim on her way out. And it was true; some old codger would be trussed up in there. I could hear her yelling at him; the walls were very thin. A bloody army general, or

a wayward judge. Always, *always* an upper-class twit . . .
Sévèrine herself was philosophical about it.

'Why worry about it?' she often said to me. 'If that's
what they want, let them have it. Who are we to judge?'

She was proud of the fact that she was a virgin.

'I've never slept with a man in my life, and I'm nearly
forty years old,' she would say. 'Men are good for two
things: flaying and paying.'

Sévèrine was the only dominatrix pro I knew. I heard
she retired a couple of years later and went to live in the
South of France. Another stripper who was a friend of
hers told me it was because she got arthritis in her
whip-hand. Apparently, that often happens to pros who
specialize in corporal punishment.

In early spring the following year I got the downers again;
I decided I'd had enough of the West End, I had to get
away from the club. Away from men's eyes. So I left
stripping for the second time. I got Henry to take me on
holiday to a beautiful five-star hotel in Cornwall. It was
magic. I had a lovely room with a private bath, phone,
colour television – there was even a big squishy cushion
for Moustique. Bliss. I felt ten years younger after that
break. I decided to go and stay with my parents, who'd
moved to the seaside. They were running a beach shop/
supermarket there. There was plenty of time before the
season really got going; maybe I could use that time to
work something out. My life was a mess.

I spent a month or so there, walking every day along
the wild, empty beach and across the dunes, in the teeth
of that vindictive east wind. You would never have
thought it was April; it felt like Siberia in January. But
the space, the solitude, and the fresh sea air seemed to
have the effect of emptying me of all the Soho shit. In a
way I *forgot* the West End; forgot it with my body, that

is. I felt as if I were still unformed, waiting. It was only when something prompted the memories – a letter from the ever-faithful Henry, usually – that I recalled my life back there, with a great jolt. Did all that really exist?

There was a tree outside my parents' shop. It was still bare and wintry-looking, but it was nearly always full of noisy crows. Every day I walked by and saw them perched there making a racket.

'Behhhhh,' they went, as if they objected to the very idea of existing.

I thought, I know how you feel.

The first grockles – holiday-makers – turned up. Ordinary people, families, who were staying on the caravan parks and camp sites all round that area. They reminded me of everything I'd wanted to get away from all those years ago when I first left Burnley. I know that sounds terrible, but it's the truth. Ordinary working-class life terrified me. I began to feel the old familiar oppression; a kind of hemmed-in hopelessness. I started to miss my old pals, the laughs we had . . . the money. I even missed Henry, and in a funny way, those idiots in the bar. What a life! What wonderful choices there were! I was back to that again. I think I was addicted to the freedom I'd had in Soho, even if it did come along with plenty of headbanging pressures. I went back for the second time.

It was 1980; I was thirty years old. Was it my imagination, or were the streets meaner, and people more wound up than I remembered? Soho was never exactly a restful environment, but I could definitely sense a change; a kind of desperate edge to the place. But then of course Soho only reflects the society which it services.

It was good to be back, see my friends again. I started at the Doll's House, and M. Emile let me have one of the little rooms over the club for a nominal rent. Whilst I'd been away this time, a new phenomenon had sprung up:

the peepshow. There were half a dozen in Old Compton Street alone. Some of the girls I knew were working in one of them, so I went round for a visit. What a surreal place!

It consisted of a hexagonal 'stage' that was nothing of the sort; just a slightly raised area of floor where the girls worked. It was dark and oppressive, bathed in dull red and amber light, and it felt like the walls were about to close in on you. In fact the walls were little more than plywood booths, in which the punters stood and 'peeped' at the show through letterbox-sized 'peepholes' with metal flaps that opened and closed. The men put fifty pence in . . . clunk click . . . that gave them two minutes' peeping time. All the girls could see were the men's eyes, and that was the spookiest part of all as far as I was concerned: pairs of disembodied eyes gazing at you from all angles. You had to actually be there to realize just how menacing that could feel.

Most of the booths were empty whilst I was visiting, since it wasn't one of the peak times (lunchtime and after five P.M., when the offices close), but the ones that were occupied were shaking like mad as their occupants jerked off.

'Doesn't it drive you round the twist in here?' I asked my friend Chrissie, who was working at the time. She shook her head.

'It's better than doing the clubs. There's no contact; you don't have all the audience to face . . . and there's the physical barrier between us and them, which suits me fine. Plus the money's better – £20 a shift; that's only six hours, not twelve. Those Noddies out there don't bother me one bit . . . except for the eyes, they freak me out a bit sometimes. They remind me of Willard's Rats; you know, the horror film?'

'I don't think I could work in one of these places,' I

said, as one booth in particular threatened to go into orbit; the occupant was in such a frenzy.

I should have kept my trap shut.

There were plenty of new mysteries about. Young girls up from the unemployment blackspots of the North. Some were as young as sixteen. The bosses welcomed them with open arms, and the punters smacked their lips: fresh flesh.

Even the winos and tramps seemed to have increased during my couple of months' absence. You saw them staggering round Soho Square, or flaked out on benches, gibbering. They swore at you as you walked by. Tattered old Millicent was still around, I noticed. The first time I ever saw her was back in 1969, when I was a mystery. She punched me in the stomach as she walked by me in Old Compton Street. She did that to people at random, just when she fancied it. You soon learned to avoid her; you crossed over when you saw her approaching in her filthy stinking rags, weaving along the pavement. Her hair was grey and it stuck up in scraggy tufts in all directions. From a distance she looked like a walking Brillo-pad. On Bad Days, days when I was in the dumps, old Millicent epitomized everything that was depressing about Soho: the tension, viciousness, and explosive undercurrent of violence.

The Doll's House was going to seed. There was no choreographer, no show, no script, no nothing. You just got up there and flaunted it. I hit the bottle again. Nobody could speak to me; I was just so bitter all the time. The punters got the worst of it, especially those crack o' dawn wankers. Every morning I had a bad hangover. I would stalk across the stage like a lunatic, ignoring the lights, the music:

'Have you tosspots had your breakfasts yet?' I would hiss at the startled audience. 'Because I haven't . . .'

Sometimes they would be so intimidated by this crazy person in front of them that somebody would nip round the corner to Mario's café and get me a bacon butty. Others went up and complained about me to the door-man. I laugh at that memory now, but it wasn't funny at the time. I wanted to kill them all, I was so filled with hate. Nothing would have thrilled me more than to go on-stage with a machine-gun, and blast the fuckers' heads off. That tightly coiled part of me, the one I'd felt like a hard knot in my belly all those years, was refusing to keep quiet any longer. I was just a walking mass of bitterness, and what made it worse was that I still couldn't articulate it.

One day I was on-stage dancing away when I suddenly realized I'd lost part of my vision. Zigzag lights flashed and burst in my head, and there were misty gaps where I focused my gaze. Help, I thought; I'm going blind. I staggered off-stage halfway through the number and flopped into a corner of the dressing-room. Even with my eyes closed I could 'see' the brilliant white flashes, like explosions in my head. For twenty minutes I couldn't see a damn thing. Then I had a pounding headache and was sick.

Migraine. I'd never had one before in my life. I had three more within the space of a month.

Get out for good, I told myself. *Do it*. Stop arsing about; try for another college, only this time do it properly. Write your book.

And then something ridiculous happened: I fell in love with the new stage manager. He was a university gradu-ate, eight years younger than me; middle-class . . . we were chalk-and-cheese. But he was like a lifeline; a way out of my hell.

'Let's get away,' we said to each other. The West End wasn't exactly the spot for new, raw love to be nurtured.

Steve's family lived in a beautiful house on the south coast. I could hardly believe my luck; back to nature again. It seemed that every time I got into a state, the countryside or the sea played a part in my rescue. But by this time I was very ill, although I wasn't really aware of it. Sick in body and spirit. For nearly a year I had a headache most days, and I was constantly throwing up. I had panic attacks, and refused to go out. I burst into tears at the slightest thing. I was still suffering with the migraines, and they scared me. Every time I had the flashing lights and blindness a part of me panicked and thought, that's it; this time my sight won't come back. No matter how many times it happened, I thought that.

Steve was great; he sustained me, let me talk, and he listened. His family too welcomed me with open arms. I think they opened up a whole new world for me. And I did for them, too; one they never dreamed existed. A nightmare world, in some ways. I felt like my whole being was crying, sobbing. And yet, and yet – 'I'm not a victim!' I insisted. 'And there were lots of good times, there was the love and friendship of the girls. Always, there was that.'

I missed my friends.

In 1982 Steve and I married and moved to East Anglia, where he was doing a postgraduate year.

'You should write,' he told me. 'You want to be a writer – so *write*.'

I did, but it kept coming out wrong. I couldn't find my own voice. What did I want to say? I wanted to tell about working in the sex industry, write about how it was for me. I thought maybe the women's movement would help; after all, they weren't all anti-porn crusaders. I plucked up the courage to go to the local feminist centre; I was a complete stranger, and didn't know a soul. I signed up for a 'Women and Creativity' course even though I'd missed the first couple of evenings. I'd been reading some women's writing during the last year or so and had found it exciting and truthful. But things didn't go too well.

When I got there the first thing I saw was a women's art exhibition: a wall-full of drawings of vaginas. I thought, oh no! I've seen enough of this stuff to last me ten lifetimes. I could hardly keep a straight face at first. But then I realized that it was a good thing for straight women to get into, since they hadn't had the benefit of being in the strip-club environment and being open with themselves and each other on the subject of cunts. Whereas we strippers were accustomed to the sight of our private parts. I recalled with a pang the hilarious times when we had daft 'different shapes' competitions and clitoris-measuring events.

The first meeting we had to get into groups of six and each of us had to talk for two minutes about what we'd done that was creative in the past week. I couldn't think of a fucking thing! All these plummy voices took turns in speaking whilst the rest of us listened in that respectful, serious way the middle classes have with each other. Part of me wanted to laugh; the other part was scared stiff. At the moment it came to my turn, I think I would've preferred to do a full striptease. As it was, I heard myself start to babble on about willow trees and a lost cat. It was terrible! Suddenly I took a deep breath and said, 'I'm writing a book about being a stripper in Soho.'

That went down really well. The women were kind and concerned, except that they kept saying 'Oh, you poor thing!' I felt like a kind of feminist Eliza Doolittle. It was embarrassing.

I went to the Women's Centre a few times; even got a friendly word from a few of the women there; but I never felt relaxed, or that I could be myself. And always, at some point, some young thing would say to me:

'Yes but – how could you do it? *Why* did you do it?' – shudder – 'I could never do such a thing.'

That pissed me off; it made me feel like I was some sort of pervert.

'You could if you were hungry enough,' I used to mutter. That met with a blank stare.

I stopped going to the centre. I felt isolated there, even amongst those women. They didn't understand; our lives were so completely different. They weren't unfriendly, but I felt we had nothing in common; we weren't 'sisters' at all. Above all, I got sick and tired of the 'How could you?' treatment, however genuine the ignorance. I thought, people just don't know a thing about strippers, or prostitutes – not even feminists.

I was determined to write the book – one day.

By the time Steve finished his course we were broke, without prospects of work. Supplementary Benefit beckoned.

'This is madness,' I told Steve. 'When I can be earning *back there*.'

We could go back to Soho and work for a few months; save up, get away . . . A feminist acquaintance came to dinner one night and we talked about my going back to stripping.

'Yes, but *can* you go back now, knowing what you know?' she asked me.

'I've always known what the sex industry's about,' I told her. 'And I *am* going back.'

'But that's disgusting.'

'So's being poor,' I said. 'I'd rather be a stripper than have to eat my head up every day worrying about not having enough money to live on.'

'Well, I've got two friends, students, who desperately need money, too; they're working as cleaners in a pub, for £1.20 an hour. But I know they'd rather do that than earn better money doing what you're about to do.'

'Now that's what *I* call degrading.'

As it turned out I only worked for a couple of months when Steve and I returned to London. It was coming up for Christmas, 1983. I felt like a different person, in many ways, yet underneath there was the same old me. I'd been away from the West End for nearly three years, and in all that time I'd been thinking, working things out. Everything that had been bubbling away within me throughout the stripping years had come to the surface whilst I was sitting quietly in the Norwich flat. All the things I'd kept hidden, repressed, the way women do. 'Blank it out', as Big Linda and the other girls used to say all those years ago. But that doesn't stop it from existing; still going on deep inside your own head, your guts . . .

I could see things much more clearly now.

We planned to work and save up some money so that we could both go off somewhere and write in peace. Steve got fixed up with a job on the lotteries, thanks to my ex-boyfriend, Rob; and in his free time he taught English to foreign students on a casual basis. I went back to the Carousel, part-time. They'd relaxed the rules a bit so that girls could 'job-share'. I was determined not to kill myself doing the old seventy-two-hour week. I knew that that was what really took it out of you.

'I'm too old for that routine,' I told Bernie. 'I'll do six hours a day. It's enough.'

Over the road the Bijou had reopened as a peepshow; a dear old pal of mine was 'choreographer' there.

'You should try this; it's better money, and for the same hours,' he told me. But I still didn't fancy the idea, even though a lot of my former Doll's House and Carousel colleagues were peepshow ladies now. I thought I'd stick it out at the strip-club.

All the old regulars were still coming in, except for the ones who'd died. That pest of an Arthur sat in the front row three times a week, just as he had for donkey's years. And he was still up and down the stairs to complain. I figured he must be about a thousand years old by now.

The dressing-room seemed like a ghost town. Practically none of my old friends were there, and nobody seemed to want to hang around in there in between shows the way we used to. The new girls were kids who just came in, did their spot, then fucked off out. I noticed a new breed: a crop of junkies. Kids of sixteen, seventeen, some even younger; doing this job because it gave them the money to buy heroin with . . . which didn't mean that the sex industry turned kids into junkies; oh no. There are plenty of rich junkies – only they've got money; they don't need to hustle or strip to sustain their habit.

It was depressing, all the same. I thought, you poor sods, you've got even less hope than my generation. You have nothing. I hated walking into the shower and finding a young lass shooting up, or puddles of blood and discarded needles in the toilets.

The management had a purge whilst I was back, and cleaned out all the junkies. They were too unreliable anyway. But I still found the place a real downer. Every day in the dressing-room I half-expected to bump into my own ghost; the girl I had been in the old days: raucous, laughing, half-pissed. I imagined I could hear Kitten singing her head off in the shower; her voice echoed in my mind . . . any second now she'd come stomping out with the steam still rising from her pink body, leaving a trail of damp footprints across the floor. I could visualize it so well.

'Where's me talc?' she would bellow.

On the back of the big, gilt-framed mirror, the one that reflected all the dazzling lights at you on-stage, I wrote:

There must be a place up in the sky
where lonely strippers go to die

Don't ask me why I did it; I wasn't even thinking at the time.

I went to see some friends at a peepshow down the road, Mandy and Cass.

'I wouldn't go back stripping now if you paid me,' said Mandy. 'I mean, if you paid me double the wages.'

It's true the girls were making much better wages now – well, not exactly wages. Their peepshow was operating a new scheme. It had only started a couple of weeks previously. Instead of the boss paying the girls £20 for a six-hour shift, he paid them nothing at all.

'Sounds like he's got a good bargain there,' I said.

'No, wait, this is what happens, see,' Mandy explained. 'The punter puts his fifty pence in the slot for two minutes' viewing time, just like before. That's the boss's share. Then the girl who's working to that booth asks the punter if he wants to see "something naughty" . . . 'course he does. So he has to shove a pound note through that little slit beneath the peephole, and that's our wages. You wouldn't believe how much we can make a shift. Because all those bastards naturally want to see our "naughty bits"!'

I had to admit, it was ingenious. The girls were making seventy, eighty pounds a six-hour shift; it took me a week to earn that at the Carousel. That knocked stripping on the head for me.

'They only give you two or three shifts a week,' Cass said. 'Because there's plenty of competition for jobs – and anyway, two or three days of this is *enough*.'

She wasn't kidding. I started there the following week, and it was a real headbanger; it made you feel like half the human race belonged in a loony bin – the male half.

I got two daytime shifts, Tuesdays and Wednesdays. The peepshow was by far the weirdest experience I'd ever had. The weekend before I started, the boss had altered the place slightly so that now there was no 'stage' area, just five seats, each one facing a booth. Velvet curtains separated you from the other girls, although you could pull them back and enjoy a chat during the lull periods. They also took out the letterbox-sized 'peeps' and installed two-way mirrors, so that when a guy entered the booth, you could see him but he couldn't see you. Then as soon as his fifty pence dropped into the slot a bright light went on directly above you and the situation was reversed. That's when you asked for – and mostly got – your 'wages'.

Just underneath the bright light over your head were two handrails. When you got the cash, you had to climb up on to the 'shelf' beneath the two-way mirror, grasp the handrails and literally hang around there, flaunting your stuff. The punter had a worm's eye view, and you didn't see a thing. You were way up there above it all, chatting with your neighbours on either side. It truly was bizarre. We girls were adept at eating kebabs as we worked, and passing bottles of wine along the line and back. At peak hour (between five and six P.M., as always) you were literally hanging up there non-stop. You couldn't hear yourself think for the babble of high-pitched voices:

'Want to see the naughty show?' – 'Are you a tit man or a bum man?' – 'Want to look at my naughty bits?' – 'If you don't want it, please piss off; this is not a charity.'

It was like working on some kind of crazy switchboard.

After my first shift I had blisters on the palms of both my hands through clinging like a bloody monkey to those handrails. My head was splitting with the noise and the lights. My hands and nails were filthy from handling grubby pound notes, many of them torn almost in two through being wrenched through the slit. I had over seventy pounds – dirty money in more ways than one, I laughed to myself. But if those bastards are daft enough, if they have nothing better to do with it, why shouldn't we have it? All those nice, respectable Mr Average-types. Don't forget – we saw them when they first walked into the booths. We knew.

I took my loot to a pub in Cambridge Circus; they were always short of single pound notes there. I got tens and twenties in return.

'A year of this would see us right,' I said to Steve, who was earning good money himself on the lotteries, in the run-up to Christmas. There's always money in money. People didn't have much hope in these days of Madam Maggie, so why not have the odd flutter on a lottery ticket, in the hope that yours would be the £1,000 prize-winner?

I did another three shifts at the peepshow, and it was good; I was laughing all the way to the overdraft. Then – disaster. We were raided.

It was a couple of weeks before Christmas; the cops timed it well. I'd just come off 'stage' and was up in the dressing-room watching TV with a few of the other girls. The door burst open and a wicked-looking bastard stood there.

'All right ladies; you can get dressed now; you'll be coming with us.'

A big groan went up.

'Where to?'

'West End Central.'

The bloody Pit!

Within seconds the building was swarming with cops; plain-clothes and 'nipple-heads', as we called the uniforms. They prodded this and poked that, and radioed up and down the stairs to each other. We were taken out, five of us, and bunged into a van that was parked in the middle of Old Compton Street. The punters vanished as if they'd never existed.

Meanwhile, back in the peepshow, the old bill were engaged in searching the premises, with sledgehammers. I couldn't believe I was off to West End Central again, after fourteen years. The prospect made me gulp.

One of the black girls was crying; she was convinced they were going to give her a good hiding once they got her in there.

'They did last time,' she said.

I remembered my 'Juliet Bravo', the macho bitch who'd belted me that first time, when I was a mystery. All the way to the station, I tried to calm myself down, stop myself from panicking. The Christmas lights in Regent Street didn't help; they were a mockery. I hated them.

I had the same feeling when they took us inside; the same as before. The door closes on you and you're nobody, just a thing with no rights, that they can basically do what the hell they like with. At least this time there were the other girls with me. We bucked each other up.

They threatened us vaguely with keeping us in overnight if we didn't answer their questions. But we were in luck; they weren't interested in us. It was the bosses they were after. They kept us there for several hours, took separate statements from us, strip-searched us . . . we told them nothing. Easy, because we knew *nothing* about the bosses, and wanted to even less. Who needs that aggro? was our motto. Bosses didn't and never have interested me; when all's said and done they're there to bleed money out of anybody they can. They're leeches – just like other bosses. I thought the same about the strip-club bosses as I did about the mill-owners who lived in luxury off the backs of workers like my own mother. Parasites one and all.

The police treated us relatively okay. They didn't slag us off or get stroppy, even though one infant rookie did a double-take when he saw us all sitting in a row outside the cells. He looked at the black girls as if they were lice.

Once we knew we weren't to be charged with anything, we could relax.

'I thought it was too good to last, that money,' Mandy sighed. 'What a pain! You might've waited till after Christmas,' she told the duty officer, who was another slip of a lad.

Just before we were finished a fair-haired young police-woman with a nice smile and a pair of dimples came up and asked us if we wanted a cup of tea! I couldn't help it; I thought, what's a nice girl like you doing in a job like this?

They freed us at ten P.M. We'd been there since four. It felt great to be in freezing Regent Street; the sky was clear and starry, and the Christmas lights looked better than they had a few hours ago. Even a short spell in that dump is enough to make you feel like nothing on earth. We stood there quivering like jellies.

'I *thought* they were watching the joint,' Beatrice said. 'Didn't I say the other night that I could smell that West End Central smell? You know the one I mean . . . sort of a . . . dirty pound notes smell.'

We had a drink together then went our separate ways. A week later the peepshow reopened with a new name and a new frontman. But I was finished. I knew I'd quit for good: had it. Steve was earning; if he hadn't have been, who knows? I probably would've gone back to stripping. But I felt that my West End days were over; those last three years off the scene had for the first time in my life allowed me the space in which to live and breathe; *learn* about myself and what I really wanted to do. I had begun to discover my own potential; a luxury denied to most women of my class and background. I had fought every inch of the way to become a person. I still had no formal education, but I realized that I had been learning all the time, starting with my life, then adding on to it through the writings of others. The little Lancashire mystery was still a part of me; I understood her better now; her and all the others like her, with our bright hopes and dreams, and our frustrations.

I wanted to tell her story; my story. I knew that was where I should begin: with my own life, and then the lives of my friends. All that remained was for me to do it.

Richard
A Stage Manager

I really just drifted into the sex industry because I needed some money and I didn't want to work in a straight job. When I left college I went along to Brook Street jobs bureau and spent a whole day being harangued about how I had to sell my personality to my prospective employer, by this woman in front of a telescreen and a battery of telephones. Then I spent the next day being interviewed in various places in the City as an insurance salesman or an office clerk or what have you, and I just thought, 'What am I doing here?' And so I didn't wait around to see if I was going to be offered a job or not.

I was living in a squat at the time, doing a lot of organizing for the housing co-op there, but that wasn't me at all either. Everyone involved in housing is deadly boring, as are council meetings and all that kind of local politics shit. Anyway I was getting more and more depressed because if you've got no money London is hell on earth. And I had this friend who was working in Soho as a stage manager and he left to go to El Salvador, and so one night I thought, 'I've got to do something about this.' Then the next day I went down to Soho to see if the post was still vacant. And that's how I came to be a strip-club stage manager. I told all my relatives I was a stage manager in a West End theatre. And at last I had enough money to be able to eat something more than just chips.

I must have been the only stage manager in the world never to have seen the show. Between the stage manager's box in the club where I worked, and the stage itself where the girls performed, there was a brick wall about two feet thick. The stage manager's place was part of the dressing-room, in a kind of dungeon underneath the theatre. As far as I was concerned it was the best fucking job I ever had, and I've done all kinds of shit work: factory work, shop work, bar work, all that sort of thing. All I had to do was shift whatever props there were for each number; completely basic, a chair or a bed or sometimes something a bit more elaborate like a dummy of Frankenstein or a paddling pool, that kind of thing. Then I had to put the tape on and switch the lights to the right setting, pull the tabs, and that was it. The rest of the time I had free, while the girl went through the number for eight or nine minutes, because I couldn't see the stage so there was no way they could get away with any fancy production numbers, it was that basic. So I just used to sit and read a book, or chat to the girls, most of whom were really nice to me. I learnt more from them than any book I ever read.

I really admire the girls, I mean, what I feel about them, my admiration and respect for them I couldn't really put into words. Of course you get the occasional wally but most of them, nearly all of them, are incredible people. They have to put up with so much shit; they really live and work under intolerable conditions, and they have such verve and guts – they really show you what it is to be human; to be able to survive all that damage and still be human. I think that's quite an incredible achievement. The ones I particularly admire are the ones like Janis who've brought up kids on their own as well. I feel privileged to know them, because in the ordinary run of my life I would never have met anyone like them. It was only by chance that I stepped out of my class for a little while and found myself in this incredibly heavy, exhilarating world.

The quality of relations between people is completely

different in Soho to what it's like in the straight world. In the straight world everybody has something to hide, and you live with this tension all the time. But in the dressing-room of the club nearly everybody's naked or half-naked, and it's a great leveller. It affects people so that they're more straight with each other. There's a greater frankness and openness and honesty, and the people are tougher because they're more exposed. Everyone's in the same boat, dealing with day to day craziness, so there's nowhere you could hide – no comfortable spaces to hide in like in the straight world. You can't crawl away into yourself because you're all there, exposed, on display. Of course I was a privileged observer, being a stage manager who doesn't have to take his clothes off; but you can't help being drawn into it, because the girls treat you like one of them and expect you to behave the way they do, so really you have to be the same way. And it made me wonder just who the hell I was anyway, you know what I mean? A jumped-up middle-class brat who thought he knew it all. I felt like a babe in arms when I walked into that club.

That's when I really began to think about middle-class morality and all that shit. I began to realize it was lurking there in my shady corners too. And that its basic principle was hypocrisy. Because when you're involved in the sex industry, you see the basic relations between people in our society stripped of all the bullshit, all the glamour and fetishization, and it really made me think about the relationships between men and women in a completely different way. I mean my ideas about falling in love, for example. They were the usual clichés, you know. But when I got involved with a woman in the sex industry it was completely different. There was none of this obsession with each other's bodies which comes with being clothed all the time, and being subjected to the most rigorous policing from childhood onwards, about your own body and everybody else's.

Again there was none of that sort of bullshit romance that you get drummed into you from books and films and so on. It was a completely raw, intense, violent, gut-wrenching feeling. I don't mean it was violent like we used to beat each other up or anything, I mean its intensity was violent – there was so much at stake, because in that situation you're so exposed. When the whole of society is shitting on you, being loved by one individual becomes a matter of life and death, when it actually happens. This feeling was completely new to me, completely unexpected; it took me by the scruff of the neck and turned me round and at a stroke it cut me off from my past life, and threw me forward into a future I just wasn't prepared for. Nothing had prepared me for it. It was really like that; like vertigo, exciting and frightening at the same time.

That's another thing about Soho. Everybody there takes you at face value – there's none of this shit about, 'Oh hello, what do you *do*?' that you get in the straight world. In the straight world people like to pigeonhole you, imprison you in some stereotype, define you according to what job you do, your function, because they can't deal with existence, the fact that you exist and change from second to second. In Soho you can be what you like, say what you like, do what you like. Within limits of course. But there's none of the bullshit. If you wanted to you could treat yourself as a total blank and completely reinvent yourself from the toes upwards. You feel that free.

It's frightening if you come from a middle-class background like mine, because no matter how much you may want to exist, from childhood you have it drummed out of you; not by force so much – although there's that as well – but mainly by the more subtle means of offering rewards for being a good boy, conforming with straight standards of good behaviour. It sounds like a prison, and it is. In Soho you have to start to exist. You're subject to all these incredibly powerful pressures, of which the place itself is just one, and you're really thrown back on your own resources. That's the only place you're going to find any strength from, not from any bullshit standards of behaviour, stiff upper lip or any of that, you know, the celebrated cool. You have to dig right down into your human core and come up with something real and strong pretty soon, or you're done for. That's what I meant to say earlier, really, about being human under such great pressure. My generation and my milieu, people are soft; they've had it easy, they haven't lived; but at the same time, and because of this, they're incredibly hard underneath. I mean a brittle, rigid hard; and that's their egoism. There are exceptions of course, but like all exceptions they're few and far between, and they prove the rule. That's what you find if you scratch the nice, polished surface; you find an insane, insatiable egoism.

But in the sex industry people aren't like that. They don't have to protect themselves against illusions. They have to protect themselves against realities, and so they're more real. And so they're more spontaneous, more generous both practically and emotionally, more fun, and much easier to get on with. Because when a whole society's busy denying your humanity, what else can you defend yourself with but that humanity? That's all you've got, isn't it?

I wanted to say something else about the morality thing, and this has probably been said before, but so what, nobody seems to have got it yet. As I said, the basic principle of straight morality, the basic thing is hypocrisy. Because once you set up a norm, and then say everybody must conform to this norm or they're deviants and criminals, or sick, you're involved in a vast, unending police operation, because norms don't really exist. Any imbecile can tell you just by looking at it, that 'normal' sexuality in the human race is a chimera. And in the sex industry the evidence of your senses is inescapable. None of that shit about reality itself being bizarre and fantastic; it's just normal for our society and our time, the whole thing, the whole craziness of it. I say craziness because it's a social system, a whole world leaning on you with its vile system of buying and selling, and its power and domination structure, and it's trying to destroy your humanity, trying to make you into a thing; passive, usable, disposable. Something you can wipe your arse with and throw away – and that's what this society is about, and that's its core. Its basic morality, a morality accepted, it seems, by everyone in the straight world, and especially those in positions of privilege and power, its basic morality is its constant pressure to turn you into a thing.

This to me is the most immoral thing. And all this policing of the conscience and of sexual practices is so much bullshit, because all it is is a reign of terror and ignorance, in the midst of a society which loudly proclaims itself as being free. So the straight morality operates on this bullshit principle. I'm not saying it goes against itself, although it does. What I'm saying is that the bullshit, the hypocrisy and double standards, that's the most important thing about it. Without them, it wouldn't exist. It has to create mystique about things, about sex and bodies and about power and about buying and selling, or it couldn't exist. But when you land in the sex industry, where all the relations between people appear naked, then you see it for what it is. In Soho you can't get away from the power of money and straight society and the buying and selling of people's bodies. There's no glamour, mystique, romance, bullshit.

Only the punters don't know that, whether they're punters for sex or punters for morality. Wankers or Whitehouses, they're two sides of the same coin. Take the punters who want to buy sex. Because they've got money they have a fantasy, and they think they can buy that fantasy. They think money can magically transform their wish into reality. But you can't buy people; and that's why they keep coming back for more, because they can't get satisfaction. What they're after is an illusion, and after they've had their little wank it dissolves into thin air. They rip themselves off willingly, the stupid sods, and there's all these people around waiting to jump on the cash they throw away in the process. Sex industry bosses have got it made. It's like heroin, it's a never-ending demand once you get on the merry-go-round.

As for the Whitehouses and the Thatchers, don't talk to me about them, they're worse. These people are evil.

It's very heavy, life in Soho. In those streets you feel as if the whole city is bearing down on you. There's no escape. It really is a ghetto. There's a tangible violence in the air, that all the straight people drifting across Soho Square don't see or feel, even though it's going on right under their noses. I'll never forget one night when we went into the Crown & Two Chairmen and Scottish Ian was there. He was pissed out of his head, and he started off doing magic tricks like sticking a cigarette through his jumper, and ended up waving his new knife around – a really nasty little weapon. I felt really uncomfortable because not only was he pissed, but he seemed to be on a knife-edge, as if he was just waiting for someone to give him a little push, and he'd go over the edge and start actually using this knife. I thought it was a really dangerous situation.

And there was that time when John, that huge bloke, went berserk in the Lido, and smashed all the optics and the mirrors behind the bar – some lovers' tiff, it was – that really put the shits up me. So the violence is always there, running along under the surface, but it's always ready to break out, and you never know when or where; and living with that not knowing, it's very wearing. The only way to cope really is the booze. That was the only way to make it bearable. Given that you could have a great time. An explosive mixture.

Looking back now, as I've hardly dared to do these past years, I'd say it completely changed me, that spell in Soho. It ruined me for straight society; I didn't like it much anyway, but now I can't stand it. So I feel a sort of exile. That's what you become when you get into Soho. It'll change you so much you don't recognize yourself any more. But I wouldn't have been without it. Without it I wouldn't have lived; I'd still know next to nothing.

Yasmin
A Prostitute Woman

When I first left school I started off working in an office; it was what I'd wanted to do; I'd even been to night school for two years, training as a typist. After about eight to ten weeks I got so bored with it – nothing to do, except type a few letters every day and that was that, so I left. I was sixteen. Then I got a job in a factory, that lasted half a day – a cutlery factory. I couldn't hack that, so I left that, because it just wasn't me. I thought it was time to broaden my horizons, so I went to London and got a job in a hotel, as a chambermaid, which lasted at least a year. It was hard work, but it was all right. Then I met a girl who'd previously done stripping and she said that you could earn a lot better money, so she put me on to that. I was a bit naïve, I suppose, but willing to give anything a try . . . and I did.

She showed me the ropes. I went for an audition and got the job. I stripped for three years. I didn't like it really; it had its drawbacks – but then again, I did have *fun*, I'm not gonna dispute that, but it was hard work, there was mental stress. What caused the stress was doing something you don't really want to do, but you've no other chance of making it. If you want money and you want the finer things in life . . . Why shouldn't we have the finer things in life? I want them. And I've not got an education; I've no career, so what is there left? Work in a factory? I'm not gonna do that. So that was that. I kept at it. I mean, there's got to be a thousand and one jobs that people don't like doing, but they do them, and stripping is just another job – I didn't like doing it but I did it, because of the money.

Most of the girls I worked with were very nice, and they were from all different backgrounds and countries. What I didn't like about the job was being looked at as some sort of lower species. We weren't classed as anything; we were looked down upon. And knowing that we were on-stage and the punters could talk amongst themselves, or jeer at you, or take the piss, and we had to put up with that sort of thing used to annoy me more than anything. And also, knowing what the punters got up to, especially the ones that were sat in the front row, with the bowler hat over – whatever – giving you the eye as if we're really enjoying doing what we're doing, and knowing that we're exciting them. When deep down, it just made me puke . . . *puke*. No it did not turn me on, not in the slightest. I wanted to be sick on them. Little do they know that when I used to dance on the stage I used to think all sorts, like what am I gonna do tonight? What outfit can I buy? What am I cooking for Sunday dinner? All that sort of thing.

What made me decide to stop stripping? I didn't think at first that it was because I'd had enough. The main reason was for my little girl's sake. I just thought Soho was not a good environment for her to be brought up in; she was my prime concern. Although, when I stopped, I did realize that I *had* in fact had enough of stripping, but it was for my daughter's sake more than anything.

I came out of the West End and went into a mother and baby home, because the guy I was going out with at the time was straight, and he got me away from the West End. But that didn't last very long because I was unhappy. But I did have a break for a few months, and then I started working on Park Lane, and I worked on Park Lane for a year. It was great, funnily enough; say for the first six months. It was a new experience and it wasn't so much frightening or anything, because we always worked in pairs. It was the fact that it was novel to me, and for me it was good because I got to go into fabulous apartments. I got to meet really interesting people from *all* walks of life, from pilots to biochemists. And we used to have a laugh on the street; it was actually funny, running away from the law; it was exciting; it was great fun – like being a mischievous child all over again. As I say, that was for the first six months, and I wasn't afraid, because – well, I was young then, and you've got a lot of bottle when you're young; you're very gutsy. You didn't think about it. But after six months went by and I got pulled by the police, it seemed to shake me up a little bit – what you have to go through when you're in the police station. The sarcasm of the law; it's always the same, you've always got some nasty jokes to put up with. I'm not saying that they treat you badly, but you can do without the sly remarks; their 'humour'.

They give you three cautions; on the third time you get picked up, you're then charged with prostitution and sent to court. That never happened to me, because after I got picked up twice, I didn't want it to happen again so I was fortunate: I met some Arabs who I got on very well with, and I stuck with them for a while, and I didn't have to go back on the street. I worked through six months without being picked up at all, and then I got two cautions within a week; it all happened at once.

I think the law's wrong. Why should it be that way? If a woman wants to go into a night-club and let a guy buy her drinks all night, isn't that a form of selling herself? But for what – a lousy few drinks? I'd rather have the cash in my purse, if you don't mind, and do without all the booze. I mean, I could go out and be picked up every night, but I've got self-respect. Now although I go and

work, and get money for it, I still respect myself because
I am not *giving it away*. *My* way of meeting someone,
and giving it away 'free', is caring for someone, and that
person caring for me. This that I'm doing is a job and it's
services rendered, I'm afraid, just like you would sit
behind a desk in an office and put hours in. I put work
into it as well; I might go and give someone half an hour
of my time: I want paying for that, if you don't mind. It's
just a different job, that's all. I basically think that
society's attitudes to people like me are Victorian, straight
out of the last century.

But the bad experiences . . . One time in Park Lane,
there was a punter. He raped me, really – made me do
something I didn't want to do. The thing was, he looked
the part. Very 'respectable'; he'd got a beard and he
smoked a pipe . . . it was the pipe that made me think
that he was a very placid man. And what happened was
he turned out to be a heartless bastard. He said he'd got
an apartment in Maida Vale, and what happened was, he
was driving me there and I suddenly realized that he
didn't turn on to the road to Maida Vale, and we ended
up on something like a motorway, or a flyover. I said,
'Look – we've passed the sign' and he said 'It's all right, I
know where we're going'. We ended up pulling up near a
golf course, an isolated spot, and I knew straight away.
I'd got a feeling that something dreadful was about to
happen. When he was driving I couldn't be brave and
open the door and jump out of the car because he was
doing about 60 mph; I couldn't do that. So I just had to
sit back and wait. He started turning, he went really
weird, like a psychopath. I got annoyed and started telling
him off, and the *next* thing he said was 'You've got a
black pimp, and isn't he from Leeds?' By this time I
thought, my God the man's *crazy*, and what's gonna

happen to me? And his eyes looked really shifty and frightening.

Then he said, look come on, you're gonna do this, you're gonna do that, and he made me do oral sex. I just went along with it, but that's still rape in my book. I was frightened to death. If the guy had left his keys in the car I would definitely have taken the car away and escaped like that, because he did get out of the car to urinate, but he took the keys with him. Anyway, I did what he told me to do, which lasted five minutes, and then he said 'Now get out of this car you bastard'. So out I got and he drove off, and as he drove off I had to sneer and shout at him, just to get the frustration out of me. And I was just totally in the middle of nowhere. It was black, there were no lights, no roads, and I thought God! I'd got a summer dress on and a cardigan, and I thought what the hell am I gonna do? But being a strong person as I am, I went on to a main road, crying my eyes out, flagged down this van, and made some cock-and-bull story up about being dumped by a guy I'd met in a night-club. He took me all the way home to Hammersmith, dropped me right outside the flat.

I didn't go to the police because – you're joking! – I wouldn't've stood a chance. For a start I'd've had to have made a story up. I wouldn't have been able to say I were a prostitute because immediately I would have been the one on trial, for what I did. And it would have been *my* fault. So it would have been pointless. That whole experience was dreadful; it knocked me back. I didn't do any work for months and months.

As for the job itself, I totally disagree with people who say we're just passive, like dolls. I will not be treated in that way at all. I'm a human being, and we're just gonna get back to the point that it's a job, and I won't be treated like an animal; I'm not one. It's the media that puts us across as dogs, as animals. They make me angry. There are many different forms of prostitution. Now, film stars aren't classed as prostitutes, but they are. They are selling their bodies to get into a good movie, to have a good script. They screw producers and directors to get the part, but they're not condemned for it. And when they're in the parts, they're still selling themselves. And TV hostesses; they sell themselves. Why do they need a pretty female at the side of videos and televisions, on those game shows? Why? To sell them.

Punters, now. They make me feel sick. They make me feel ill. Imagine having to lie with somebody you don't want to be with, with no feelings whatsoever. Some of them are grotesque; fat – horrible. But I must say the majority treat me like a human being; I *make* them. You'll get the odd one that's flash, but most of them are all right. A large percentage I would say are married men: eighty per cent easy. Most come to prostitutes because they don't want to form a relationship; they don't want to get involved with another woman. They want to get what most men want – a bit on the side, which they get, and then they want to go home and forget about it; turn their backs on the sauna or the girl they picked up on the street, and go back to their wives. They just want no involvement at all. It suits them very well.

Society will never be able to stop prostitutes as long as there's punters. And there will always be punters; there's always men that want sex outside of marriage. And with us, they have always something to fulfil their needs. As long as we need the money.

It's the posh ones who have the weirdest requirements. I used to have a regular customer, ex-public school, and he used to want to be caned, and he also used to want to spank a woman. He was about forty-five, married. I've got a customer now who is 'happily married', he says, but he's bored with his wife. He says she's a contented housewife who's done a good job bringing his children up, but she doesn't want to know about sex. They sleep in single beds; he's still raring to go, wants an exciting sex-life; she can't give it him. She does not want to know. Maybe she's too tired after doing all the fucking housework. So he comes to see me.

Some of the punters are all right, but the majority – well, I suppose I don't like them because I don't like doing what I do, but sometimes you can talk to them and they're all right. Some of them are nice people. And you get some that are really young as well. What explains an eighteen-year-old coming to a sauna for a massage? You get all ages. But the customers are nearly *all* middle-class. Ninety-nine per cent. Not the working class. And you do get the ones who come in for psychology; they want a shoulder to cry on; someone to talk to. Then there's the odd old gentleman that can't do anything but cuddle you. They just want that bit of comfort. They've probably been married for forty years, and their wife has died, and so they come for a bit of love and affection. And you really don't mind giving it, because the old folks are no problem at all. They're so gentle and loving. Society abandons old people, and then they become lonely.

Basically, I think you are pushed into prostitution. You're *pushed* into doing it, because if you come from a working-class background, and your father's worked in the mill all his life, and put in twenty-two hours' overtime to keep a large family, and you're the eldest, you then find that you leave school early, as quick as you can, to earn money to help the family. So then you've got no education behind you. What sort of job can you do? Go in a factory . . . who wants to go in a factory? If you like wearing nice clothes, being feminine . . . People say we're degrading ourselves, but why is that? Because I take money? See, I'm getting back to *that* again. I'm 'degrading' myself because I take money from customers, but if I want to go and lie on my back after I've picked up a guy from a night-club, I'm *not* degrading myself, because I've not taken any money. It's the money part of it that gets up people's noses. I would like to pay taxes, because at least if I paid taxes I could stand up and say what everybody else does: I'm a citizen, I'm paying my taxes, so therefore don't come and dictate to me. It doesn't matter *what* I do for a living. I harm nobody. I wish it were legal – but I wouldn't like to work in a state brothel; oh no.

If you want to talk about 'degrading', well, I say that it's degrading to have to work in a loo, cleaning somebody else's shit from the bowl, washing the bowl out, things like that. But that's not 'degrading', is it, to people that are not prostitutes?

It annoys me that I'm classed as a leper, classed as being thick because I do this work; it is annoying. I certainly wouldn't have gone halfway round the world if I hadn't been a prostitute. I wouldn't have been to Barbados, I wouldn't have stayed at the Ritz in Paris, all the best hotels everywhere I went, like Monte Carlo . . . and be bought the finest clothes, and eaten the finest food. I've been all over the place; I wouldn't have done all that – no way.

Another thing that annoys me is that, okay, a prostitute earns a lot of money, and at the end of the year, she earns what for example a surgeon might earn. She's on thousands. Yet you can't go and get a mortgage on a house; you can't get bank loans and things like that, and yet there's more guarantee of getting the money back from a prostitute than there would be from somebody working an ordinary nine till five job.

I mean really, deep down I wouldn't like to think that I would be lying on my back and half of what I earn is going to be paid in taxes, but you're forced into saying you want to pay taxes through what society has built up around prostitution. You want something to throw back at them. Because, okay, when it comes down to it, you're already paying taxes for everything you buy: food, drink, cigarettes, clothes. But you want civil liberties, like other people.

Doing this job makes you a lot wiser and a lot less naïve; you just won't be taken in by bullshit. Because you *know* men; you know the crap they come out with; you know that, in straight life, they are only saying to you what they know a woman wants to hear. Which is a load of bull, generally. You see, you are with men *all* the time; you know exactly where they're coming from. You're always one step ahead of them. And the only time you can be taken in by a man is when you're deeply deeply in love with somebody, but even then, in the back of your mind you know where he's coming from. It's just that you're so madly in love that you can't do much about it at the time. Until you get over it.

People think 'prostitute' – and that's it, you can't be anything else. But I don't act like a 'prostitute' when I am a prostitute – the stereotype chewing gum, looking brassy, overdoing the make-up – suspenders, black stockings. That's the media again; that's the man's fantasy anyway. It's what the media have made a prostitute out to be.

If I were to walk into a room and there were half a dozen people in that room and I said to them I was a model or a hairdresser, they would take no notice. But as soon as I said 'I'm a prostitute' they'd either be shocked and wouldn't believe it or they'd think well, she could be – but the whole attitude of every single one in that room would automatically change. They'd like me until I said I was a prostitute, then everything would change. But why should it? I am *me*, not my job; and I'm still *me* at work. I'm the one who draws the line at work; I decide what I will and will not do, most certainly I do. Nobody rules over me.

Having said that, it is true that the job gets to you sometimes. Oh definitely. I carry a lot of stress, mental stress, and nobody, but nobody, could ever understand that, except me. Because – I don't know about other girls, there must be thousands of them that feel the same – when I was younger it was different. When I was nineteen or twenty and I worked that year on the Lane, it didn't bother me one bit; I was having a good time – making money, spending it. *Now*, as I'm doing it, all I think about is what I am doing, and why. I think that is because I don't want to do it, but I just don't see a way out at the moment. Sometimes I have gone and cried in a corner on my own. My daughter's been in bed, and I've cried for an hour. Because if I don't let it out of my system that way, let it escape that way, God knows what would happen. And sometimes I've had to have a break for a couple of weeks or even a couple of months, because I can't handle it. And I never know when that's gonna happen, because it's a slow build-up. I probably might walk around one day, and I'm feeling all het-up, maybe it's the day I've had. But all these days add up into weeks and months, and then all of a sudden I might be at work one day and I just freak out, and I might just leave. I take off. Because at that particular time I don't care whether or not I've got a job to come back to. I just want out, and when I want out, I've got to have out. I've got to go. So all this bullshit about how people say that it doesn't bother us, for us to do it in the first place means we've got no morals, no respect – that's a load of rubbish;

that's a load of codswallop. Because nobody has got more respect for themselves than I have for myself: I've got a lot of self-respect.

There's nothing I would like more than to be in the company of a caring man, to meet somebody, and to be loved by somebody. Why the hell haven't I been going out, raving-up, looking for men? It's been a year, and I can honestly say that in that year I have slept with *one* man. It was for one night – and it might as well have been a punter, for what went off. Now you tell me how many of these strait-laced bitches can do that? And they can condemn *me*? They can condemn me, because I work as a prostitute, and I've been almost celibate for one year? And it's not the fact that I'm working as a prostitute that's made me go out and look for somebody, because my work doesn't turn *me* on. I'm not saying I've not had the odd client that I've wanted, that has been good-looking and had a decent body, but that's rare and it's when *I've* wanted to.

It's all right for a man, a man can get it off whenever he wants, but for a woman it takes more than just a man being undressed. A woman's got to feel stimulated; she's got to be loved and emotionally involved. And she can only feel like that if she feels for that person that she's with, so it's not my job that's made me not go out and look for a guy. Men can cut themselves off from their bodies. They must be able to if they can walk into a situation, walk into a sauna where they've never met a girl, she's a stranger, yet five minutes later they find themselves in the situation where there's two bodies naked and you find that you're having sex with them . . . and a guy can do it; a guy can get it off like that. Women need more than that.

What choices would I have had if I hadn't become a stripper and then a prostitute? Not a lot, my dear, without any qualifications. Not a lot. Probably stacking shelves in a supermarket, or let me see . . . some other really exciting job like that. I have no regrets about my life at all; it's made me a woman of the world. I've had some fantastic experiences that I would not have had otherwise. Straight society? I think that they should leave us alone to get on with what we want to do, and they should think that without girls like us, the number of rapes would multiply like you wouldn't believe. Probably child-molesters would increase, because as stupid as it sounds, you get punters that come in and they talk about children. You tend to think that it's one of their little fantasies, to go with a child. Though it's annoying there's nothing you can do about it; you either tell them to shut up or – it depends how you feel about it. Lots of things would happen without prostitutes. Lots. And what's more, it's the people that condemn us most who are the ones who're coming to see us, so what's all the fuss? I don't know why they make out it's so bad. There's a damn sight more punters than there are prostitutes, I can tell you that.

I like to feel that in doing the work I'm doing, I'd like to have something at the end of it – a house, some security. I might still be doing it in six months. I might still be doing it in six years, who knows? It just depends. I mean, if there's nothing better around the corner, well I probably will just hang on to a few regular punters and keep it that way. Just keep a hundred pound a week coming into the house.

There's a lot more girls working now, because of the unemployment. It's high; so high, and it's not getting any better with Thatcher in government. We're not gonna get anywhere, because she's not working for us, for the working class at all. Not at all, she's not doing *anything*; she's doing it all for the right-wingers, the middle-class and upper-class people. People that have got money already. So she will make the prostitution scale go high: sky-high. In fact she's already doing it.

And it's all so hypocritical, because the judge can sit there on the bench and fine a girl £400. Then if she comes up another time, he'll fine her a few thousand pounds. And how's she gonna pay those fines? He's sending her out on to the streets, because you've got to go and earn it that way to pay the fines. It's a vicious circle. So that makes the government a pimp, because the money that's going into the courts is what *they* call 'dirty money', isn't it? Hypocrites. So really, the girls are paying *well* over the odds, never mind taxes. And the judges themselves go to prostitutes, some of them. As a matter of fact, I'm seeing a barrister at the moment, who works in Crown Court. Now that's hypocrisy to the highest degree, isn't it just?

We work damned hard, and we get a lot of stick. People say 'easy money', but how can it be easy money when you don't want to do what you're about to do? You take it home with you, you think about it. It's all right saying 'I've switched off; I'm home now' but you don't switch off. It's still in your subconscious or buried somewhere. Sometimes I've been made to feel dirty. I have. Why should I feel like that? It's only because of what society has made. Why should I feel dirty if I'm watching a programme on TV and they've got prostitutes on it, in the little squalid rooms, and they're being really brassy? That just does not go on. People don't realize that some of our customers love to wine and dine you, take you to expensive restaurants; they don't just leave it there. And they want to talk, about anything *but* your job, and just act as normal human beings. Which is what you are.

Men call us 'whores' and 'slags' but really it's them. They are condemning us for the job that they make happen. Because without them, there wouldn't be us.

I'll tell you what the most common question is, from the punter to the prostitute: '*Do you think it's a fair size? Is it average?*' Until I did this sort of job I never knew that the man had such a hang-up about his size, but believe me, ninety per cent of the men ask that question: 'Is this average? Or what would you think; is it big or small or what? Please tell me . . .'

From every age, that is the most common question. And the second most common is: '*Do you enjoy it?*'

And you say – well, I tell them the truth: 'Look, it's a job, and that is it.'

And sometimes I lose them; or the man might have had an erection and it just fizzles away through me saying that. Now that means more hard work for me, but I won't lie; *I will not lie to the prats*. I tell them the truth.

The punters really do think that we are so experienced sexually, but do you think a prostitute gains sexual experience from lying on her back and blanking her mind off? Because I don't. Not at all. You do not gain experience of sexuality from being a prostitute; as far as I'm concerned, you've either got sensuality or you haven't. It all comes from within you. It's not just how you screw. It's as simple as that. You don't gain experience by lying on your back and going with men you don't want to be with. It annoys me when customers say that to you; when they expect that you're going to be what they call a 'go-er'; that you're gonna be good in bed. It really riles me. Men are beginning to feel inferior as times move on, because it is getting a little bit better for women – but not much. Men are gullible, and I mean men of all ages; there's no age limit to being gullible. And they're also stupid, and illogical. When two people get together and have sex, I mean *real* sex, it's always the woman who gets condemned for it, but not the man. Why should we get called 'slag' when we're both doing it, the man and the woman?

The usual way of doing the sex at work is you just lying on your back and doing nothing. But sometimes they ask you if you would go on top, and that annoys me. It is good in a sense that there's not that much physical contact because they're not lying all over you, but if you're on top, it's you that has to do all the work, and I personally don't agree with having to work and giving him that much pleasure. That's getting too involved. And when sex is finished, and they've still got an erection, I take great pleasure in getting my own back in a small way. What I do is, I slap it really hard; I slap their penis, and the initial shock starts sending it down; it starts withering. Then the punter goes: 'Ow! That was a bit strong, wasn't it?' And I say, 'Well, you can't walk out there with an erection now, can you?' I tell them: 'It doesn't look very nice'.

And when they're doing it I'm counting the money I've made so far. All the time as I'm going along, I'm calculating what I've made up to that point. On the odd occasion I feel, I think about the actual person on top of me, but if I were to fix my mind on that all the time, then I really would go crazy. I wouldn't be able to cope. You've got to be able to blank it off. But from time to time it just hits me about the person that I'm with, although I do try to keep up that mental barrier. So that it doesn't get to you every single time you're doing it with somebody. Your earnings keep you in spirit.

There aren't any time limits in the sauna; it's entirely up to you, from the minute they enter the room. It's your shrewdness that decides how long they're gonna be. I give them forty minutes at the most, from the massage through to whatever, and if by that time they haven't achieved anything, it's just a case of me picking the money up and saying 'I'm sorry'. But there are ways you can do it; you don't just say, 'Well, fuck off, I've had enough now'. You have to be a bit more sensitive than that: 'Look, I'm ever so sorry; it's really got to stop.' You can do that, and get away with it. You always get away with it, so that's no hassle. They're at your mercy, regardless of whether they actually make it or not. I don't mind spending a bit longer if I'm being paid for the time. But you don't get a lot of them like that in any case; it's normally about twenty minutes, from the beginning of the massage right through. Sometimes you might chat with them for five minutes after; I do anyway. That's when I know them and they are regulars that come in once or twice a week. To a certain extent you do form a relationship with those types – a working relationship. They talk about their wives – complain, usually – whatever.

There's just a massage-couch in the room, and there's also a chair that can be pulled down into a bed, but it's not often you use that because that means there's more involvement. Before you know it, you're in a position where they can take more advantage, in the sense that they can try to be loving or want you to put a bit more into it. Whereas if you're on a hard massage couch, it's very slender, and there's not a great deal you can do on it; you're restricted. And it's better that way.

Two years ago, when I first started in the sauna, there was this guy that used to come in and we nicknamed him the 'Courgette Man'. Anyway, he used to come in, week in week out, with panties, stockings, suspender belt, waspie: all brand new every single time he came in – the full kit, the biggest size you could get, because this was a pretty big, stocky bloke. Another middle-class wally. And when you went upstairs he always used to ask: 'Can you give me ten minutes on my own?' Then you'd walk into the room and he'd be there in all the gear, in the basque, in the stockings, in the suspenders. With a sanitary towel strung in between his legs. He'd have a bottle of Atrixo hand cream; he'd have his own Durex; he'd have a couple of courgettes – this is all the tackle he used to bring. And he'd even have pads – falsies – in the bra part. He used to want to caress you and that, and he'd put your hand on this basque thing he'd got on, and you didn't know what the fuck to do . . . whether to caress it, or am I stupid doing this, or what? What do I do? And he wanted to be messed around his backside with the courgettes – Brown-Eye, we called it.

Well, I did him a few times and then it was really puzzling me, and I thought 'Sod this; the very next time he comes here I'm really gonna ask him *why* he wants all this'. And I did. I said, 'Look – tell me to shut up if I'm being too personal, but what sort of reaction do you want from me when I walk into this room and see you dressed like this? Do you want me to be startled, or act normal, or what?' And we really got talking, and I'm telling you, this was one fucked-up guy. He says, 'Look, this is my fantasy. I'm not gay and I never will be; I love my family. This is what I want. I don't want to go to a doctor, then get sent to another doctor, then on to a psychiatrist . . . I just want to do *this*.' And he thanked me for talking to him, but then he never came back to me again, because I believe my knowing his little secret, well, I got too close, that's what it was.

I worked at another sauna before this one, and it got raided. They'd planned it at the right time, when the shift was due to change over, so they'd get a lot more girls. I was working at the time and honestly, I'm not exaggerating, there must have been at least twenty police – at least. They came from every exit – there were about four customers in the sauna at the time – and they just charged in like the Sweeney. It was as if we were armed robbers or something. They sectioned everything off and officers came to each of the girls and made sure they were hovering over us and all that rubbish. They went running around, looking upstairs in the bathroom for proof. If I'd've been a little bit wiser I'd've gone straight over and picked the phone up and rung a solicitor, and said to the officers that they were not taking me unless they charged me with something, because under the law I'd be free to go otherwise. But no, I let them walk all over me; it all happened so fast; you're not given a lot of time to think, 'what can I do?' My handbag was searched, and we had to put up with the policewomen with the medical gloves on, fishing down the toilets for used Durex . . .

I got taken to the station at five o'clock, and I didn't get out of there until twelve o'clock that night – because we were all separated, put into rooms and interviewed. All they wanted was your boss; to try and catch him for pimping. 'Come on, how much money has he took from you girls?' that sort of thing. But it wasn't so much a question of being loyal, because the boss wasn't worth being loyal to; but who needs the police and the courts on their backs? And that's what would've happened to me, so it was through not giving in to them that I was there so long. Till eventually there wasn't anything they could do. I did make a statement, but it wasn't the one they wanted me to make. And immediately the next morning I rang my solicitor and asked him if I could have my statement retracted, because what they had got from me was under duress. So we filed a complaint, and the statement was retracted.

Nobody needs to tell me how much the sauna boss made out of us. I'm not stupid; I worked it out for myself. But there's nothing we can do about it as the law stands now. That's the price you have to pay for not working on the street. You've got a lot more security; you feel safer. It's much less dangerous. Where I work now it's not the case that we have to pay so much anyway. We pay just fifteen pounds a week to work there, and that is to cover advertising, things like that.

My daughter is the number one in my life. She is – well it sounds unfair to say that she's the reason why I do what I do, because she isn't. But then again, she is. And, as much as *I* want nice things, I also want the best for her. I like coming home from work and coming to my daughter, being her mother, playing with her, cooking for her, and keeping a lovely home. I like to sit and read with her, and she's really a loveable child. I won't spoil her even though she does get the best; she also has to learn the value of money. I just don't throw everything on her as if money grows on trees; I'm not going to make it as easy as that, because I work bloody hard for it.

If somebody met me, and got to know me for a couple of weeks, and didn't know what I do for a living, I can guarantee he would say to me 'You're a nice person, and you're a lovely mother, and I think you're bringing up your child in the right way'. Because there would not be the prejudice. I do not lie to my daughter, in the sense that I tell her I work in an hotel; I meet some people, and I help them, and it's true. I do lie by omission, though, obviously. Let's just say that now, I'm working as a prostitute in order to give my child a good education, so that *my* child has got something to look forward to. Because it's education that counts in this world, if you want a decent life. Which brings me back to what I said at the beginning: the choice that we've got in the working class; the life that we're forced into.

We prostitutes might all be different in our own ways, but I think the main thing is that we all give each other love and kindness. Little things like kindness, generosity, consideration, respect – we give each other all those things. It helps you get through. We don't do what we're meant to do, toe the line as working-class women, but – why the hell should we? We're not just brought into this life for – what? – reproduction and to cater for men? Why? Why can't we go our own way as well, and be independent? And earn money, and make a better life for ourselves, and our children.

Cathy
A Peepshow Dancer

I've done the lot: stripping, the peepshows, and nude encounter. Right now I'm in the peepshow. I don't want particularly to talk about my personal life, because that is private. I keep my home life very much independent from this; well I try to. I will say this: I first came to the West End when I was a kid, fourteen, actually. Yes, a runaway. I'm twenty-nine now. I kept getting taken back, put in homes, and so on, but I kept leaving them, running away again. I hate institutions. They put me in a borstal at one time when I hadn't even done anything wrong. It was just that they had nowhere else to put me, so they shoved me in there. What a liberty!

There is no common denominator about liking or loathing a club. I think it's universally accepted that you hate the punters. It's funny because I didn't mind the Carnival. But I couldn't go back stripping again. I never minded the Carnival; maybe it was the stage wasn't so close to the punters; the lighting, or something. I didn't mind the Doll's House because they were such little imbeciles in there, it didn't matter. Their opinions and views on you were irrelevant, because you thought, well they're such cretins anyway. The Sunset, though, I really hated, because it was meant to be like the poor man's Paul Raymond's – and all that crap about rehearsing. But at the end of the day, they were just wankers sitting in those seats. They weren't there to see an 'up-market' show, they were there to see tit'n'arse and everything else.

But I never liked stripping. I always felt self-conscious,

and – maybe it's the way you're brought up or something, I don't know what puts these ideas into your head – I felt perhaps it was wrong, and why was I doing it, and at the end of the day was it worth it for the money? And you just look at those people and you think, 'God, what am I doing here with people like you watching me take my clothes off, masturbating in the front row?' Yeah, because I wouldn't tolerate it on a bus or anything, I'd get up and hit them! I'd kill them! So why am I on-stage tolerating the same thing? Because they paid three quid to get in and they're paying my wages.

I used to get on the Sunset stage and the lights were bright, and it was a big, weird stage, and you could see your customers. Like a half moon. And I used to get on that stage and I used to – you know when you can't stop yourself sweating? It's a subconscious thing, and not my body, but my whole face used to pour with sweat. And it got to the stage where it was so bad there, I hated that place so much, that I had these ruses. I used to walk on the stage and go 'OW!' – make out I'd trodden on a bit of glass so that I couldn't carry on and they had to pull the curtains. Or, I used to pay the back-stage manager half of my spot money to write that I'd done my spot in the book when I hadn't done it. It was that bad in the end. I didn't like the management there, didn't like some of the people who worked there, and I don't have to mention *them* (the punters), they were the pits. They don't even come in the same breath as staff and those you work with, do they? Oh no.

We used to earn a better living in those days. We used to have two or three wage packets. You could always put a pay packet away. Can't now, it's survival money. Because of the 'Clean Up Soho' campaign. In the old days, you had a lot of strip-clubs, so if you had any trouble in one you just walked round the corner and got another job in a different one. That's why people here don't want to be interviewed by the media, they don't want to talk, they don't want their photo shown, because now, basically, you've got three strip-clubs left, and some peepshows, things like that. So if you get the sack or walk out of a job you can't just easily walk into another.

You know what you feel inside, and you also semi-dislike yourself for not standing up and saying, 'Well shit! I'm not going to take this!' But the other half of you says, 'Don't be such a silly bastard; you've always been known for having a big mouth, but you need the money you're going to get at the end of the week.' You've got rent to pay, you've got to live. I mean, what I'm earning now, in the peeps, I could probably go and earn in Tesco's, and half of my head says, 'Do it.' Maybe you lose confidence when you haven't worked in a straight job for a while, or you think: you're going to go for this job and they're going to say, 'What have you been doing for X amount of years?' And you're going for a job behind a till in a supermarket, saying, 'Oh well actually, I've been dropping my drawers for the last eight years' . . . 'Oh yes, Mrs M., don't call us, we'll call you!'

Always, stripping, you get two questions from men. They say, 'Does it turn you on?' and, 'How much money do you earn?' Or they say, 'How much money do you earn?' then, 'Does it turn you on?' And you say, 'No, it doesn't turn me on – my pay-packet turns me on.'

Another thing, the thing that's always levelled at you is, 'Oh well, there are other ways of making a living.' Yeah, there are – but they're no, better. At least when you're stripping you're your own boss. I think that probably had a lot to do with it. It was an incentive, to have a better income. And there was a lot of friendship amongst the girls. There was sort of bosses and workers – you

knew which side you were on, and there was always this
sort of camaraderie amongst the workers. We had the
odd fracas now and again, because you get a lot of women
sitting in a dressing-room for long hours, bored . . .

I reckon the best strippers were out-and-out exhibition-
ists, of which there are maybe one or two. Or sex-
changes, they were good as well. They'd always wanted
to be women, you see; they became women, then they
had the chance to show off what they'd got. So they'd be
grinning like morons because they'd achieved that. I think
they wanted to be women, they thought they should've
been women, so they became women.

From my point of view in life, money can be a great
pain-killer and a great incentive. If you're earning enough
money you think, 'Shit, this is horrible, but I'm getting a
good return at the end of the day.' You can blank part of
it off. When you really start to think about what you're
doing . . . That used to slaughter me because I used to
get on that stage and think what I was doing; that was
maybe why I used to shake and sweat. If I could blank it
off, I could just breeze through it, and I could blank it off
when I was stoned. I'd be out of my head, and I'd just be
working to the music, and I'd just look at the lights,
above the punters' heads, didn't connect the one with the
other.

There's a hell of a lot of plain-clothes about. There's that
Soho magazine, that community magazine; there was an
article last week, about these three wonderful squash-
playing PCs who work in Soho. You know, all nice family
men and women, they're playing squash and netball and
that. They're always trying to put them across as being
nice little bobbies on the beat, as if Soho were a village,
a community. Perhaps we should take up squash and
badminton, then people'll think we're a nice class of girl.

This is just my shit luck. The other week, this journalist from *Woman* magazine was doing an article on why men pay for sex, and she wanted to talk to some prostitutes. So I was walking round Soho and there were some of the girls down there, on the batter, so two plain-clothes had gone into this club; they hadn't taken any notice of the girls. I wondered why. And the girls said, 'It's all right, they don't bother us lately; they've had this crazy knife man going round stabbing some of the girls.' So the cops have been reasonably off the girls' backs, they haven't been harassing them so much. So I'm chatting to them, trying to get a couple of them to talk to the woman from *Woman*, because they tried to do this article last year and they couldn't get enough information. Anyway, these two plain-clothes came out, and what we didn't know was that there was a van round the corner. Then a uniform walked up and they started cautioning the girls. And they pulled me! I said, 'Look I'm not on the game, I work round the corner in the peep.' They said, 'Oh come on love,' and the other girls said, 'No, she really doesn't hustle, she was just talking to us.' And I didn't take much notice at this point. I thought, 'It's all right, it's only one caution, they've got to caution you three times before they nick you, haven't they?' Then this policeman said, 'You don't believe that, do you? We can take you down right here and now.' Everything I said made no difference. But they didn't take me away.

It wasn't till I got stopped and cautioned the other day, that a few days later I found out about the new police powers, about how long they can keep you. It's something ridiculous like ninety-six hours, if the magistrates say so. And they can keep you for thirty-six hours without access to a solicitor, which is a long time. It's horrible being nicked, taken down to the station. Spewed out of a Maria in an underground car park, actually.

Once they thought that I was somebody that I wasn't, and I must admit the woman was almost my double. Anyway, she had eight different warrants for her arrest, and they were convinced that I was this woman. Originally I was in the station on some minor charge – footway. It was incredible: they let me out and suddenly these coppers came out, there were four or five coppers, who got my arm up my back, pushed me into a brick wall, told me that I was under arrest. And I said, 'Well, what for?' By this time I was babbling like an idiot. Well, I took out a complaint against the police and I was seen at Bow Street, and they talked to the officers involved. I was bruised up, scratched up, kept in the nick all night, then a copper came in at eight o'clock the next morning and said, 'No, it's not the same woman.' And when I filed the complaint I got a letter, months later. I've still got it at home, I should frame it. It says: 'Due to the absence of civilian witnesses, we do not feel that we can proceed with this case.'

If I *had* been that woman, there is still no way, even if she had eight warrants out for her arrest, she should have been manhandled, kept like that, pushed up against walls with her arm half broken up her back. It happened to me and I was the wrong woman, and I thought, 'Bloody hell – I feel for her when they do nick her.'

Then there was the time this boss of a peepshow I was working at – I had a big row with him and he pushed me, gave me one big shove, and I hit the wall, my head split open and I got great gouges out of my arms, where I fell on this chair. I thought, I'm just going to fuck off home. He said, 'I'm going to nick you for being drunk and disorderly,' and I said, 'Come off it, I'm not drunk, I'm not disorderly, you've got to nick somebody for that in a public place, and I don't call a peepshow dressing-room a public place.' I didn't believe it – all of a sudden the police had come, nicked me, put me in the van, and I spent the night in West End Central again. No doctor to see me.

Anyway, I went to Horseferry Road Magistrates' Court. There was this old boy on the bench. I said, 'How come I'm getting done for being drunk in a public place? I was in the dressing-room.' And he was a real doddery old bugger, and he was going to me, 'Women that do your job should be very careful if they're under the influence of drink. There's a lot of nasty men about.' I said, 'You're telling me,' and he gave me a fine.

The other thing that gets me is they're trying to close everything down. The council, I mean. Yet half of them depend on people like us for their living. Like Dr —— whose wife's a councillor who's trying to close the places down. So last week I walked into his surgery to pick up my normal shopping list, and I said, 'Will you please tell your wife to stop objecting to club licences, because so far, I'm down forty quid this week, thanks to her objections.' So he said, 'I'm sure if you were out of work or in any difficulties, my wife would be one of the first people to help you.'

I said, 'Thank you very much – when I've got nowhere to live and no money in my purse, no job, Doctor, I'll remember that.'

Yeah, I'll be round there. It's back to Victorian values, isn't it? We'll have to go round begging. Everything she's got, like her jewellery and furs and stuff, is through people like us. All the strippers go private.

Victorian values!

Anita
A Prostitute Woman

I was working straight and it was crap, crap . . . horrible.
Just boring cleaning. Then I lost that job and we knew
this Rita who was a stripper. But we knew that she had
money all the time. We kept seeing her in all these
beautiful clothes, and when she went to the night-clubs
she'd got drink after drink after drink, and we'd only got
six quid between us. And I says to Rita, 'I need a job.'
She says, 'Go down West End, you'll get a job down
there.' At first I thought, no no. Rita says, 'Listen, let me
get you this interview, just try it. You'll not be taking
your clothes off in front of nobody, except the choreographer, and he'll tell you if you've got the job.'

So we went, and he told us to go and watch the show,
but when we did, we said, 'No, we distinctly can't do it.'
So we went away. But then we thought about it: nobody
we knew would see us anyway, blah blah blah – 'We'll
just try it.' So back we went, and we picked some music
for a tape, and then we did this number in the rehearsal
room. Just got it all together, when to start taking off our
clothes . . . and then – it was the first time on-stage. It
was horrible. I was scared; I wanted to go to the toilet all
the time; my nerves just *went*. But we couldn't see the
audience because of the lights, so I couldn't really see
anybody. Good job. I knew we were shaking, they must
have seen it was our first time. And I remember all the
other girls sneaked to the back to watch us, have a laugh,
crawling on the back.

When we'd done the first show we were scared – 'I
can't do it again' – then it came to the second time. Two

hours had passed and we were due back on-stage. We just did it. The second day was better; we just got into it. It was great at the end of the week when we got paid – no, even before that when we got a sub. Because we were broke, they said, 'You can sub some money off your wages.' And then we got other spots at the other clubs, Sunset and so on. But the money was brilliant.

I'd take stripping to factory work any time; any time. I loved all the girls, every one of them. Some I knew I didn't like really, but I still enjoyed working in there; just being in the dressing-room, I loved it, the whole atmosphere. Everybody's close; just everything about it I loved. I think after a week I got sick of the job, but I loved the money. I couldn't have gone back to a straight job, and get up at six o'clock in the morning, all that shit: no chance. No, because I still had my own time, in between spots. I could go to the market, meet my friends. It took it out of you, it was still work, but it was good money.

The punters? No; I never even looked at them. I couldn't be bothered with them. I couldn't talk civilly to them, even in the street, or in reception.

Well, when the 'clean-ups' came, a lot of the clubs closed down, and we were getting sacked right left and centre. Again, I met somebody else who was hustling; she worked in this escort agency down on Windmill Street. She says, 'Listen, the money you're earning in the clubs you can earn in one day without having to run round; come down and see the guy . . .' But I said 'No' at first; that was really against my principles; I was *not* hustling. But then after a bit, being out of work, I went down there, to the escort agency, and I got picked straight away by this guy and we went out, had a slap-up meal and, that was it: back to the hotel. And as soon as I'd seen the money – I had £120 off him the first time. But then it was an agency, different from the street; it was big money. It was £60 before he even started. But the agency got raided, we got busted, closed down, what a drag!

And by then I'd got money coming in; I was used to it, and so I went on the Lane, Park Lane. It was horrible. Horrible. I hated every minute but I had to do it, because I was getting my week's wages in a straight job off one guy. I did three or four a night. But it was bad – I had loads and loads and loads of weirdos, honest to God, people just don't know. Sometimes, you *do* know who's gonna be funny, when you look at him, and you think, 'No: no way am I taking that one,' and you advise the other girls, 'Don't take him.'

Then again you can get into a car and think, 'Oh he's all right that one' and then the bastard drives you off somewhere, and you go, 'Where are you taking me?' and he says, 'To my place,' and then you start panicking. There was this one, and his 'place' was a long street with one door in it . . . all that came past were some lorries and trucks. And he took me down, it was like this railway station place but it was deserted. And I remember him saying, 'Take your trousers off,' and he threw them. He just changed his attitude and said, 'Bend over.' I thought he was gonna do it backwards, up my arse, but he just went normal, doggy-fashion, only I were stood up. And then he turned me round and went, 'Listen: don't follow, don't come back up here, don't come out till you've heard the car pull away; otherwise I'll come back and kill you. You can't go nowhere round here.' And I knew; and I waited till I heard the car go, then I just got me trousers and left.

This lorry picked me up. Oh, and the punter asked me if I'd done any other men and I said, 'No, I've only just come out,' because he wanted to take my other money off me.

But even in the escort agency you're not protected, *not one bit*. I got one guy where the cab-driver came up into the hotel with me, got the escort fee and I went into the room. There was this fashion show on TV, so I sat and watched it, and the client said, 'Have you come to watch television or to make me happy?' So I says, 'Well you asked for an escort,' because *we* weren't allowed to say 'Sex?' straight away as he could've been police, undercover, and if I put it to him first he could nick me. I'm supposed to be an escort, for company, not sex. The client's got to put it to me first. So I said, 'Well, what do you mean, am I supposed to be making you happy?' I said, 'You've got a drink and you've got the TV on; I can't help looking at it.' He wasn't talking to me anyway. So he turned the TV off, and then he went funny. He says, 'You know the Prime Minister? Well I'm gonna go to the Prime Minister about you.' Then he pulled my wig off, took my money back, threw my bag away, took all my clothes off me and hid them.

I tried to lock myself in the bathroom and he kicked the door in. Then he's saying to me, 'Wanna drink? Wanna drink?' and I said, 'No, I don't want no drink; I want to go, just let me go now, keep your money, do what you wanna do, but just hurry up and let me go home.' He said, 'No, you're having a drink,' and you know in hotels when they give you all those miniature bottles of drink in your room – whisky, gin, brandy, vodka? – well, he put every one in one glass and he said, 'You're drinking that,' and I tried to spill it on the carpet.

Then I remembered if you ring 'O' on the phone it went down to reception, so I dashed over and tried to do it, and he even pulled the phone out of the wall. I was scared, scared stiff. And he was messing about, screwing me screwing me screwing me all the time, he wouldn't let me sleep, pouring his drink in my mouth, so I was drunk and didn't know what he was doing. He put a fork to my throat; I'll never forget that. In the end he crashed out, because he'd been drinking too. So I just waited till he'd really gone to sleep, then I tiptoed around, got my clothes together. I got dressed on the landing outside. You know where this was? On Park Lane – the Intercontinental.

I went back to the agency straight away and I said, 'Listen, you don't know what I've been through last night, and I haven't got paid and I've just got away from that one punter you sent me to.' So the madam says that I should have attracted attention to the hotel room by putting a window through. I said, 'Yeah, but if I'd put the window through, he could have thrown me out after,' I didn't know. I kept thinking of all the things to do, but you can't do anything because you want to survive, and even in the five minutes that it would've took for the management to come up to that room, he could've stabbed me or something like that. I was just scared; I had to let him do it.

But a lot of punters tried to come clever: 'You're nothing but a slag, give us your money,' and 'I'm not fucking paying *you*.' They scared you to death, but then again you had the good ones, who kept perking you back up. I remember once I had this airline pilot, I'll never forget it. He said, 'How much is it?' and I told him, 'Sixty,' and he went, 'All right then, here, count that.' And he threw me this big wad of fivers. I counted three hundred and eighty quid. And he went, 'Take it, I'm going back to America tomorrow, it's no good to me.' And he was great, no trouble; I wasn't with him two minutes and he was gone, and I had three hundred and eighty pounds. It's types like him that make you keep on. There was another one, from the agency, a gun collector. Some Arabs had got shot in Earls Court, and this guy had come over from America to buy the gun, he wanted that gun that somebody'd been shot with. He gave me a one-er, that was it, and I told him I'd got a little boy and all that, the rent to pay. Then, when I was in the bath I could hear him counting some money out and I thought, 'Oh, he's ripping me off, he's ripping me off!' – taking my money back again. But then I remembered that I'd hid it. And when I went back in that room there was another hundred and twenty pounds there.

But most of them, two-thirds of them, are wanking *bastards*. Men superior? Oh no, no, no, not a bit. Every one's different, you don't know; young, old, you don't know what you're gonna pull next. There's even boys out there looking for prostitutes, for the first time. You don't know how many virgins I've taken, and they couldn't do it, because they were too nervous. And I've had to tell them, 'Go, go to a girlfriend. I can't show you any loving, it's just a quick whatever-you're-doing.' It's honest, what I say: 'Get on with it,' and, 'Will you hurry up, because I want to be up and out, I've got money to make tonight.' They don't mean sod-all to me; I used to feel sorry for them, because one of them cried once, he was that embarrassed. I had to say, 'Well come on, come on, hurry up, if you can't do it, out out out.' Why should I feel sorry for them when they're wanting to use me?

We had hassle from the police loads of times. We even got chased. They chased us to catch us, to take us down to Vine Street. Chased us, and I mean about sixty get out of the vans to chase two girls down the middle of Park Lane. They get hold of you, and because you've run, that's it, you get *thrown* in that van. They take you down and, oh my God, it's the women police that treat you bad; they're just bitches. They call you anything they wanna call you. You're a lump of shit, that's all you are to them. You haven't got no respect from the police anyway, not one bit. 'How long have *you* been *bagging* it then?' – that's their words, their way. And down at the station they just give you this little caution; they *chase* you to warn you not to go back on the street, it's pathetic. We used to call them 'Batman and Robin', they think they're so flash.

It's mainly street hustling really, that you get a lot of stick from the police. But you have to work on the streets sometimes, because there's safety in numbers. Two of you can't work in a flat, or you get done for brothel-keeping. It's *wrong*, so wrong. It's safety in numbers, because there's plenty of guys out there that ain't nice guys. You take your life in your hands out there. God knows how many times I've looked back and I can really shiver, and I think, 'I was nearly dead then,' and it's not because I nearly crashed my car, or I nearly did something like that; it was somebody else killing me. I was doing it for money, but I was nearly getting killed at the same time. I've had to run for my life. I've even rung the police up, told them the registration number, and the next day there's been that same punter driving round the beat.

They tell you, 'Of course you're covered, you've got police protection', they don't do fuck-all about it. They're dead sarcastic: 'All right, all right, what's he look like? We're writing it down, see, blah, blah, blah . . . oh, it's a *yellow* car is it? Registration number?' But then you'll go round and you'll see that *same guy*. The only time the police even come and ask you if you've seen certain punters is if a girl's really been attacked, or murdered. If you've only been scared by them, even though that scaring could get worse, they'll not do *nothing*. Because some girls will not take it from punters; they will back up to them, and then it can get worse. But if you just do what the weirdos say, you might get out alive.

And there's plenty of weird punters. You don't know

how many briefcase men, with suits and ties on, that wanted the whip and the leather boots. Not *him* spanking *me* either; *me* spanking *him*, and I mean *really* spanking. I had one, I'm not joking, this one guy came in, and he had this big box under his arm. God knows what I thought was in that box but I took him anyway. When I went in the bedroom and said, 'Are you ready?' there was this wedding-dress laid on the bed. So he said, 'Can you put that on please?' I did, and then I asked him what he wanted me to do next. He shoved his hand up the skirt part and started stroking the tops of my legs, and he went, 'Do you know my wife?' This had *nothing* at all to do with the wedding-dress, don't ask me where this came from. 'I seen her one day getting strapped to this chair, by these three black men, and they were tugging at her petticoat.' He was saying all things like that, and, 'I saw they were gonna start *fucking* her, fucking fucker fucker fucker fuck her.' It turned him on, fantasizing about these black guys screwing his wife. God knows where the wedding-dress came in on it.

I nearly died, what he did next. He got a little cassette recorder out of his bag, put it on his ears, the earphones, and it had Scottish music coming out of it, highland fling and all that. I had to ask him what these black men were doing to his wife. 'What did they do next? Did she like it? Did you see her smile?' Blah blah blah, and I had a wedding-dress on. You tell me what kind of kink that was, but he had a briefcase, and he was *really* posh. And he would give me any money for putting that wedding-dress on. I told him 'No' at first. 'That's extra money, you've come here for straight sex.' He give me the money; he loved it. Loved it. And when he'd finished, he wouldn't even look at me. *Wouldn't even look at me*; couldn't wait to get out of the door, as soon as it was done. Then he did, he looked at me in disgust. But it was *his* disgust, he got rid of it on me. *He* made me do it; it weren't me saying to him, 'Let me wear a wedding-dress, listen to Scottish reels and talk about black men fucking your wife.' It was all *his* idea – I did it just for the money, not for my pleasure. Yet afterwards he would not look at me.

But they're like that, horrible. As soon as they've had their orgasm they are HORRIBLE. You'll say to them, 'There's a sink over there if you'd like a wash.' But they don't want to look at you, yet they've just been right intimate with you. I'm not saying that I want them to, I hate them just as much as they hate me. I hate them as soon as they walk through the door, never mind when they're finished; I hate them while they're doing it. They don't know that when they're doing it to me I'm laying there looking at the ceiling; we used to put pictures up there, nice pictures, so that we could look at something different every time. Because *they* meant nothing to me, nothing at all. To him it was everything, but as soon as it was finished – my God . . . And they used to come back and all. I mean, you don't want them to be nice as pie with you, but then again you'll still get some that'll say, 'All right?' and so on. I hate them. Hate them. Because of what I have to do to get that money. Some of the things you get asked to do . . . They don't treat you like a human being, not one bit. *That* is all they're interested in, nothing else. Some of them will ask you questions – 'Are you married? Have you any kids?' but they're only formal questions, idle conversation, meaningless. They just want to hurry up and get you undressed, that's all. No, you're not human to them. Not at all.

But I don't think I'm pathetic; I'm strong. You've got to be. As soon as I leave work, it doesn't even enter my head. There's no way I'll take my work home with me. Of course there's a barrier between what I *do* and what I *am*, of course there is. I don't even think about it – I never remember one distinct punter, unless he's paid me particularly well. I'm not 'having sex'; it's a job. No way is it sex, in my head. I do not let them kiss me; no, I do *not*. And some of them'll say, 'I'll give you extra money,' and you say, 'No, no. No chance.' Or they'll say, 'Well that girl does it,' and they don't, that's bullshit, so you'll say to them, 'Who are you, like?' You have to keep something, don't you? Something of yourself. With me, it's my mouth.

After the Lane, I stopped altogether, and I was trying my hardest to live on the Social, back in Sheffield. I couldn't get a job because I'd got the kids, so I just kicked that in the head, and I ended up shoplifting. I used to nick the things I couldn't afford, what I'd got used to, living off that money, and I wanted that lifestyle. And it wasn't flash, I was just living normally; I had the normal things in my house. But the DHSS money, oh, you must be joking, with the kids – it didn't even last me two days, three days. And it's not because I lived expensively, but I wanted the best for my children – they wanted to wear what every other kid was wearing at school, not hand-me-down shit. They want new clothes all the time, and money – not that I'm saying they're greedy kids but even twenty pences add up. So I just ended up nicking, getting caught, nearly going to prison. So I went back on the game, in the sauna this time. It were hustling, but you couldn't get sent to prison for it. So I worked at that for a bit, but I was lucky if I was coming out with thirty pounds a day, and that to me was bad after working an eight-hour shift, for what you were doing. It was horrible, knowing what you'd been doing for that little money.

So then I went to the lowest form of hustling – that's what I call it anyway, and that's working the flats. It is terrible. The sauna was *crap* – it started costing me more to get to work, and pay my babysitters, than I was earning. Anyway, this girl says to me, 'You can earn £400 a day.' I said, 'Shift!' and she says, 'Honest to God, you can walk home with that money.' I still didn't believe her, so she gave me this number and said 'Ring that,' but she never told me the details. I rang this woman up, went down there, and when I walked into the room, I remembered seeing the signs – 'Busty Susan' and 'Young Model' – and I always used to think, 'It's girls working for themselves,' but it was organized. It was all run-down, and I thought, 'Oh *no*.' Well, I got the details: you get so many knocking on the door and it was ten pounds a time, straight sex, eight minutes. Then the maid would knock on the door and if he wanted to stay longer it was extra money; plus, if he wanted you to take your top off it was an extra five pounds, oral was an extra five pounds, everything was always extra. No talking, just, 'Hurry up will you.' You always had six or seven waiting to come in, the door never stopped, and it was a twelve-hour shift. The insides of my thighs used to *kill*.

The first day, my shift was from three to three, and by one o'clock I was shaking; I wanted to scream, I wanted to run, forget the money, I wanted to go home. No breaks. You had a maid who'd make you a cup of tea, that's all you got, there were no cooking facilities in there, nothing. With every client you had to get up, get dressed, go out and meet him, go in the bedroom, tell him, 'Take your clothes off please,' right clinical, no bullshit. I mean, I was what I was, you know, fucking – a *hustler*. Just get on with your job. You couldn't stop the door from knocking. It was really horrible. And I came back home after two days. I'd got £600. And then I had to sit in my house and weigh it up, because there's no way I could have got that money any other way. I earned double that really; *they* took half of my earnings. I don't know who it was and I don't want to.

The maids were brilliant – they were like my Mum; there was affection. I got close to about two, and it was really nice. Sometimes I used to say, 'I *can't* do no more. I *can't*.' I was using tubes and tubes of that KY jelly, I used to get sore off the fucking Durex; I used to buy them by the gross. There's no way you could go to work with twenty or thirty Durex and think that was enough; no chance: you needed forty and fifty Durex a day. Sometimes I used to go to sleep! And I'm not joking, I was in bed with my guy one night and I actually said to him, 'Do you want any extras?' It was on my mind all the time. I couldn't leave it behind. But then I wanted the money. And some nights after work I'd be in my own bed and I could *feel* the banging on the tops of my legs, like I was still at work, like they'd not got off you. Horrible, horrible, horrible. It really was the lowest form of prostitution. I couldn't stick it. I did it for four weeks, two days a week; and you couldn't sleep when you went back to the hotel, you were past exhaustion. It made me sick. In fact I was sick once, while I was working. And I kept getting paranoid – 'Oh please don't let that door go.' You're like that when you're laid there, you've to write down how many you do, otherwise you lose count: 'Ten plus one, ten plus one,' and you think of how many guys you've took. But then again, I had that money; I stuck it in the bank, and I felt great.

And even there, you used to get all the business types – hundreds of them; the posh ones, on their lunch breaks or even after work, six o'clock, before they go home to their wives, the dirty bastards. Mr Straight-Nice-Guy. And you had to go to the clinic every week, you went off your own bat, and you can guarantee every few months you've caught something off those dirty bastards.

* * *

Back working on the streets . . . I know girls with £4000 *fines* outstanding. They all know if they don't pay them, they're gonna go to prison – £4000 or a nine-month prison sentence for hustling, for going with guys, who if she didn't go with them, they'd fucking go and rape some bastard, to get their kink, or take it out on kids. If there weren't prostitutes there'd be more rapes, but they even slag you off for rape; they take it out of you when you've been raped, and stick up for the man again. They try and prove that it was the woman's fault – 'She's a pro so she can't have been raped,' or, 'She was walking near a district that's used for prostitution, blah fucking blah.' And that bit gets me and all, when you're called a 'common prostitute' when you go to court. 'She has been charged with being a common prostitute? That's *wrong*; even a murderer doesn't have a label stuck on him in court, they don't bring up previous convictions.

My friends Denise and Ava were both working on the beat the night they caught the Yorkshire Ripper. Denise got pulled by this one guy, and she looked at him and she went, 'No.' She said he was too *eager* to get her in the car. He went, 'Hurry up! Hurry up! Get in the car!' She said he was scared; he must've been scared of the police doing the rounds. And he went, 'Do you want it or not?' so she went, 'No, it doesn't matter, I don't want it.' So then he went further on to another corner, where Ava was stood, and he says it to her. Well, she'd had a lot of fines off the courts, thousands, so she wanted to get off the Square, to get a punter to get her off Havelock Square, so she got in his car. Denise tried to warn her not to go as he was too pushy, but she jumped straight in the car before asking him the usual, 'Want a girl? Business? Ten pounds, all right?' She just wanted to get off the Square, away from the police.

So he took her down the usual place where they took

the punters, they don't go down there now; and this cop car was doing its rounds, telling the girls to go home or they'll nick them. Anyway, they ran a check on his number plate for some reason, I don't know, but luckily, they came up to the car, and the police knew Ava straight away. And they told the guy to get out the car, and then he went for a piss. When he went for his piss, he must've had them in his jacket, but he dropped a hammer and a screwdriver, or something like that. And this policeman took it upon himself to go back to where the bloke'd had a piss, and he found the hammer and screwdriver, and Peter Sutcliffe was caught.

I'll never forget because they had to keep Ava and Denise in the best hotel in Sheffield, and they had to have police guards round the clock, because of the press hounding them; the press were killing them. Hounding them and hounding them. They couldn't sleep at home, they had to stay in this hotel; they had to keep taking the phones off the hook.

And when they were called to identify him, both of them reacted, they were sick and sick and sick in the police station; it was nerves. They must live now in nightmares, thinking they were in that car with the Ripper. Because that was every girl's fear. Even in Park Lane, where you knew it wasn't his territory, you still kept thinking every guy was the Ripper. It was horrible, but you had to go out there, you *had* to. I mean, look at them girls with £4000 fines; they know they're still gonna get another fine, but they've gotta take that chance. Not because they've got ponces, but they had to even go out there and do one for ten pounds, so that they could live for another day, and go out and do another one.

But at the same time they're getting nicked. Some girls I know used to come out of the police station after getting nicked, and they'd go straight back on the beat because they knew that they couldn't go home with no money; they've got kids, OK. Some of them did have ponces, and I used to feel sorry for them, but not many. I can honestly swear over the years I've been hustling, the majority have been independent, like me. I've never, ever held a ponce. Just through principles anyway – *never*. I'm tight – not tight, but I have to think, 'Well I might not get it again tomorrow,' because it's not stable money. It's not always there; you might go out and you might stand there all night and not pull a punter, especially if there's a new girl on the beat. Well then you've got no chance; they all want the new one, all the regulars. And most of the punters were respectable married men, I know for a fact. I know my uncle's one. Men get away with it, there's nowt you can throw at them is there? They can pick and choose what to call us, a horrible name, or call us every single one at a time.

I've learnt loads, and I'm *thankful* that I've been to the West End. I feel I'm a lot wiser than other people; I just won't trust certain people. Nobody could bullshit me now, take me for a cunt. Nobody. I've gone hard as well, that's my defences. I'm independent all the way. I rely on nobody but myself. I don't think I've ever met *one* bad woman hustling; they've all got hearts of gold, they're not wicked at all. As for me, if I hadn't done this, I'd be stuck in a house now, with about ten kids. I'd've been married to some big, fat bum, I know I would; but I'm not.

Straight society thinks it's better but it isn't. It's one big routine, they live every day like a routine. The women do; the men don't. The men have it all ways really, don't they? Don't they just. If there weren't a punter, anyway, there wouldn't be a prostitute. And if there were no guys who wanted to see a woman with no clothes on, there wouldn't be no fucking strip-clubs either.

'Sequinned' Sid
A Male Prostitute

I was from a regular working-class family, grammar-school education, three O-levels, and then into the bank. Straight jobs, yeah, boring. I realized that I was a bit of a weirdo in the bank. You weren't allowed to take your jacket off, and I did, so they suspended me for the day. It was quite funny. So then I used to come to London. That was where I could get rid of my sexual frustrations. I came from Kent, near Gravesend – and I met some guy and fell in love. He whisked me off to London.

Then I was doing straight jobs. I started in a building society, commuting at first. Then I worked in Soho at this dental place where they used to work gold, for the fillings. And from there I saw a job going in what they call a discotheque now: 'Beat City' – great big place, where people like Tom Jones started. This was in the mid-60s, I was twenty-three. I got a job there, but it all fell through when the guy who was running it went into liquidation. I had to look for another job. And there it was, staring at me in the *Evening Standard*: 'Male Dancer required; no experience necessary,' and I thought, '*There* you go Sid, you're a good old jiver, mate.' So I went along for it: 'West End Theatre Club', nine Old Compton Street. And I arrived, and it was a *strip-joint*! I nearly died. But I thought, 'No, fuck it, go on.' So then I went in there and I met this little Scots guy who was the choreographer – pissed out of his head. As soon as he saw me he just wanted to get into my pants. He took me for a drink and told me what the job involved, which was going on-stage with these girls. So then he took me home to his place and got into my knickers, and I got the job. Casting couch, love.

I remember my first time on-stage. I had to mime to 'I'm Married to a Striptease Dancer', and there I was in a pair of pyjamas, and this beautiful girl just danced around me and took her clothes off. She was beautiful. I was nervous as hell, but after the first day, after doing six shows I thought it was a piece of cake. Really I was just a prop, I felt like a prop. Those guys in the audience weren't there to see me; it was the girls. I had to strip off down to my pants – no more. Not even a G-string.

So then they gave me another number, which was quite horrific. I mean, I *had* been with girls and stuff, but I preferred men. They gave me this number with this German girl; she had to kiss me a couple of times. Her tongue used to go down my throat. If she was in a bad mood she'd show it! I felt a bit intimidated by the girls. Absolutely. The girls were much more self-assertive than straight girls outside. Oh, yeah. Well you have to be in that sort of work. They could tell; they were always getting approached by men, so their defences would go up immediately. Whereas straight women, I think, they don't know about this. They're more gullible.

The money was good, too. The money was great compared to straight work, and it was more *fun*. There was a lot more happening. You met a *real* sort of people, people were more *real*, and it was a helluva lot of fun. Great fun. Straight people, I can get on with them to a certain extent but then they become dull after a while. I think they haven't really seen life. They know nothing about life, and they're all the time trying to portray this image of whatever they are, or whatever their professions are. I recently went to this party of all these psychiatrists, and they were the most boring farts I've ever seen. Rave? They just stood there and drank wine. 'Oh hallo Felicity, yes, how are you darling?' 'Oh look there's Nigel, wonder what he's doing. Nigel, what are you doing?' A load of crap.

It's not all working-class people who take their clothes off; I've met some really well-to-do people who've done it. Okay, it's circumstances led them to it; although it *is* basically working-class, it's just when you do come across the posh ones, they stick out a mile. Rifts with their families and that. Once they're in the business, though, they lose all that.

The management's what I liked least about stripping. They did nothing, they were exploiters, they knew nothing, they were as thick as ten lavatory planks. A Mafia, in a mild form. But they were just exploiting other people's bodies and brains, because you need a certain amount of brain, to put across a number, work things out.

Probably one of the reasons why I did enjoy the strip-club so much was also because you can be yourself. This was it. I mean, working in the bank, I led a double life, you had to keep up the pretence. I think there's something about being naked. You put a whole load of professional men in a room, and a whole load of wallies in a room, and you strip them all off, and everybody appears to be the same. There's something about clothes, they're a barrier. It strikes me too that in the straight theatre, when you're in the audience, it's the same sort of thing almost as the strip-show. You're not people, you're like voyeurs. And you know, they call the audience 'punters' in the theatre too. Just like we call them in the clubs. In the straight world it amazes me when I listen to the radio sometimes, and you hear these fourteen- and fifteen-year-old girls who're still afraid to talk to their mothers about menstruation. It's nearly the year two thousand, right? But that's unbelievable. I find it very hard to fathom.

Right, getting on to what I do now. Well, I do a *service*; prostitutes do a service. But it's a headbanger. And I'm not surprised that people age so fast in this job. Because it's not the actual doing it, it's the build-up to it. Okay, so the punters have this – whatever they feel for – they come; they don't know what to expect, but they know what they want. But *you* don't know what to expect either. It's not that I'm worried about being beaten up or shit like that. That doesn't worry me, it's just wondering what sort of person is gonna *be* there, how long he's gonna take . . . You know you're gonna get the money, you fucking throw them out the window, otherwise. No, it's just the build-up to it that's disturbing. I work from my flat. I've been out on calls and stuff, but I don't do the streets. The punters have usually been okay, going out on calls.

I think as regards laws, it should be legal; prostitution should be legal. I think we do the punters a great service. There's so many old men who, probably because of their looks, can't find sex, and their sexual drives, their preferences are such that they'd never meet someone in their normal lives who would satisfy them. They need people like masseurs, prostitutes, whatever, to relieve them of their desires. But they haven't got power over me, no, not at all, I can just turn around and tell them to fuck off. They come from all walks of life, all ages, all backgrounds.

Most of my clients are those that work in offices, and just want to get their rocks off before they go home. A lot of bisexuals – a *lot*. Going home to their wives later; probably haven't had a decent fuck for months. I think from my own experience these people are basically homosexuals who want to lead a normal life, want to bring up children. It's sad really. It's like the other day, some old boy whose wife had died phoned me up for a massage and he said, 'Ooh, I must tell you, I'm a bit queer.' I said, 'Only a bit?' Those punters out there, they can't get satisfied by their partners, that's the truth. So they come to us.

It's really incredible how many more of us there are now, really amazing, the numbers, all in the last couple of years. You just wouldn't believe it. *Now* you find if you look in the papers where I advertise, there are *so* many male masseurs. Once upon a time there used to be about half a dozen, now there's more than a hundred, because there's no work. Some guy at the gym last week, he was saying to me, 'Have you seen all these adverts for male masseurs? What sort of people are they?' Well, I didn't let on, but I says to him, 'I should think they're just ordinary people, who're out of work. There's no work, mate.' They're just on the gay scene . . . it's working-class boys, of course. *That's* when it's sad. But you're not selling yourself, you're selling a service.

If somebody comes along and they don't like my set-up, they take one look at me and they think, 'What's this?' Then you get, 'Oh, I've left my money in the cab,' something like this. I get really angry, so angry because they've actually been into my little home, and I've got nothing out of it. Soiled, that's the word, you really do feel sort of cheap and . . . no, not cheap, soiled is the word. And also when they come, of course I put a blanket on my bed, a great big red towel, special for working. That goes on the bed, and I have a little pillow for them too. Yes, so that it always stays my own bed when I remove them.

What my clients basically want is just to get their rocks off. A wank. Some of them demand a bit more. It's just somewhere to get their rocks off, and their biggest kick is, I feel, from the moment they make that phone call and make the appointment with me, until they arrive. They're going into fantasy-land.

I find you don't get the types who want to come along and beat you – they want to be beaten by you. You invariably find that the ones who're into CP, corporal punishment, are public-school educated, from every age group. These are the fluty-voiced ones, the ones who've got on and done well, successful men. I give them the slipper, and I hit them as hard as I can. Yeah, I've got a nice Chinese slipper, which is basically just a rubber sole. Or the cane; some of them like the cane, because they were caned at school, and it brings back memories. They say over the phone, 'Are you into CP?' And I say, 'What do you want, the slipper or the cane?'

I can't get into the head part. I suppose if I was a really successful whore, if I was younger, really into it, yes, then I'd have to play-act. I'd have to act out the role, but I'm laid-back; I'm not into role-playing, scenes. I want them in and out. I mean, if it takes more than fifteen minutes I get angry. I get really angry.

I always start with a little massage, then I just turn them over, do their legs, then I move on to the stalk. And most of them like a finger up the bum; I would say ninety-nine per cent want their bum interfered with. I think I've had a couple of really straight het types, but even then I wouldn't say that they'd *never* had a homosexual experience before in their lives, maybe as kids. Well, isn't it like that with girls, they interfere with each other when they're kids? I know boys do.

Gay men should have the right to adopt kids, why not? They'd make wonderful mums. I think people are basically bisexual anyway, but society forces you into roles. When I go out on my own, not working, and I meet some guy . . . it's like last week, I met somebody and he was going, 'God you're sexy,' and I said, 'I know

I'm sexy.' Of course I'm fucking sexy, I've been in the sex business all my life. I'm more open and I express myself. Having said that, when I'm with clients, it's work, for me. I don't let people kiss me, there are certain things I won't do, no, no; but if someone comes along who I fancy, then I can bring some pleasure into work. But that's rare. In my head, I just think of the money, I really do. When we refer to ourselves as 'whores', men or women, we mean the job we're doing, not an insult: the service we're doing.

I once had a punter who didn't think I was worth it because he didn't tip his barrow, but I've never had threats of violence from guys, touch wood. I'm pretty big and tall, and I always wear something that reveals my muscles and lets the punters know that I am strong, and they'd better not try any fucking rough stuff. You know the 'dominatrix' professionals? I think there's a lot of transvestites who go in for this stuff, who go in for this chaining up and so on. I reckon there's more boys doing that, boys dressed up as girls, than there are women. Dominatrix for the geriatrics! And the best of it is, the punters don't even know; they wouldn't know that it's boys not women, not even the regulars.

I personally haven't had any real hassle with the police, just a brush now and then, but I know it does happen if you're gay, you get trouble from them. They've got these pretty policemen who go round the clubs and cottages, *agents provocateurs*, yes. It's terrible. I suppose I've been very lucky in that respect.

I've met so many girls in my life that want to put me straight, they think, 'I'll get him into bed and I'll make him heterosexual.' You can't do that. I had het experiences when I was young, up to the age of twenty. I first realized that I was homosexual when I was about sixteen. I knew that there was something 'wrong', but I didn't want to be gay. Because all I knew about gays was that they were old men who dressed up as women; I never knew that there were people actually my age. I only saw what they portrayed it like through society. I felt awful. I used to do things like going into the toilet at home and jerk off with men's magazines, and *make* myself come over a picture of a naked woman, rather than a picture of a naked man. You see you're being pressured into being something that you're not. This is why coming to London and going into the striptease business, it was like somebody lifting a world off my shoulders: I was *free*.

Now, I don't give a fuck, I honestly don't. People can take me as I am, or they can fuck off. In any case, I do believe straight people are the problem, of course they're the problem, absolutely. They have so many values to keep up to, whereas if they would all be themselves, it would be a better world.

If there hadn't been this business, I don't know, maybe I would've turned out like one of my clients, gone into banking and – no; what am I talking about? No, I'd've done something else equally bizarre. Mind you, there are a lot of people like me in mundane jobs, oh yes. I could've carried on like that maybe, settled down with a bloke I liked, but the prospect is unappetizing. I need excitement in my life. I've got lots of nice memories – but you can't live on memories. I reckon I've lived a very full and interesting life, that's been through stripping; I don't think I would've had that opportunity any other way.

Generally though, I think we're people who're different, in this business. We're people who have no inhibitions, and we see fit to do as we want to do, and *fuck* the rest of the world. Seriously, you have to conform as a kid, but once you're grown up and you get out there, you know, the world is your oyster and you do what you want to do. And okay, you may upset a lot of people, but you

give a helluva lot of people pleasure when it boils down
to it. At least we're honest; I feel that the people I've
met in this business are so honest. They're *straight*, they
talk to you *straight*, whereas basically society is always
trying to get all round corners and stuff.

I resent the majority of punters, if I come clean, oh, I
resent the bastards! Absolutely. I feel I do a decent
service and they ought to tip me, but they'd never think
of doing that. Sometimes when you see what turns up at
that door, when they take their clothes off, it's awful.
But it's difficult at the best of times to get back into
straight work, after what we've done, and these ain't the
best of times. In any case, you can't win in that way,
because then you're back to square one: boring boring.

I've had women ring up, but not often. But invariably,
when women are involved it's usually their boyfriend or
their husband who phones you up. They say, 'Do you do
couples?' and I always say no. They want to watch you
fuck their wife or girlfriend, it's pretty crass. But it's the
same with women prostitutes, they get blokes phoning
them up for a threesome because they want to see a
lesbian scene before they can get it up. There's a lot of
that goes on. It's just the man's selfish fantasy. But
generally, punters are selfish – they're absolutely intent
on their own pleasure, that's the key. They're not concerned with you getting anything out of it. You're getting
the money. They think, 'I'm paying him for it, so why
should I worry?' It's not making love, oh no. Quite
honestly, they'd be better off having a wank. They might
just as well save themselves the money. Mind you, you
do get the wankers too. You learn to suss them out: they
just want you to talk, then they don't pay. The customers
ring up and they say to me, 'Describe yourself'; 'What do
you look like?'; 'How tall are you?'; How big's your
dick?' Oh yeah, they want to know the whole works. I do

get the odd woman ringing up; they sound pretty sure of themselves. They say, 'How much? Do you do extras?' I tell them it's £70 or something to put them off. I wouldn't be able to do anything for them.

I'd say that punters will try to get as much out of you as they can, the good time and everything. They'd just bleed you of your personality if they could, if you let them. Just like the ones that hang around the strippers; they come along because they have a good time, enjoy it. It's a release for them. Okay, *you* may be the one that's providing this good time for them, but you yourself don't enter into it, when all's said and done.

Christine
A Stripper

I started at the Carnival seven or eight years ago. I went round the clubs for three days with my friend Jane. She was earning the money and I wasn't, so I thought, 'Why not? I might as well.' Before I came down I was unemployed in Scotland, but I had been working, in a factory. But the money wasn't so good and it was boring. When I came down here it was to meet people, and there was a lot more freedom, nobody breathing down your neck like in the factory. And the money was really bad compared to stripping.

I wasn't living at home anyway. I was living with a boyfriend and his parents and I felt that I wanted to just get away. I thought, 'Bollocks to this,' and I got a ticket and went, came down here to see Jane. Aye, I remember the first time I went on-stage. It was Dee and Jane and somebody hadn't turned up for this treble number. This was the two o'clock show at the Carnival and Rusty says, 'Go on'. I was going, 'Oh no, God,' and first of all I thought, 'They'll all see my stretch marks'. You get conscious of things like that! And the girls were saying, 'Aw, go on, you'll be all right,' so I said, 'Okay – I will.' So I went downstairs and on the stage, and there was this black backdrop and three stools. We were supposed to sit on them for the first part of the act; and I didn't know, but Jane and Dee went and hid behind the backdrop so when the tabs opened I was just sort of left there all on my own and oh my God! I saw all the faces there! I didn't know what to do, and there was nobody there, and I went, 'Oh NO!' It was really awful. They came out from behind the curtains, and then that was the first show, those two taking the piss. A baptism of fire!

And then somebody else didn't turn up, so they shoved me on on my own. Jane said, 'I'll stand at the side by the curtains so that you'll not be alone,' and they gave me the *Star Wars* music! And that's good for dancing really so I could handle the dancing bit, but as for doing anything else . . . Because I'd watched Jane and Dee sort of mimicking a lesbian number, and that had really embarrassed me. Then when I saw little Debbie, flashing, I thought, 'Too much! I can't handle this, I can't do that!' You could see things she'd had for breakfast a hundred years ago. I thought it was awful. But you get over it. I felt after a fortnight like I'd been doing it for ever, and I'd become really bold, within myself. But the first time was really awful.

Now, when I'm up on-stage I'm very positive with the punters. I really make fun of them. It's no good if you let them know they're bugging you and that you're upset about having to come here. It gives them the advantage, the ball's in their court. I let them think that I'm really bold about it. It obviously works. They sit there and they don't know what to do. You go up there and leer at them, they just don't know how to handle you at all. I've even had punters write to me saying that I seem positive about myself on-stage, that I'm not frightened. I'm not the victim, oh no, no no – *they're* the victims when I get up there. Whatever's gonna happen, they get it!

When I came here first I thought I knew a lot of things and I didn't really, but *now* I could teach my mother.

Punters . . . I don't think anything of them at all, apart from they're a bunch of creeps, actually. They're only nice when they give me something, but they're not nice people otherwise. Why are they here? They pay to see you. What's nice about that? I ignore most of them except the young ones; they come in and take the piss and I don't like that at all. I just don't work to those people. I'll just walk off the stage, and those mugs who think they're clever'll see nothing. They start shouting things like, 'Ya whore,' and all that so I say, 'Well what about your girlfriend, she must be a whore as well, she takes off her clothes for trash like *you*.' That's all they can think of to say, 'slag'. They think it hurts your feelings. It's even the same when you're out walking in the street, minding your own business, and some fella goes, 'Gissa smile darlin'.' If you tell them to get lost it's, 'Oh well, you're an old slut anyway.' So I just ignore them, because if you answer back you're giving them attention and just encouraging the stupid bastards.

As for the ones that say, 'It turns you on, stripping' – they're joking! Looking at them greaseballs?! What!! They've gotta be kidding! If anybody says that to me I tell them, 'What? – Gedoff!' Imagine, you're going on-stage first thing in the morning to a load of old men! So what am I gonna do, walk out of the dressing-room and get one of them to muff-dive me or something?! Oh leave off, no, God! I'm amazed that people can think that!

I think about it sometimes, why men go to strip-clubs . . . it troubles me. When I see young guys that are on their own and that are regular features I think, well there must be something wrong with their willy or something like that. Whereas the old men, I can accept because obviously they're past it; they don't get to see much young skin now so they come in to see us and remember. So when it comes to the middle-aged type, you always can recognize the married kind; they're obviously not happy with their wives so they come to get off on you, then they go back and fuck with their wives after! Oh, what a terrible thing to happen, but it's true. They go into some seedy joint to watch a chick that they think is a slag anyway – but if they think you're a slag why are they watching you? I think it's very disturbing, actually. I think most men are disturbed. They used to say that women were, but I think it's the bloody men that are. I think they've got a bloody cheek, because I'm not a nymphomaniac; I'm quite happy to have sex at home with my man and that's that.

My boyfriend doesn't put me down for doing this job, but I think he's a bit jealous. He doesn't like to come and see me, although he works just around the corner. And he hates to see those greaseballs, he hates the punters. I think he thinks I'm too good to do this job. I mean I'd feel unhappy if he *didn't* think I was too good. He's told me so. He accepts. He doesn't say to me, 'Don't do it,' although I think he would prefer me not to do it – what man wouldn't? But really I think he respects me. After all, it's just a job I'm doing, and it's *me*, the person, he respects. I mean, I just couldn't be a little housewife-thing passing time in a little house – no thanks! Just sit at home, do your housework – I'm sorry, but that's not me. I said, 'I'm sorry Tim, but I just can't.' I came back to be with the people I can relate to; I want to be with my friends, people I know, that understand me, not in those narrow lives at home. Here you're free, in the way you dress and the way you talk and everything. No bullshit, everybody accepts you for what you are, warts and all. I go out and be what I want to be. And my little girl, I bring her here and she likes it. She likes Rachel and she likes all the other girls and I don't think she understands straight people!

I don't know what would have happened to me if I hadn't come here and started stripping. I don't know . . . I'd probably just be stuck at home like everybody else, and I didn't want to be. I just didn't want that. And I'm glad I did come to London. I don't regret that, oh no!

Because I could never go back to Scotland and live like that again. And everybody pressured me to be like everybody else. It's sad for my other sisters. They have not learnt anything; they just got married and had bairns. And I've learnt a lot. Things that I can talk about, like what's going on in this world, nuclear wars and how much money's being spent on weapons. I didn't know any of this till I came here and met people. But back home they're ignorant and it's like I say to my Mam, 'Why do you buy that rag? [*The Sun*] It's not fit to wipe your arse on!' and she goes, 'I buy it for the bingo.' I had to make my own choices for myself, and I did. What were the others, really? None at all. And it's not been that bad except for the rough periods.

Well the best thing about it is meeting the girls, the girls that I've met, because they're genuine – well, most of them. There's one or two that ain't, but I know they're people I can trust and I really like them. They've all been in the business, some a lot longer than I have, and I think it's good because they're really nice and I feel I can belong somewhere when I'm here. When I'm at home I don't feel I belong anywhere, except with Tim, but I do feel I belong here, like it's a community, and it's great. And I respect any girl that strips. I respect them even though I may not like them personally. Because I know what they go through.

I don't profess to be better than anyone else, and I don't think anyone else is better than me, because we're all the same. Why should I be ashamed? Why? You know what I think is more obscene than anything else? Picking up a page three in the *Sun* with a girl's picture on it and then right next to it some horrible story such as a mother losing her bairns in a fire, and the've got a girl sitting there flashing off her tits. And some dirty old wanker's reading the paper, loving the tits, but the poor woman who's lost her kids . . . everything . . .

I can walk out in the street any day and see somebody's thrown the *Sun* or whatever paper on the ground and there's tits all over the place, on the floor. People are walking all over that. It's lying in the train, lying in buses everywhere you go, in the road, and you see the car wheels going over it. She's a pretty girl, right, but that's obscene to have her picture thrown all over the place so that anybody walking up and down the road sees it, walks over it like a piece of shit. That's not fair to that girl. I'm not slagging the girls off, I'm slagging the paper. At least when I'm here, I'm on a stage and it's not going any further, so it's more private. I know those chicks make good money, but I feel sorry for them because I think they're being more exploited than a stripper. But I still think I'm being exploited because every time the man on the desk or the stage manager says to me, 'It's your turn, you're on next,' he's exploiting me because he's telling me to get down there and get my knickers off. That's a man, and they're men that are exploiting me.

And the bosses, they don't respect us. They think they're superior, but they are full of shit. Like 'B'. I don't think he's a decent man. He's a pimp. I've seen him sometimes in the bar. He sits there and takes a wad of money out of his pocket, and I think, 'He's got all that money in his pocket, he could give us another quid more each time we go on-stage.' And if you go into the bar and a punter offers to buy you a drink, 'B' will go, 'What do you want to drink, darling?' and if you ask for a Coke he gives you a real dirty look as if to say, 'You should be fucking drinking something expensive,' as if you're a hostess. And I'm *not*; I'm not paid to do that. If I want to drink Coke, I'll drink Coke.

I think the thing I dislike most about this job is the

men. Like I said before, not so much the old guys, because I can handle them. They're past it, they're old and they wouldn't see a woman unless they came here, but it's really just the fact that men come here. I mean there was one guy here the other week and he was pointing at my belly and going, 'Fat belly,' and laughing, and I thought, 'Why is he laughing at me?' I just got right angry and I thought, 'I'll either kick him or I'll walk off the stage,' so in the end I did both. But I think the men, basically, are what I hate most. I *do* hate them. Because to them we're just objects – sex objects, that's all.

Well, to be perfectly honest, I suppose it is degrading in a way. But I'm not with the argument that I'm degrading any other woman. I may be degrading myself . . . When people say I'm degrading other women I say, 'Bollocks'. Whereas I think the real hypocritical whores in this world are the office workers you see round these pubs, sleeping with their bosses and pretending that they are so superior. And there's us lot here, we've got plenty of opportunity to sleep with men, we've got opportunity every day of the week, and to get paid for it as well, but we don't do that. But the office twats hide behind their little nine-to-five job, their respectability. And sometimes they come downstairs after they've been drinking – oh I hate that! And they sit and laugh! And I say to them, 'Right, well, as it's so funny, YOU get up and do it.' But they're not brave enough, they're only brave enough to sit with their men and take the piss. I'm brave; I get up there and take my clothes off – believe me, that's brave. Those women are full of shit.

In this world, a man can go and fuck whoever he wants and that's fine. But a woman? She does it, and she's a slag. Men think we're underlings to them, but we're not. I'm no underling to any man. The men out there in the audience, they are nothing to me. What are they? Just a bunch of tossers. When it comes down to it, we don't respect them any more than they respect us – and we've got more reason to feel like that. And that's another thing. Ever since I started this job I've learned so much about men, what twats and pricks they are! I respect Tim because he's a nice guy but generally, there's no way will I respect men. I don't even respect my own Dad because I know he's a real shit. I know he's been a real shit to my Mum, left her and all us lot, and the way he's behaved . . . and he thinks he's a 'respectable' member of society. He's friends with the police. Two men I respect and that's Tim and my Granddaddy who's dead now, and he *was* a man. He was good and he never hurt anyone or swore. . .

What I definitely wanted to do, was to pursue the career of being a singer. Then I'd give up this place like a shot. But it just didn't happen. Not yet anyhow.

Mariana
A Stripper

I don't like saying that I was a stripper, but I do say sometimes, it just depends on how I'm feeling. Sometimes it's easier not to, because people tend to say, 'Oh yeah, wow, what happened to you? What did you feel when you were actually doing it?' And you try to say, 'You know, I'm thinking is the costume gonna hold up? Is the make-up looking all right? Is it gonna be the next break when I can have my dinner? Or, is there any problem at home?' These things go through your head; it's like any other job – but people think that you're there *doing* it. We take it for granted because we're more blasé about it and the general public are not. People are so fucked up about sex anyway. And that's why I really do have to measure and see can this person take it if I tell them what I do? Because once they see they're talking to a stripper their whole attitude changes. The men go, 'Ah, you're laughing all the way to the bank,' but at the same time they think you're thick and stupid, or sex-mad. That's the picture they have in their heads about us.

But in a way I was lucky when I first started, because I couldn't speak any English at all, so really I was engrossed in getting the work together. It was terrifying in a way, but in another way it was much easier to get on with the job. At least I knew that I had the job and I had the money coming in. All I really thought then was how to keep this; learning how to be a *good* stripper, the *best*, so that they are not gonna give me the sack. Because I couldn't do anything else. Because if you cannot speak the language and you don't know anybody, you're fucked!

It was winter when I first started. December. God, it was a crazy place to me; I thought it was gonna be like this for ever – the cold, you know! I didn't know what a pub was, and the first time I went in there, oh! I'd never seen so many white, red people before. Like they'd never seen the sun in their whole life. Really red faces! And everybody drinking, squashed together. Nobody had their own table, like in Brazil. The whole atmosphere was crazy. Everybody was just drunk! Drunkards. And then all these men, the ones in the audience. I started at the Paradise, in Brewer Street. Now that was ridiculous, that beginning. I was so disillusioned about everything. The stage was so big and vast.

I had the whole day to think about it. I had a quarter bottle of whisky. I hate whisky! I didn't even drink. I needed something, I couldn't do it. I just couldn't face it. I went and watched my sister, Titia, and I thought, 'She looks like a prostitute, you know, offering herself', being so – ugh! I was *so* ashamed and really, I felt terrible. I tried to tell her my shame for her, but she was always in a hurry because she had to do all the other clubs, the way they had to then.

Then she came back and said, 'Okay, you saw; now you do it,' and I went, 'Aaaargh! I can't do this, this is not right.' She says, 'You either do it or you go back.' Back to Brazil. So I thought, 'Well, I have to pick up the cards.' So that was when the bottle of whisky appeared. Everybody was being quite nice to me. I'd never seen so many naked women in close-up, all in one day – the whole thing freaked me out. Everybody just changing, their bums stuck up your nose. It was such a tiny dressing-room. So eventually I did get up there and it was *terrible*; those lights in your eyes and them all staring at you. Oh my God! And to me, the picture that I have is that the men didn't have any shirts on. Everybody was wearing the suit, the jacket, and it was all dark out there, with the little heads on top. I couldn't discern that much, just the dark suits, and they were all sitting there *staring*. I really felt like I was in the zoo. So I take the clothes off and it was a very nervous thing, with Titia backstage shouting: 'Keep moving! Keep moving!' and me shouting: 'I can't! I want to go home!' in Portuguese to her. Poor little thing, shrieking: 'I want to go home! I changed my mind, I don't like this!'

Then I had to find my way to all those clubs with everybody drawing maps and me having to be on time. I was so cold, too; all the time, cold. I went for an audition at the Nell Gwynne and they spoke in Italian, trying to get through to me. Up on the stage they put me, with the footlights on . . . very professional. They said, 'Take your clothes off,' and I had so many layers on, it took a long time! There was no chair and I thought, 'How do they expect me to take off all the tights and the boots?' so I sat on the floor! And they said, 'Move! Come on, dance!' I said, 'Dance with no clothes on? – How stupid!' I couldn't imagine myself in a discotheque with no clothes on. So first they gave me a number with about five hundred pieces of costume to take off, and I would just stand in a spot. And I guess that's how I learned – it was a good way of learning right from the beginning how to use the stage, back, front, sides, then the whole routine.

The first time in Soho I worked a whole year, which was great. At the end of that year I got married, so I took my husband back home to show my family. They hated him, his long hair, and all that. I'd met him at the Sunset Strip. You know, people say, 'Good for the strippers, poor things' – they really think so much of us – 'they can have all the men they want.' You don't have *time* for relationships! You have to make do with what you've got around you. First of all I had a taxi-driver, which was very practical for the late shift; no hassle. I think with stripping a girl cannot have any extra hassle. No sick children at home, anything like that. The pressures are so much that I don't think you can sustain a real relationship. It just sort of turns around the clubs, because you are both there. It's like you aren't real people.

Now, when I was with David, who is my husband now; when I first split with him, it was really because we just didn't fit together, with me being home so late all the time. So he had his own social life without me, and then Sunday I just wanted him to give me his whole attention. But since he already had his set-up, I was expected to fit in with *his* social life, and that was impossible. It just does not work. In the clubs, it's everything, your family, everything, you just cannot get away from it. It is no good being snobbish and saying, 'I've got my own life elsewhere,' because you don't! Okay, you don't choose your family, but in the clubs, those people you work with are from all over the world, not just geographically, but different races and set-ups. There is no way you can *not* be involved.

Sometimes you go home and you think, 'Christ! How did I get into all this?' For instance, when a girl gets beaten up, or someone has an abortion . . . But the good thing was the unity. The women were so together, and that was the nicest aspect. It's solidarity. Even though you didn't *always* get that family feeling running through. Like, I can remember at the Nell Gwynne, there was this girl who used to go and visit her boyfriend in prison, even though he was in there because he killed her child. And so nobody liked her attitude, because of what he had done. But it didn't mean that she was actually ostracized. Also with the one who was a heroin addict. I mean, even though she *was* ostracized, she wasn't *really*, because nobody was gonna do her any harm. But at the same time, she knew that we didn't like her taking the heroin. There are more heroin addicts around the clubs now, but that's like it is in society as a whole. The drug is much cheaper now, and these are poor kids who really have no other escape; they can't handle it. They are dying after –

how long? – fourteen days. They have no hope in this society.

There is a lot of loneliness in the West End. Even with all the people around, you still get lonely. And that's why, for a lot of the girls, the dressing-room is like a home. On Sundays, when it was all closed, it could be very lonely. That's why I split up with the cab-driver – he was never there on Sundays, he still worked. It was fine for the sex – I needed that, because I've *never* worked that hard in all my life. I mean, to actually work thirteen hours a day, and at the beginning, it's really non-stop, you rehearse in between. I couldn't believe it! So we took speed on the Friday and the Saturday – Newton's* – that was the beginning of the speed. You could control it. It was so you could go to a discotheque on Saturday night after work, because you just hated to spend the whole week working and not having any fun. Sunday was really for washing, going to the launderette, getting all your housework done, your place together, getting everything in. Because you don't have time during the week. So that was Sunday. Big day of rest! And so you had to go to the disco on Saturday; you had to take speed. You had to have fun, somehow.

The first year everything was so new to me. I had so much to learn, and I was determined that I was going to make the job as solid a career as I could, because I just didn't want to lose the money. I would've gone back to Brazil, if it didn't work out. Gone back to university to do law, which is just a continuation of the office. I'd done one year, and at the end of it I thought it had got so boring. And what you learn anyway, you're not going to practise. That's the worst thing. And all the law is from here, English law. It's all very hypocritical. So I would've gone back, and been a bilingual secretary, which would pay for the books and feed me. And

---

* Dr Newton: Harley Street supplier of amphetamine.

also the money stripping, that I was putting under my mattress, I was gonna buy a flat, so I didn't have to wait for men to marry me to give me the house and all that. That's what was going to happen, but then I got married and I thought that's even nicer, to go home with the husband. He was a stage manager, then he started selling dope, to make the money to go to Brazil. Then he didn't want to stop and I thought . . . well, I don't mind being naughty but I didn't like giving my rights to the police, you know. You can do your thing without giving them your rights, and by selling dope you're giving them your rights, whereas by taking it, it's you, it's your fault, it's not other people. Nick didn't agree with me, so we got caught. They came in the morning and I opened the door: dogs and everything. I couldn't leave him alone in this trouble so I shared it, 'for better for worse' and all that. We got fined and went to court and the place we were living, the owners found out about the police and so we got thrown out. They threw us out. It was really bad.

But then the second time round, when I came back from Brazil, was a bit of a mess. I began to get in a mess because after that session of the first year's work, the money all went. And so I went back to Soho and – I really felt bad when I went back, because I *left*. Because I got married I thought life was gonna change, I was gonna do something straight, and then we came back and we really needed the money and all that, so I went back. That's when the drinking started. You should call your book 'We work in this business because we need money!' It was not fantastic money but a *good* income. Even now, when I get really depressed I'm thinking, 'My God I could be making that much money if I just went back.'

When I went back to college I found the whole transition was just incredible and the people after Soho freaked me out. So hypocritical and they play games with you; it's the big ego. In Soho it was good really, it was nice to see the girls on the streets with all the make-up and the eyelashes, flaunting it all and feeling proud and having cash. Not 'Excuse me' like the English women usually are. I never even thought about it, having the money, it was just there. I always thought that one must work and you get paid and that's it. I never thought that if I tried to get out it would be difficult to get somewhere, but it *is*. Money means your whole independence.

It's incredible sometimes the feeling of power you get when you're actually on-stage, and yet you're the one nude, and they have their clothes on, and you look at them and you think . . .!! And if it was a bad crowd, like the football supporters, because of the language I really learnt to feel a glass wall between the stage and the audience. Because I'm quite sure that, at first, when all that shouting and screaming was going on with really rude things, I was smiling away, you know, saying, 'Thank you thank you'. I think that really built something inside me. I always felt that, with the football crowd and those types, you are the clown, the jester, and so you're there for the egg on the face and all that. But with the stag party it was better. You *did* have the power because you were the sex that they required. That man didn't have enough to give to his wife the next day, so you were gonna dare him to show how much, which they never do because it's not just that they are drunk, but because when you size one of them up they cannot do a thing. In a crowd they're great, but if you just pick on one then that poor sod has you and the whole audience against him; so I could handle that situation, I could turn it. I could use my power then and really give them the show!

But I felt more animosity from the older guys than the young ones. The young ones to me, I felt clear about what went on in their heads, but the older ones, I just couldn't read their minds at all. I didn't know what the hell was going on inside their heads, I thought they were mad. I didn't think they had any sexuality, not like the younger ones, whose balls are full, who don't know what to do with their cocks and they were just . . . you knew about them. Whereas the old men were really creepy. That gave me a horrid feeling, I just could not understand why they were there – apart from 'Poppa'. It was really that we were his friends; his children. He really treated us as that, going and eating, it wasn't just because we had pussies and tits, it wasn't like that. With some of them I knew it was their loneliness.

Then there were types like that man with the bowler hat, 'Willie the Wanker' we used to call him, in the front row, jerking off under his hat! And the one with the fruit and the glasses, Ken, he used to roll the fruit under the tabs, and he was really happy, you could tell him anything and he was smiling even if you swore at him! He pretended to all the other punters that he knew us; he had these wild fantasies! Then the person who picked me out was the one who kept asking me to take my shoes off, 'Footsie', that was funny. He gives money and then bars of chocolate. Then there was an old one who used to give a pound, that's in the time when a pound was like five pounds today.

But with straight people I think, they make love in the dark, it's just a case of finding the hole and the woman being very Victorian and just lying there and they think of God and all that, just the obligation. So the sex industry is all for the man just like everything else, even marriage; to fulfil *his* needs, not really to fulfil hers. He needs a home for himself, he needs to have children for his name to go along, it's all his. Father-to-son, and the women just get used. We were just talking other day, that it's not illegal for a man to rape his wife, and I couldn't believe it. It's disgusting! If you realized that before you got married . . . But everything here is so old, so archaic and entrenched and you can't change anything. I mean it takes ages. Nothing changes.

Chloe
A Prostitute Woman

There were three of them, three American diplomats, living in one of those houses near Park Lane that cost three, four hundred quid a week to rent. What happened was, the guy picked Sandy up on the Lane, and how he laid it on her was, 'Listen, I'm over here, I don't know much about London, and I'm gonna pay you well. But I also wondered if you'll stay for a drink for half an hour. I'll pay you extra.' *He* knew that none of this was gonna come off: 'Even tomorrow, maybe you can show me round London, I'll pay you; I'll buy you summat.'

So Sandy thought, 'Great' – gets back to the flat and the other two's hid behind the door, and as soon as she came in, they went for her. And the guy who's picked her up's crowing: 'Ooh, she fell for it, didn't ya?' – threw her on the settee – 'Coming out wi' me tomorrow are ya?' – whack! – 'Shopping as well, you cunt?' – slap! That was their thing, as soon as she were in the flat, right, whack across the face; threw her on the bed, tied her up on to the bed, and they did the lot, up the backside, the lot. She were in a right state. That's the truth. And we all kept saying, 'Go to the police,' but no, none of us would ever go to the police, because we knew we'd get, 'Well, you lasses, you know; you know what you're doing out there. You're taking your own risk.' All the crap.

It was the same with Jody and me, when we were in London. We were working the Lane and this car stopped; we were walking down. Two guys in it there were, and we were two girls. We did the business and they said, 'Back at your place?' so we agreed. That's what we wanted to do anyway. We got in the car, in the back, then the driver pulled off, went round the corner, he put his foot down – the car made a right racket – he shot to this corner, and another guy jumped in the car like *that* – in the back, with us. I put my arm over to push the door where Jody was, and he fucking said, 'Look, cool it'. Straight away, he got the knife out. And at first I thought they're not gonna do nowt, because you don't think it's ever gonna happen to you. They took us out on the motorway, and we were miles out; I wanted them to dump us, I thought they were going to. That wasn't all, they started waving knives in our faces, grabbing hold of Jody's hair and saying, 'I think we'll have you first,' and all that stuff and then they were saying it amongst themselves, 'You have her first and I'll go with her'; they were squabbling. And Jody's going, 'Ya not fucking having none of us, ya bastards!' – really freaking out, and I thought no way, if you go off like that, you get it worse, so I'm going to her, 'Cool, it, Jody.' She's going, 'I'm fucking not! *You* stand for it if you want to!' I *didn't* want to; it were just – I know what she was feeling; she was panicking that much. It came out, and she couldn't hide it any way. I was trying to think logically, keep cool: 'Right; I've got to get it together for the both of us; I don't want to end up dead; let them do what they want to do, and go.'

We stopped on the motorway, and I mean, on the hard shoulder; they dragged Jody out of the car and said to me, 'You fucking stay here, cunt,' and I says, 'No, man, I'm coming an' all,' and Jody's shouting: 'Chloe! Chloe! Don't leave me, come wi' me!' It was down on the grass verge; I'm telling you, he pulled her tights down from the back, and I thought he was going up her back passage, but he wasn't. And this is on the grass, by the side of the motorway, with a drop down the side of it; a dip, and

Jody were there on her stomach, and he made her have sex like that. And then they dragged us both back into the car and took us to this flat, near the bloody Elephant and Castle. It was above a shop, and there was an Indian guy asleep in the doorway. The place was filthy; it stank. There was just one single bed in the corner and a mattress on the floor. I got pushed on that. And because Jody all the time was nervous and screaming and carrying on, they were trying to get her most. I tried to calm her down, and she did in the end. But two of them went with her, because of the way she was going off, and one of them went with me. And I just laid there and did not move, no motion at all, and the guy was going, 'Come on – fuck! Fuck! Come on! Show us what you can fucking do! Acting fucking pretty – show us how good you are at it!'

When they'd finished they says to us, 'Stay here and don't fucking move.' I'd got the registration number in my head, honest to God, because I thought, these bastards aren't getting away with it. Oh, but I'll tell you the worst thing, when we stopped at these traffic lights on the way to the flat there was this fire engine, firemen looking at this house, but there was no fire. And I wanted so much to wind down the window and shout: 'Help!' But I thought, would they speed after us? They can't run after us in the fire engine, can they? Will they be quick enough to get the registration and come after us? Or, if they don't, we're dead. So I didn't do that.

So they said, 'Stay in this room,' and they pissed all over the bed where Jody was, all over her feet, and she was crying, in a state. They'd kept us *hours*, from about ten o'clock at night, till we got away about five in the morning. And as they fucked off these two Indian guys were coming upstairs, the other blokes must've said, 'You can have them now,' and we just ran past them down the stairs, and they were shouting after us.

It's horrible, really horrible, but I knew if I'd've started carrying on and creating, and screaming, we would've had it *right*. Because he really did have the knife up to Jody's throat and he was going to kill her, and she's going, 'Well fucking do it then ya pig,' and he was really getting mad, as if he was gonna stab her, she was hysterical. I went, 'Oh leave it, she's upset, she doesn't know what she's doing.' I tried saying *anything* to calm them down, and keep *us* alive. It was horrible.

Well we didn't go to the law. Because the first thing we did when we got home, and it's the wrong thing in the eyes of the law, is have a bath. You're not supposed to do that if you get raped. But I got home and scrubbed – you want to, honest, it makes you feel horrible – dirty – somebody smarming on you like that, doing that . . . ugh. I wanted to. Because it was against your own will. And then if we'd gone to the police after, we couldn't have proved owt. Because we'd both been in the bath. And like I said, if we *had* gone to the cops, it would've been, 'Well, you're that sort of girl. A loose sort of girl. What do you expect? Forget it.' They would take the particulars down as a formality, then they push the file into a rack and that's the last you see or hear about it.

But what's the point in taking it out on other guys? Maybe you say, 'Harden up, and start treating other guys like shit,' but what good is that? He might be a genuine gentleman. I mean, I did meet some, one or two, in this business. But half of them I wouldn't believe shit what they say about what comes off with the wives and that. 'She's left me,' or, 'She doesn't go to bed wi' me.' I think they're just making excuses up; they just want a change, most of them. A change is as good as a rest. Can't be bothered to get into other relationships, or they don't

want to because they're on to a good thing with their
wives, and don't want to lose them. They just want to go
to bed with somebody else *different*. Some of them *do*
want to go, starting from licking your feet upwards and
that, but others don't, they just want to get on top, and
get it over and done with – and so do you.

But no, I didn't like hustling really. I didn't like it one
bit, to tell the truth. I was frightened, on my guard, all
the time. You get so you don't want to believe *anybody*.
A lot of lasses that you work with; you're on the street
together, and you get to know faces that come round
there often, and it's, 'Oh don't go wi' him, he's rubbish;
he's a time-waster.' That's one good thing about it: all
the lasses stick together – that's one thing I *do* like. But,
listening to the girls you get to learn things, like never
trust a man that smokes a pipe, that looks cool, calm and
collected, because it's wolf in sheep's clothing, things like
this. Because of the experience of other lasses. I've talked
to load of girls that have had bad experiences with
punters. They still continue doing it, not just because of
unemployment, though that's got to do with it now, but
also because it's not *easy* money, but it's *good* money,
compared to straight work. Your time's more your own.
I've worked in a factory, and there your time's *theirs*.

But really, all I've wanted to do all my life is work with
kids, or work with old people, helping old people, and
I've done it. But the only reason I got that job in the first
place was because I was a prostitute. Now, I'm classed as
a child-care worker, and I'm qualified, and that's because
I have been a prostitute and I've got a criminal record. If
it weren't for prostitution, no way would I have got that
work. And it was the probation and aftercare service that
helped. If you get an application form to fill in for a job
nowadays, you have to fill in the part that says, 'Have
you ever been in trouble with the police?' and if you put

'Yes', they ask, 'When and where and why?' I'm telling you, if you put 'Yes', forget it. You don't even get as far as an interview.

But I was put on probation, and they were interested in my aftercare, and they got me on a one-year course, like a YOP scheme, and you can better yourself, get on from there. That was how they helped me. So I got on a three-week college course, and then I got a job in the kiddies' home, and from there, the old people's home.

Now I've been working with educated people, the ones with all the qualifications, O-levels, A-levels, and all that. I haven't, but I've got experience. I worked with girls with these qualifications, yet at the end of the course they just kept two students on, me and another guy without qualifications. The ones with the exams got sack, because they just didn't have the common sense. It was all out of text books.

I did hustling for one year, all of us lasses together. We survived. We lived comfortably. We were young, and we thought, 'Easy come, easy go,' so we earned and spent. We always knew we could go out and earn the next night, because there's always men out there that want it. To tell the truth, I have met some nice people, good-looking guys, and I have then reversed the usual fanny you get from punters, the 'What's a nice girl like you doing in a job like this?' I have said that, only to the guy, to the punter; 'Why have you come out to look for a girl, why?' And the response I get? 'Well, where I go, where I live,' – I'm talking about the middle classes now – 'there's lasses round there but they want all roses and romance, and each time you go to see them they want a bouquet of flowers, or the Big Romance and all that, but I don't want to be bothered. I'd rather come out and pay a lass like you, who needs money desperately.' And I say, 'Oh, big-hearted, eh? How flattering.'

I don't know why this is, but it's the same outside prostitution. In straight life as well, you get a lot of people that think because you've got a different-coloured skin, you might be a bit different underneath; your blood might be a different colour, or you might be a bit different, you've got a different shape. Damn ignorant! I think it's sad for people like that, I really do. I feel sorry for them, more than anything. I feel sorry that they're so damn ignorant. And you get people that say, 'I've never been with a black woman before,' and I've said, 'Now what made you say that?' and they go, 'Well, I haven't. I've heard black girls are different.'

'In what way?'

'I don't know . . . sometimes I've heard they're *better* in bed.' Then it's, 'And black guys are better than white guys, because they're *bigger*.' And then it's, 'Oh, I think you're very pretty, *for a black girl*.' Now, it's things like that that niggle me, and many a time I've gone, 'Look, forget it pal; I don't want to know.' Even when I've needed the money badly. And I've thought, 'Forget it. I'd rather stand out here another few hours, and wait until something better comes along, than suffer that shit.' What niggles me is that they can be like that. How can they be so ignorant towards *life* in general? And these are 'educated' people. I'm telling you, it does annoy me. I've had all that kind of thing: 'Well you're not really *black* are you? Because you are *quite* light-skinned. You're what I'd class as half-caste; you're not *really* full black, and you haven't *really* got the features. Your nose isn't *really* that flat, and your lips aren't *really* that big . . .' And sometimes, honest, I feel I could slap somebody across the face and say, 'Now listen: you're a very sad person; I *really* feel sorry for you.'

Of course I'm black; I'm not ashamed of that. And I've said to many people on purpose, 'Well, do you know this year when you go away, to get the colour I am, how much is it gonna knock you back? It's gonna cost a right bomb, innit, for you and your wife? To get nice and brown like I am; like I am *all the year round*.' Then you get, 'Oh, but that's different!' and I ask them, 'Well, is it different because you know you're not gonna stay like that, or because you haven't got the nose to go with it, or the thick lips, or what is it, frizzy hair? Is it that, you ignorant bastard?'

'Oh no, I don't mean it like that. *Don't take offence*. I've nothing against *the blacks*. I'm good friends with *one*; my wife knows *one*; *one* lives down the road from me.' And these people, I have not got the time of day for. And I feel sorry for them; they needn't pity me; I think their lives are so sad.

I've got lots of straight friends from all walks of life, who like me, say what a great person I am, and so on; but if they found out I was a prostitute, they wouldn't be my friend for much longer. And *that* to me is very sad, also. But again, that's prejudice and ignorance, because I've heard it lots of times: 'Oh, a prostitute,' nudge-nudge, or, 'What slags'; it's like the ones that wrote up after Nickie's article in the *New Statesman*. Don't know fuck-all about it; they're just talking from the tops of their stupid heads. All this crap about doing it because you must like it; well I never liked it. Never. To me, it was like doing a job, like being a typist in an office, or a cleaner, or whatever – collecting a wage I think I damn well deserved. But some of the insults that you get . . . Okay, you get some people who do treat you respectfully. They know you're doing a service for them; they just want to chat, go to bed with you and that's it. But on the other hand you get some right pigs that come in. On the whole, you are looked upon as just a slut, just a bag, just somebody dirty, and the only reason for *that* is because you take money for it. Now, that's crap in itself, isn't it?

You get them coming in and saying, 'I just want a good time with a lass who's got a good sense of humour; my wife isn't interested; she takes her make-up off and doesn't want to know. She won't do what I want her to.' No wonder, the state of some of them! They always put it down to the wives; it's the wives' fault. And I get them that say to me, 'I bet you get some right cranks, don't you?' And I just think, 'You're a crank.' I've had some right weirdos, all right – 'Talk to me about flowers . . .' Really! This punter wanted me to talk to him about nice things, colours, 'But mention flowers, all different flowers, and colours and that.' On my life! A very posh type, he was. And I had to say stuff like, 'Bluebells, roses, lilacs . . .' Definitely a posh bloke – but that was always the case, though. You might get a working-class bloke that's come, right, but for straight sex. He prefers to spend fifteen quid to come out and just go with one of the lasses, for what he wants: to use your body, really, and then go home. He's gotta get up early for work in the morning. And he'd rather not bother going out to the night-club, buying drinks for the girl and trying to flatter her, pull her, that way. Apart from these types, which are few and far between, it is really your upper and middle class, that has got money to spend, that come. And sometimes you do feel degraded. Let me be clear on this. *Personally*, I don't feel degraded, but they can *make* you feel it for that ten, fifteen minutes that they're with you, by all this, 'I'll give you a bit extra if you'll do so-and-so,' and that is terrible. You feel like you're begging; *bartering*.

In our job, some of the girls say, 'Lay back and think of Britain.' Who wants to think of Britain in the state it's in anyway? Then you really would be a masochist.

But I'm telling you, it is the middle-class men that are keeping the girls on the street, because they are the majority that use prostitutes. If I could have a chance now to exploit *them* back, you know I would, I really would. I'd give names, to show that it is the middle class, the upper class that's keeping the lasses on the game. Like politicians and that. I would not feel any shame to show my face to society – I'd say, 'Look: this guy has been keeping me on the street or in a sauna. He pays me well, but he's the same guy that's condemning me in the open.' I really wouldn't give a shit who saw my face. My friend has been seeing a judge from Magistrates' Court, and sometimes she was actually up in front of him for prostitution, and when she was, she never gave him away – but he never, ever gave her a heavy fine or sent her down. And she always said, 'I've told him the first time I'm up in front of him and he *does*, I'll shout it out there and then in Court.' What I would like to do would be to go on television at peak viewing time, with a lie-detector strapped to my arm, and look straight into the camera; and I'd say, 'Hello, it's Chloe. You out there, you know who I mean, don't you. You're the barrister that pays my friend to piss on your face. And you know who I'm talking about – you know who you are, don't you?' The *top* barrister in this city. And he'd be shaking in his shoes.

But it's never the working-class guys that want all the crazy stuff; well I've never come across any that do. It's always the posh ones, the really posh ones who want all the plastic macs, leather, whips, laying in coffins . . . I know this one guy, and he lives in a mansion, he is absolutely *loaded* – big director of some firm, president, or something like that. An old guy, getting on. Now he got my friend and he told her to get undressed and just lie on the bed. Then he went out. And he was watching her through the door, it was ajar. And he waited till she was totally naked then he sent his Alsatian dog in. Now, this dog wouldn't hurt anybody, wouldn't do anything, but when he sent it in, it started barking, and the *fear* on her face! And he was stood at the door masturbating. He shot his load, then he came in and he give her fifty pounds. And she said, 'Ya mad bastard what ya doing, I thought that thing were gonna have hold of me.' And he says, 'He wouldn't hurt a fly.' That weird bastard wanted to see the *fear* on her face; that is what he got off on.

But then I remember one guy, this was when I was working Park Lane, who got off on watching me watch a video of his mother's funeral! He put the film on, and, my life, it was his mother's funeral. I swear, honest to God! And then as soon as I saw it my heart was beating; I kept looking at the door thinking, 'Can I make a run for it? Because I *know* something's gonna happen . . .' But nothing did happen, and I sat there, but he was getting turned on by me sat there watching in *horror*, with me mouth open, his mother's funeral, his mother's coffin going into the ground. Now, he was some diplomat or summat like that, and it was me panicking, my shock . . . 'Well I think I'd better go,' and him going, 'No no, just watch this bit.' And he *told* me it was his mother's funeral. And you know when you get something like that? – I was a nervous wreck – you get them kinky like that, you just want to go home. You can't cope with the rest of the evening; you're too shaken up. And the next day I thought, 'Shall I go out?'

I suppose compared to working on the street, the sauna would make me feel more secure, with a lot of girls around me, knowing that I can scream out. You suffer a lot. And most women out there *have* to do it to look after their families, because they *can't* get a job elsewhere because they're not adequately educated or qualified. Some women have really got to do it, to survive. Gotta pay this, gotta pay that; and they are doing it for their kids, to feed them, and everything. Whose husbands have pissed off, or maybe they're one-parent families, whatever. And I feel I'm just glad I'm not in their shoes, that I could say, 'Right, this is it; I'm stopping it; I'll try and get another job.' And I think it was dead sad that I could only get another job through being in trouble in the first place.

But there's that many weirdos, guys that want tying up and dressing up that you find it hard to remember. You remember one or two. The other day Julie told me about a punter who came to her house, quite well-to-do. Sharon was there and he said, 'Well, I'll take your friend as well.' And Julie was laughing, she's saying to Sharon, 'Wait for it, wait for it!' He gets this bag out and he takes these boxing gloves out. They had to box with him! Julie was telling me this the other day at the bus stop. And they had to box with the guy, and say, 'You're not hurting me, come on! Come on!' And he'd punch them, not really hard, but each time one of the girls was knocked down to the floor, he put another pound down. He'd got fifty quid in pound notes, and coins. They'd gotta do this until all his coins had gone, and then they soon fucked him off – sharpish. And that was all he wanted; just to box with them; no sex. He got his rocks off – just with that.

I had this guy once, he was quite nice to talk to when he was being sociable, before any sex. He lived in a beautiful big house, drove a white Porsche, really wealthy; his wife was a fashion designer. He was a good-looking guy. His old lady was in France, at this big fashion show; it was being televised and everything. He was one of those Hoorah Henries, Eton and that. He paid me, and I mean he paid me well, beforehand, then he says to me, 'Please, please, I feel embarrassed over what I want to do. I don't really want to have sex with you as such, and I won't ejaculate in you or anything like that, don't think it wrong but – I wanna shout at you and abuse you verbally. It feels like I'm getting all my frustrations out.' And he's calling me a fucking bastard and a cunt and 'ya slut, ya slag!' and, 'You're all the same you women, you're whores!' you're this, you're that.

And as time went on I was getting a bit fed up with it, because he was really getting all his aggression out, his frustration; he was scowling so much. He was nearly frothing at the mouth, swearing at me and abusing me. And I said, 'That's *enough*,' and straight away he changed, and said, 'Yes, all right then, thanks ever so much.' And I felt sorry for him. I thought, 'You pathetic man.' Dr Jekyll and Mr Hyde, you know. And I thought afterwards, it was that his wife was away a lot of the time, she was a very successful woman, so I reckon he must really have been swearing at her, abusing her. Now that's all very well, but I think you have to draw the line somewhere; you don't always suffer this shit. Tell them to piss off or whatever. Now there's the other extreme; where the girl has to abuse the client. My friend Pat had one and what she had to do was she had to wee in his hands; he used to cup his hands, she weed in it and he drank it. And I've said, 'Pat!' and she goes, 'So *what*? I *love* it. I *love* it – *he*'s drinking it; it's *him*.' But me, I wouldn't piss in his hands, I'd tell him to piss off. I wouldn't give him the time of day. And she says, 'No! He gives me fifty quid.'

I've a friend who was up here the other night; she has got a child to a famous football manager, and she's let him know. She was a prostitute; he's gone with her, and she's ended up pregnant to him. She apparently phoned him to let him know, *not* to say, 'I want some money off ya,' but to let him know she was the prostitute he went with nine months ago, and she got pregnant. And she says she wishes to this day that she hadn't bothered, because she didn't want money off him, she just wanted to tell him it was definitely him the father, and he's said to her, 'Don't come that with me, ya fucking trollop – it's not my fucking kid; how many other men have you been with, ya slag?' and put the phone down. Now if that'd been me, then I *would* have done something about it, for all that.

You'd be surprised how many guys you see – 'Oh, he's great, him on TV and that' – but there's chicks sat there and they'll say, 'Oh, I went with him, he was my client.' Or this or that politician on with Sir Robin Day: 'My punter.' And you'd get people that'll say, 'No, you're joking,' but it's the truth. Sad world we're living in, innit? But I'll tell you; it's the upper class that's keeping the lasses on the street. Keeping them in this job, but yet condemning them at the same time: 'We want rid of them; this that and the other.' They'll NEVER get rid of prostitution, not whilst *they* still want it. But the sneaky bastards'll find some way of getting the women together one day, taxing them would be another thing, wouldn't it? Something just as sneaky as now, with the courts. The state's pimping off these girls.

In the afternoon you get the businessman, the middle-class businessman and he's coming it: 'Well, let's make it snappy darling, I've got to get back to the office, I've got a board meeting.' And I'm thinking, 'Me too, pal; I've got a *bored* meeting.' So they come out in the day, they're feeling dead fucking horny and they just work off on you. 'There's so much stress on me, you don't know how much you're relaxing me, and then I've got the wife to face at dinner time; I'll find a way to get out from the wife tonight.' And they make me sick, these characters;

it's like they're using the women in a circle; they're using you, then going back home to use their wives. All races, all classes of male just use women throughout anyway, for working in the house, being a housewife, to the office with the secretaries, to coming to us for their sexual relief. Nice world, isn't it?

They say we are demoralizing, degrading the man, but you wouldn't have prostitutes without men. But it just all boils down to the same old thing: these same people who're trying to condemn us girls and yet, what would they do without us? There'd be a lot of screaming then, when there were no prostitutes, when the rape statistics have gone up, the child molesters increased.

Look at the way the world sees us anyway: *he* is the customer, he's classed as the customer, but *she* is the 'whore'. I've never put on any airs and graces, but I think in this world there are wider horizons than men's antics. You can drop a man like *that*, tell him he's crap in bed and that'll do him for a start. Now if a guy comes to me and says he's crap in bed, I couldn't give a shit. But a lot of these men come for their ego; they want to be reassured that they're good, they're fair-sized, and they're doing quite well on the job; they've lasted a bit longer than five minutes: 'Am I average? Am I under-average? Am I over-average?' But I think it comes naturally, when you're with an old dude, to tell them that they're doing quite well. It must be a turn-on, because they get it over and done with quite quickly then. And that's all you're looking for. The majority of girls prefer the older man as a client, and I'm talking about fifty upwards. There is no hassle; you know they're not gonna turn on you and slit your throat and beat you up. I just think that generation respects a woman a bit more, though not always. But mostly. It's either the very young lad, I'm talking about eighteen to thirty-five, or it's the middle class that slag you off. It's always the barrister or the director; it's always them that's the worst. They want to demoralize you or they've got kinky scenes in mind.

I don't believe that it's pornography that brings it out in men, though. I honestly don't. I think it's that most of them's on such a big ego trip; it's wanting to know that they're the best. Or this abusing people, they're lacking in their own self-esteem, so they take it out on us. And I think they feel threatened by us, because they see us as *sexual*, and it scares them.

We girls stick by each other and respect each other, because we've all experienced what the upper class and the middle class have got to offer, and what they've got to offer is a load of abuse and using women. What we've got amongst ourselves is a lot of love and affection. They've got a lot of abusing women, slagging us off, that's it. We're prostitutes, full-stop. We're not women, human beings, who've got feelings, or children, or other lives, in their eyes. I've just got a lot wiser through being a prostitute. I've never regretted one moment of what I've ever done or ever been, or what I will be in the future; and I won't regret it if I go back to doing that. I may be sad that I've got to go back on to that scene to make some more money, but I've met some lovely people, made some good friends on the game, amongst the girls. Like all the lasses I've stripped with when I was a stripper in Soho. I'm thirty years old and to me, that is the highlight of my life so far because I'll never forget one of them. We had the best laughs, the best fun. I'll never forget the love that comes from them. There's only one other person I think of with love like that, and that's my Mum. We stuck by each other through thick and thin, and if you ever needed anything you could guarantee one of them'd be there. It is lovely. To other people we might be all strippers, all prostitutes, but this is where the real respect lies – feelings, loving. We carry a community in our hearts, really.

Sex, Class and Morality

'What makes a prostitute is the nature of sexual relationships as they are viewed, created and practised by men.
And the other thing that makes a prostitute is that this
same society provides the 'goods' needed to fill this
demand, through unemployment, poverty, low pay or
bad working conditions – the list is endless. In the end,
what makes a prostitute is an ideology of commodity and
consumption. Once the body is transformed into an
object, metamorphosed by a mutilated, handicapped,
repressed sexuality, the next thing is to consume it.'

(Claude Jaget, ed., *Prostitutes – Our Life*)
Falling Wall Press

As soon as I approached my friends with the idea for
this book they understood what I was trying to do, and
were enthusiastic. I was encouraged by their response.
There could have been many more stories in this book.
Since the participants knew and had worked with me
over a number of years, they trusted me and they knew I
would not betray their trust, or distort what they had to
say. So, I was glad of my friends' support, especially after
I began to have some articles about the sex industry
published and they said 'That's right: that's exactly how it
is.'

Just as well, really, since the reaction I got from
straights was nothing but cruel abuse; a real slagging-off
from all quarters. From the political left, the right; from
some 'feminist' puritans, and other moralists . . . the

oodle. I was shocked by the response to my
How naïve of me.

I was accused of attacking the sex industry. I was
accused of defending the sex industry. One particularly
bilious man accused me of simultaneously attacking *and*
defending the sex industry. It seemed that some people
couldn't get it through their thick skulls that I was in fact
– and still am – *attacking* the sex industry and *defending*
its workers.

A 'feminist' informed me that the sex industry doesn't
exist; it isn't an industry and what we do isn't work.
Maybe she thinks it's a hobby . . .

More than anything else, I was accused of being
immoral. Nothing new there, I suppose. Except to ask
whose 'morality' were my accusers referring to? Why,
their own, of course. These paragons tend to forget that
we strippers and prostitutes are all too familiar with what
lurks beneath the surface of straight society's 'morality';
we have been on the receiving end of it for too long. We
know that the notion of 'respectability' is nothing but a
sham, and that underneath the sham, the facts are pretty
slimy. And when we refuse to keep our traps shut, the
knowledge we possess then represents a real threat to
society's attitudes and beliefs. That's when the moralists
start screaming. Too bad. The cover-up job has been
going on for too long; all the myths and lies about women
like us being 'whores' who just love what we do, or can't
help ourselves, or both.

Think of it – all those Lulus and Nanas and Camilles:
sluts who couldn't stop even if they wanted to. Figments
of male literary imagination. *That's* where all the 'It must
really turn you on being a stripper' crap we all get
at some point originates. Men's nudge-nudge-wink-wink
fantasy that women who work in the sex industry are
little more than raging nymphomaniacs.

It's also why to this day male writers, critics, and journalists persist in referring to prostitute women as 'whores'. They use that word with lip-smacking relish, almost with glee. Men love the fantasy of the 'whore'. They prefer that word, with all its connotations of greedy rampant female sexuality. Writing 'prostitute woman' would spoil all the fun, because that brings economics into the picture, raising some very uncomfortable questions about men and women, and power and sex . . . questions that have to be answered.

Female writers, I've noticed, appear to be more at ease with 'tart'. It's a much more genteel way of putting it; a way of metaphorically handling the subject with a pair of tongs, so that the 'good' female can dissociate herself from us baddies. She's not 'immoral', like us.

Back to that again! The question of 'morality'. But in any case, it's high time the whole concept of what is moral and what isn't was redefined; broadened a bit, to include the views of others who might not subscribe to the middle-class Christian version. For instance, there are those of us who would argue that a society which uses the services of women in the sex industry, yet at the same time condemns us for providing those services, is immoral and hypocritical. And is it not immoral that the source of the supply for these services should be working-class women whose only other 'choice' would be a lifetime of drudgery and poverty? Unpaid drudgery in the home, or low-paid drudgery in the factory. Both, more often than not.

Working-class women are expected to accept the life of a drudge without a murmur of complaint. What I and others like me left behind us when we ran away from our home towns was the grey life. Many of us found some *freedom* when we landed in the sex industry. To this day I do not regret what I did; and neither do any of my friends. All the labels we've been given – degraded, exploited, victims – those are the labels I've left behind on the path that was laid down for me originally. As far as I'm concerned, working in crummy factories for disgusting pay was the most degrading and exploitative work I ever did in my life. I'm aware that, in a sense, it was a Hobson's choice for me. I see that now, but I still maintain that I had more control over my life as a worker in the sex factory than as one in an ordinary factory. When I left Lancashire, I was rejecting the whole ethos of living to work and working to live, that had been the lot of my predecessors. I think there should be another word for the kind of work that working-class people do; something to differentiate it from the work middle-class people do; the ones who have careers. All I can think of is *drudgery*. It's rotten and hopeless; not even half a life. It's *immoral*. Yet as I say, it's *expected* of working-class women that they deny themselves everything. Above all, a sense of your own worth as an individual; an awareness of yourself as being a person in your own right, which is something that middle-class people take for granted practically from the moment they learn to speak. *Nowhere* are working-class women allowed the space in which to develop as human beings. We are trained from birth *not* to have any real sense of ourselves as anything other than the work we do: the servers and servicers of our 'betters', whether they be from a 'higher' class or simply our husbands: men. We are not supposed to feel; we are supposed to function. We are not supposed to have any notions about whatever potential we might have. At school, at work, through the media, we get the message loud and clear:

This is what you're worth.

This is all you're going to get . . .

So make the most of it; don't question it; this is the

way it's always been. Don't rock the boat. And as for having any aspirations of your own – forget it! Don't bother . . .

So when some of us rebel against our life's 'prospects', why should we be labelled *immoral*? Why should I have to put up with a middle-class feminist asking me why I didn't 'do anything – scrub toilets, even?' rather than become a stripper? What's so liberating about cleaning up other people's shit?

But that's what I keep hearing; time and time again. It drives me round the bend. It seems it's okay to do shitwork and stay poor: that's not immoral – but being a stripper or a prostitute and earning good money *is*. Sometimes it seems that one of society's biggest preoccupations is with the relatively high income women who work in the sex industry make, especially prostitutes. Nowhere is this more clearly evident than in the gutter press's obsession with 'the wages of sin'. It's one of their favourite subjects – 'exposing' prostitute women who are making high wages from their male clients. It seems it's fine that those men should have all that surplus loot in the first place, but it somehow becomes *immoral* when 'Vice Girls' get their greedy mitts on it . . . Never mind the fact that the journalistic pimps are making big salaries out of their 'exposés'; pretending to be prostitutes' clients, acting as *agents provocateurs*. But they're cleaning up society; doing the public a big favour! To my mind, those creatures are the *real* sleaze.

Women's prisons in this country are full of working-class women who have fought back against poverty in one way or another; by shoplifting, DHSS 'fraud' – or by turning to prostitution. Their crime is being poor and being female. But it is prostitutes in particular who receive the most vicious treatment at the hands of the law since they can be convicted on the word of *one* police officer.[1] And since custodial sentences for soliciting and loitering were officially abolished, in January 1983, the number of prostitute women who have been sent to prison has actually *increased*. To get round the law, magistrates simply upped the fines to two, three and four hundred pounds for every court appearance. So the girls are now being sent down for non-payment of fines, which is a particularly vindictive move on the part of the courts, in view of the fact that it is poverty that drives women on to the game in the first place.

'It's all so hypocritical, because the judge can sit there and fine a girl £400, then if she comes up another time, he'll fine her a few thousands. And how's she gonna pay those fines? He's sending her out, on to the streets, because you've got to go and earn it that way to pay the fines. So that makes the government a pimp.' (Yasmin)

It's important to remember in all this that prostitution itself is *not* illegal in this country – although just about everything surrounding it is. 'Loitering' or 'soliciting' in a public place is illegal, and once a woman has been cautioned twice – even if she has not been convicted – she is labelled a 'common prostitute' for life.

The law prohibits women from working together from a flat or a house for safety's sake. Two prostitutes or more constitute a brothel; *that's* why women work from the streets in the first place. It's because of their very illegality that prostitutes are so much more vulnerable to men's violence than are straight women. It's no coincidence that, of the prostitute friends I interviewed for this book, the only one who had *never* experienced violence at the hands of clients was the male prostitute. All the women had experienced rape and/or other abuse. That gives some food for thought. I believe it reflects this

society's attitudes about violence towards women generally: that it is not unacceptable. All men may not be
rapists, but they do appear to have *carte blanche* in the
eyes of the law and the rest of society, as far as beating,
robbing, raping – even murdering – prostitutes is
concerned.

When I sat and listened to my friends' tales of rape and
violence, their total lack of protection from abuse, I was
chilled. Anita, describing how her friend got into the
'Yorkshire Ripper's' car because she desperately needed
the money *to pay off her court fines*: 'She just wanted
to get off the Square, away from the police . . .'

Away from the police – into the car of a murderer. It
made my blood run cold; it also made me wonder how
many of Peter Sutcliffe's dead prostitute victims got into
his car because they had the *legal* pimps to pay off . . .

But so what? – they're only 'whores', seems to be
society's attitude. In January 1980, the English Collective
of Prostitutes issued a statement to the Metropolitan
Police Commissioner:

To the Ripper *and* to the police, prostitutes are not decent, we
are not 'innocent victims'. What are we guilty of to deserve
such a death? 70% of prostitute women in this country are
mothers fighting to make ends meet and feed their children.
But because we refuse poverty for ourselves and our children,
we are treated as criminals. In the eyes of the police we deserve
what we get, even death.

Yet even during the Ripper's trial the Attorney General
saw fit to declare that in his view, the fact that some of
Sutcliffe's victims were not prostitutes was 'perhaps the
saddest part of this case' (a remark which in turn
prompted some of us to observe that even 'sadder' was
the fact that some were not attorney generals).

That Sir Michael Havers could make such a crass

statement with apparent impunity, *and* be quoted uncritically in the press, speaks volumes about attitudes towards prostitute women. They somehow *deserve* to die, because they are 'wicked' women. Now that's an immoral attitude.

And what about the clients? The men who use the sex industry, in all its guises. Punters. Where would we be without them? Out of work, for one thing.

There would be no sex industry if there were no customers (*men*, with their higher wages and greater spending power). And the fact that we women can make good money as strippers or prostitutes *only* because of that basic inequality is somewhat ironic and definitely immoral.

It's also immoral that men want to use women's bodies without relating to us as human beings, without considering our feelings – I'm not just talking about within the sex industry, now. It happens throughout society, at home and at work. Everywhere, men expect to be serviced by women – to be looked after, cleaned up after, by wives and girlfriends, and to be sexually serviced by them too. And the sex industry is part of that system; it's yet another service for men that's provided by women. It's exactly as Chloe puts it:

All races, all classes of male just use women throughout, anyway; for working in the house, being a housewife, to the office with the secretaries, to coming to us for their sexual relief. Nice world, isn't it?

The fact is, men run the whole works. It's men who use the sex industry; men who nick the girls on the streets or raid the clubs and saunas; men who make the laws and then carry them through, by fining us or putting us away. Those are the real scandals, yet where is the outcry from straight society? I don't hear a whimper.

Money, sex, power . . . that's what it's all about. In this society, where everything is bought and sold, it stands to reason that those of us who are at the bottom of the pile are going to sell our one remaining 'asset': ourselves. But make no mistake about the fact that *everyone* sells and manipulates in this culture; that is how you survive. And sometimes you don't.

When I first began to write 'My Story', I thought I was out on my own, that nobody from the sex industry had spoken up before me. I was glad to find I was wrong. Many have. I discovered that in the last decade a new movement had blossomed; there were organizations and support groups composed of women who work in the sex industry and women and men who do not throughout the world. Making connections. Now there's a network that links us as far afield as the USA, Canada, Australia, New Zealand, the West Indies, as well as most European countries. A whole chorus of voices who have for so long been silenced, denied human status, denounced as immoral sluts . . . But now we are getting our chance to speak up, *tell what we know*.

The work of those who had begun to fight before me – the French prostitutes who went on strike in 1975,[2] and the English prostitutes who took over the church at King's Cross in 1982[3] – inspired me and gave me the courage to start speaking for myself. Then came the voices of those women and men I had worked with and respected, and loved. Strong voices; the voices of real human beings, not stereotypes, 'victims', or figments of men's imagination. And, when I listened to them speak, that's when I realized what a *true* morality is – the network of courage, support, and caring that all of us recalled in our accounts. As Chloe so eloquently described it:

To other people we might be all strippers, all prostitutes, but this is where the real respect lies – feelings, loving. We carry a community in our hearts, really.

Every time another of us speaks out about our lives, another connection is forged between us, sex industry workers everywhere. And we hope also to reach and make connections with straight women, too; so that they can know that we are not the evil 'Vice Girls' beloved of the media, but ordinary women like themselves . . . mothers, daughters, sisters. And we hope to one day touch men's consciences . . .

Working in the sex industry is one of the myriad ways in which women struggle to survive all over the world; we are not outside of society; we are a part of it. As more of us gain the courage and confidence we are finding from each other, we need no longer hang our heads and feel shame for the lives we have been forced into; just as society can no longer deny us our humanity and dismiss us as 'immoral' creatures who do not deserve to be listened to. We have voices, we can speak up, and we *will* be heard. And with our life's story, each of us refutes the concept of 'whore'; the 'whore' of men's fantasies. Now it is their turn to feel ashamed. One day men will change; they'll have to because women are changing. Becoming visible is part of that change, and that is what women who work in the sex industry are doing – becoming visible as human beings.

As for the male sexual dinosaurs, the stupid buggers who persist in clinging to their tired old myths and illusions; they will die out eventually, taking with them their warped ideas about what they think is 'sexuality' – using women as commodities.

In the meantime, Victorian Values prevail, and poor working-class women continue in ever-increasing numbers to sexually service the affluent middle-class men who call them 'whores', and condemn them to the rest of society. But that is *their* 'morality', not ours.

Now, having written this, I can look back on my own

life and see my 'escape' from the harsh Lancashire life into the 'freedom' of the Soho sex industry as the blind alley it was. Yet I have no regrets about the choices I made, and I am not ashamed; not any more. I know that the sex and class wars have not abated in this society. Women are still the poorest, and men still expect to be serviced by us in every respect. Until that changes, there can be no true armistice between us.

Notes

1. Information from the English Collective of Prostitutes' Fact sheet 'Rules of the Game'.
2. *Prostitutes – Our Life*. (Claude Jaget, ed.).
3. *Hookers in The House of the Lord* (Selma James).